EUROPEAN PORCELAIN

EUROPEAN PORCELAIN

A
Handbook
for
the
Collector

by

MARIA PENKALA

CHARLES E. TUTTLE COMPANY
Rutland, Vermont   Tokyo, Japan

PREFACE TO THE SECOND EDITION

Since 1947, when the first edition of this handbook was issued, no pains have been spared to make the book still more useful by means of the new material added to this edition. The whole book has been thoroughly revised and enlarged in order to incorporate the results of the latest researches. The marks have been numbered and many more added.

Sincere thanks are offered to the Victoria and Albert Museum, London; Rijksmuseum, Amsterdam; Staatliche Kunstsammlungen, Dresden; Bayerisches Nationalmuseum, Munich; Dr. Ernst Schneider, Düsseldorf; and private collectors for permission to reproduce photographs of the wonderful pieces in their collections.

Amsterdam, May 1968   M. P.

PREFACE TO THE FIRST EDITION

This book is the result of many years of exhaustive study. More than three thousand marks of factories and signs of painters, modellers, etc., were collected, compared and catalogued before it was possible to offer the finished work to the public.

With very few exceptions all marks included in this volume have been reproduced in actual size.

It would be impossible to give a complete list of all the sources used but a short bibliography will be found at the end of this volume.

The author wishes to thank all those who kindly supplied information, in particular the officials of the Print Room of the Rijksmuseum at Amsterdam, the Boymans Museum at Rotterdam and numerous other public and private collections and libraries. Grateful acknowledgment of their valuable assistance is also due to the Manufacture Nationale de Porcelaine de Sèvres, the Royal Worcester Porcelain Co. Ltd., Messrs. Josiah Wedgwood & Sons Ltd. of Barlaston, the Royal Copenhagen Porcelain Factory, Messrs. Bing & Gröndahl of Copenhagen and the Rörstrand Factory in Sweden.

Amsterdam, February 1947   M. P.

CONTENTS

8

ITALY

As early as 1575 Francesco de' Medici, Grand Duke of Toscana, was operating a factory making soft paste porcelain, established in the Boboli gardens. Vasari mentions that Francesco was assisted in the factory by Bernardo Buontalenti. Records show that the tickets of admission for a court ball at Florence in 1613 were made of porcelain bearing the Medici coat of arms.

The discovery of Medici porcelain is attributed to Dr. Allessandro Foresi, who announced his discovery in the newspaper "Piovano Arlotto" in 1859. Only 36 pieces of Medici porcelain are known to be in existence.

Medici porcelain cannot be claimed to be the first made in Europe. Baron Davillier, who made a special study of the origin of Italian porcelain, quotes a letter from Pater Guglielmo de Bologna, written from Padua, and addressed to Maestro Antonio, an alchemist in Venice, who worked a kiln at San Simeone, thanking Antonio for the gift of a small bowl and a vase of translucent porcelain which he had made. This letter is dated April 1470. In a document found in the archives of Venice, a certain Leonardo Peringer, "specchiarius in marzaria" (merchant in mirrors), states that he has discovered a new artifice, never before used in the Illustrious City of Venice for the making of all sorts of translucent porcelains like those of the Levant. ("Ouer uno novo artificio deficio non piu facto ne usitato in questa illustra cita de Venezia per fabricare ogni sorte de porcellane come sono quegle de Levante transparanti"). This document is dated 4th June 1518. Baron Davillier quotes a letter written by Jacopo Tebaldo, Ambassador of the Duke d'Este in Venice, addressed to the Duke Alphonso, in which he mentions the gift of a small dish and bowl made of porcelain. He wrote to the Duke that he had asked the maker to come to Ferrara, where he would find all possible facilities for manufacturing china and could earn much money. This offer, however, was refused because the inventor did not want to leave Venice on account of his extreme age. This letter dates from the year 1519. Unfortunately no specimens of this early Venetian porcelain have come down to us.

The Medici pieces are beautifully shaped and ornamented. Various bowls, jars, ewers, a gourd-shaped bottle, dishes, double bottles and pilgrim bottles are among the thirty-six pieces preserved.

VENICE, VEZZI 1720–27

Hard paste china was made in the "Casa eccellentissima Vezzi" in Venice as early as 1720.

Pieces marked Ven[a] in red or blue originate in the Vezzi factory. They are very rare. They are usually painted with grotesque Chinese figures and masquerades, sometimes with decorations in relief. The oldest are decorated in black and gold, but on later pieces the decoration is usually in Venetian red. After the Vezzi factory had closed down a new factory was established by the Saxon porcelain maker, Friedrich Hewelke in 1758, who was granted a licence from the Senate for himself and his wife, Maria Dorothea. Hewelke failed to make the factory a financial success and, when the Seven Years War ended, he abandoned the factory and returned to Saxony. All Hewelke china is marked with the letter V.

In 1765 the Senate granted to Geminiano Cozzi the right to establish a hard paste factory "Contrada di San Giobbe" and subsidised the undertaking. This factory proved a great success. The pieces produced by Cozzi were marked with an anchor in red, blue and gold. Cozzi's paste was very white and well glazed, and his gildings in particular were exquisitely fine. He produced coloured and white tea-sets, services, figurines, groups and vases, all beautifully executed.

This factory was closed in 1812.

NOVE

The porcelain factory at Nove was established by Pasquale Antonibon in 1750. Pieces executed by him can be traced back to 1752.

Antonibon worked with Sigismund Fischer, a German who was in possession of Saxon porcelain secrets. Pasquale Antonibon manufactured china up to 1781 when he took into partnership Parolini. This association was ended in 1802 and the factory was afterwards leased to Baroni. The factory closed down in 1835. By way of mark the Antonibon factory used a comet or sometimes a star in red, blue or gold. Some of the produce was decorated by the painter Giovanni Marconi.

CAPODIMONTE

The porcelain works at Capodimonte (Naples), which operated from 1743–1760, were founded by King Charles III of the Two Sicilies. The King took a great interest in the factory and even worked there himself. The chief modeller was Giuseppe Gricci. At first the factory produced very fine soft paste ware, in imitation of Japanese porcelain and Fukien ware.

Beautiful tea-sets and coffee-sets were made, as well as fine vases and snuff-boxes in highly elaborate rococo-style.

The pieces were ornamented with coloured reliefs, the subjects usually being mythological or allegorical. The gilding was well executed. Small snuff-boxes with miniature paintings were a speciality. Figures and groups of very high artistic merit, representing peasants, shepherds, pedlars, beggars, jesters etc. were produced. The mark used exclusively is the fleur de lys, but many of the early pieces were left unmarked.

Capodimonte porcelain was and is still being imitated in Italy and elsewhere.

MODELLERS AND PAINTERS

Stefano Gricci, modeller.
Basilio, Macedonio and Carlo Fumo.
Arcanist Gaetano Schepers.
Johann Sigismund Fischer from Dresden, chief painter, 1757–1758.
Luigi Restile, chief painter 1758.
Maria Caselli, painter.
Giuseppe della Torre, painter.
Giovanni Caselli, painter.
To replace the original Capodimonte factory, which was closed in 1760,

King Ferdinand IV established the Naples factory in 1771. Francesco Celebrano was appointed as director. At first soft paste china was produced, but from 1780 onwards hard paste porcelain was made. The factory turned out beautiful services, very artistically decorated, as well as vases in classical and Pompeian style. In a later period the influence of Vienna can be discerned. The beautifully modelled groups in white biscuit-ware, are exquisitely executed.

In 1806 the factory was taken over by Poulard Prad.

The Naples mark was a crowned N or the monogram FR (Fabbrica Reale) crowned in red or blue, under or on glaze. Imitations bearing these marks are very frequently encountered. The works were closed down in 1820 and the moulds were taken to the Doccia works.

DOCCIA (near Florence).

The Doccia factory was established in 1735 by the Marchese Carlo I Ginori. At first soft paste was used, but later the factory switched over to hard paste. A number of wax models were purchased from the Florentine sculptor Massimiliano Soldani, who died at the age of 82 in 1740. Fine vases, urns, services and groups, in imitation of Meissen models, were produced.

From 1821 on, when the old moulds of the Capodimonte factory were brought to Doccia, this factory flooded the European market with perfect reproductions of the old Neapolitan products. Various marks were used, in red, blue and gold under glaze (see plate).

The modellers at Doccia included Giuseppe Ettal, Gaetano Lici, Gasparo and Giuseppe Bruschi.

The painters included Rigaci and Fanciulliacci (miniatures), Valleresi (flowers), Ristori (landscapes), Smeraldi (figures and landscapes) and Giusti (flowers and landscapes), and Anreiter from Vienna.

Marchese Carlo II Ginori went into partnership in 1896 with Jules Richard of Milan and, accordingly, the style of the firm became Società Ceramica Richard and Ginori.

TREVISO

The Treviso factory which manufactured soft paste porcelain, was established by the brothers Giuseppe and Andrea Fontebasso in 1795. The marks (see plate) were executed in red and blue.

VINOVO 1759–1840

Gian Victor Brodel of Turin and the Marchese Birago of Vische, assisted by Peter Anton Hannong, a brother of Paul Antoine Hannong of Strasbourg, established a hard paste porcelain factory at Vinovo in 1776. The factory went bankrupt within a few years, for Peter Anton Hannong, although a talented artist, proved to be a very bad business man. The factory closed down in 1780, and the plant and stock were sold by auction.

The factory was reopened in the same year by a chemist, Dr. Victor Amadeus Gioanotti, with the very talented Tamietti as modeller. The factory continued operations until Dr. Gioanotti died in 1815. The productions, coloured or white, were beautifully modelled and executed, and included figures, mythological groups, and services with rococo ornamentation. The latter were painted in Sèvres style or decorated with German flowers. The factory imitated the Sèvres marks and the Meissen swords. Vases with exquisitely painted rural landscapes were produced, as well as groups and statuettes in Capo di Monte style and busts of famous personages, emperors and philosophers, in biscuit ware.

The marks were either impressed in the moist paste or painted in underglaze blue or in red, grey or black on glaze.

ESTE

This factory, located between Padua and Ferrara, was established in 1780 by Varion, a Frenchman, who had previously worked at Nove, in Antonibon's factory. It produced porcelain of superior quality, equal to the Doccia products.

VICENZA 1793–1800

A porcelain factory was operated here toward the end of the 18th century.

ROME

Captain Filippo Coccumos had established in 1761 a porcelain factory which was in operation until 1781. Artistic biscuit figures were produced.

ROME

Giovanni Volpato operated a factory from 1785 to 1803. He was succeeded by his son, who died in 1818. The produce of this factory consisted mainly of biscuit figures.

ROMA I MAG 1760

TURIN

From 1824 to 1846 a porcelain factory was operated by Dortu and Richard.

TURIN

Toward the end of the 18th century a factory was operated here by Giorgio Giacinto Rossetti.

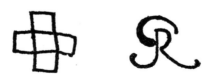

FLORENCE
Medici porcelain

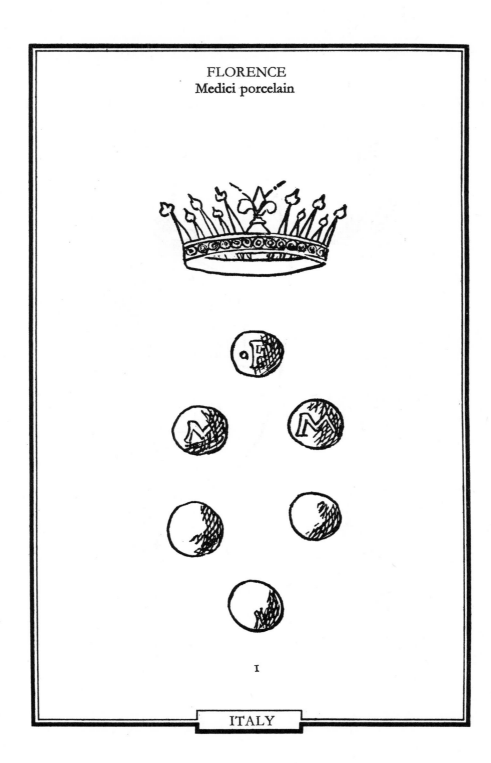

I

ITALY

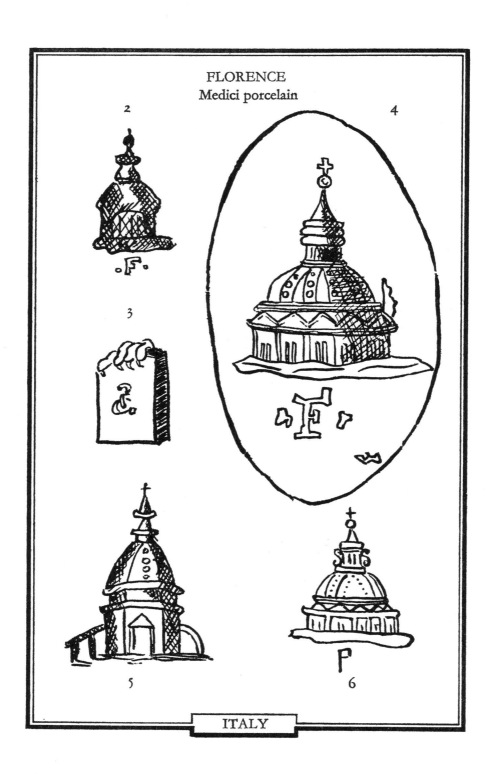

FLORENCE
Medici porcelain

ITALY

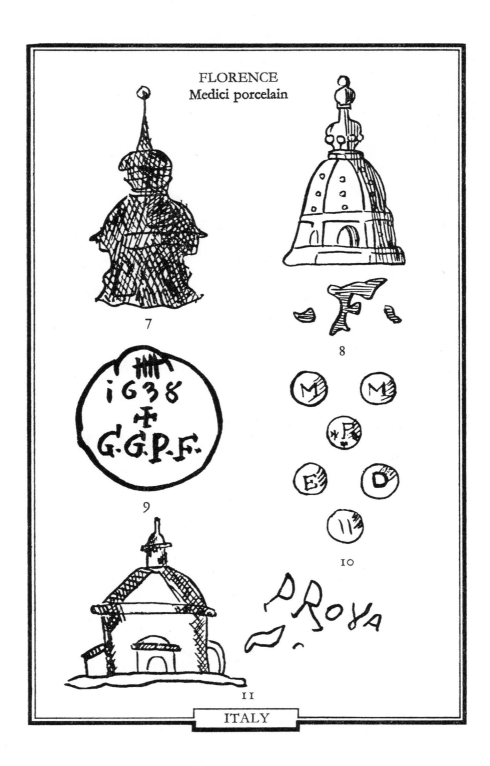

FLORENCE
Medici porcelain

7

8

9

10

11

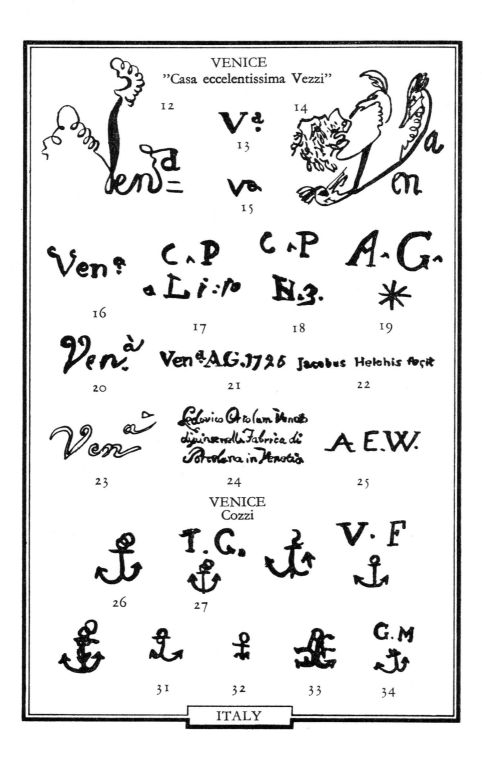

VENICE
"Casa eccelentissima Vezzi"

12

V.ª
13

14

va
15

Ven?
16

C.ᴀP
ᴀL.i.ᴘ
17

C.ᴀP
N.3.
18

A.ᴀG.ᴀ
✳
19

Ven.ª
20

Ven.ª A.G. 1726
21

Jacobus Helchis fecit
22

Ven.ª
23

Lodovico Ortolam Veneti
diqui servella Fabrica di
Porcelana in Venetia
24

A E.W.
25

VENICE
Cozzi

26

T.G.
27

V.F

31   32   33

G.M
34

NOVE

No: ue ❀
GBAB:
35

Noue.
Antonio Bon
36

NOVE
❋
37

Nove
38

NOUE.
39

Nove
❋
40

41

42

GB
NOVE
43

Gio: Marconi pinx:
44

1810—1824

45   46   47

48

TREVISO

Fabrica Baroni
Nove.
49

F.F.
Treviso. 1799
50

ESTE

G.A.F.F.
Treviso
51

ESTE + 1783 +   D. B.
52   53

ESTE
54

ITALY

19

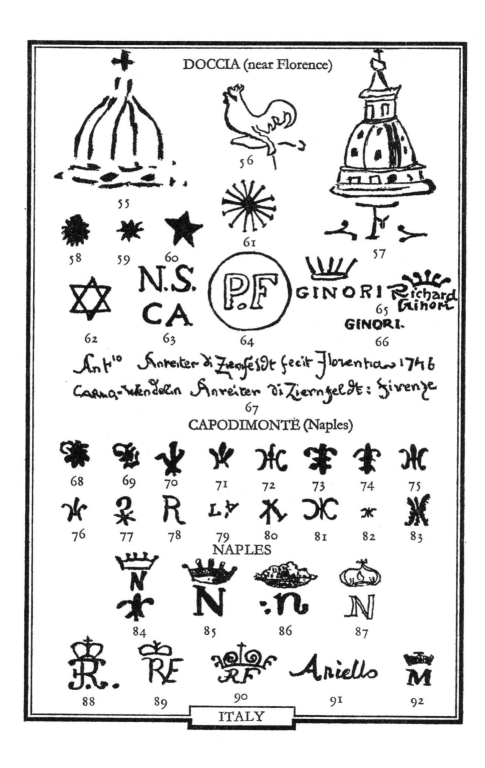

DOCCIA (near Florence)

55   56   57

58   59   60   61

N.S. CA   **P.F**   **GINORI**   **Richard Ginori**

62   63   64   65

GINORI.

66

An.^{to}   Anreiter di Ziemfeldt fecit Florentiae 1746

Carmg-Wendelin Anreiter di Ziernfeldt: Firenze

67

CAPODIMONTE (Naples)

68   69   70   71   72   73   74   75

76   77   78   79   80   81   82   83

NAPLES

84   85   86   87

88   89   90   *Ariello*   92

91

ITALY

20

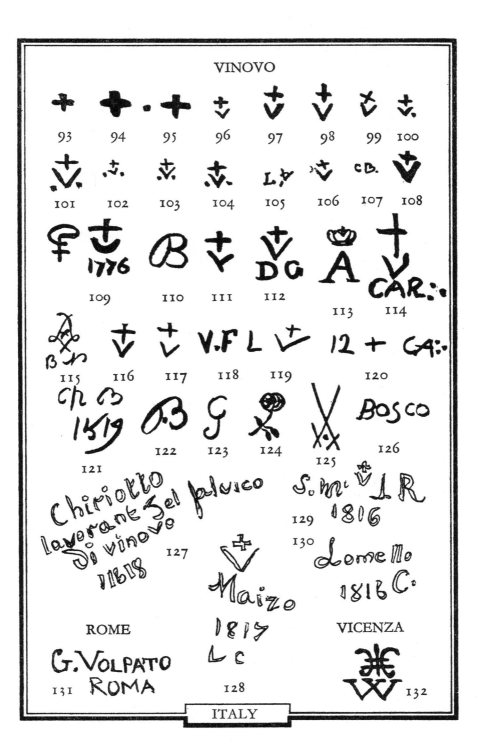

VINOVO

93 94 95 96 97 98 99 100

101 102 103 104 105 106 107 108

109 110 111 112 113 114

115 116 117 118 119 120

121 122 123 124 125 126

127 129 130

ROME

G. VOLPATO
ROMA

131

128

VICENZA

132

ITALY

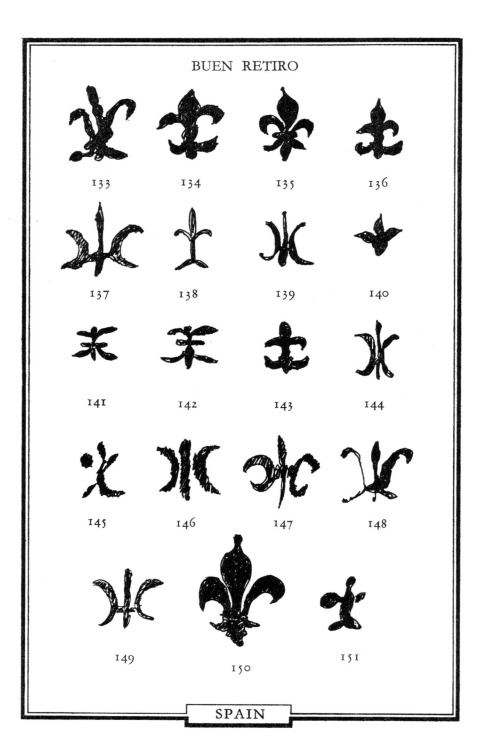

BUEN RETIRO

133   134   135   136

137   138   139   140

141   142   143   144

145   146   147   148

149   150   151

SPAIN

SPAIN

BUEN RETIRO 1760 to 1812.

This very interesting factory was established by King Charles III of Spain, who secured the services of workmen and painters from the Capo di Monte factory. At first soft paste services and tea-sets were produced, and later beautiful vases, bowls, groups and figurines. Pieces produced during the first period of the Buen Retiro factory bear a great likeness to the Capo di Monte products.

Among the most notable specialities of the Buen Retiro factory were porcelain tiles. These were used to decorate the salons of the palace and are still preserved. Among the beautiful groups and statuettes are many which were made in antique style. They were made only for the Royal Family. In 1789 a few specimens were made for sale. At the end of the 18th century biscuit groups and figurines in Sèvres style and medaillons and plaques in the Wedgwood manner were produced. After 1800 hard paste porcelain only was made at Buen Retiro.

Until 1790 Giuseppe Gricci was chief modeller. After his death Spanish artists influenced the style of the production.

At first the Bourbon lily was used as mark in underglaze blue and sometimes a double C with or without a crown. Impressed and gold marks were also used.

First director Gaetano Schepers was responsible for the quality of the paste. In 1803 Bartolomé Sureda, the newly appointed director, introduced a formula for hard paste. In 1808 the factory was transformed into a fortress, and was destroyed in 1812 by Wellington. In 1817 the factory was rebuilt at Moncloa, and was in operation until 1850.

ALCORA

The count Aranda established in 1726 a faience factory, assisted by workmen from Moustiers. In 1750 M. F. Haly was attached to the manufactory (See European Pottery). He made soft paste porcelain delicately modelled and decorated.

In 1815 Ramon Girona acquired the works. The produce of the factory has much likeness with pieces made at Buen Retiro, but the paste is greyish and the glaze greenish. Ramon Girona imitated the 18th century pieces of Buen Retiro and Alcora.

In the 19th century a small porcelain industry arose in Spain, at Sevilla and Sarcadelos.

GERONA

A porcelain factory was established here in the 18th century.

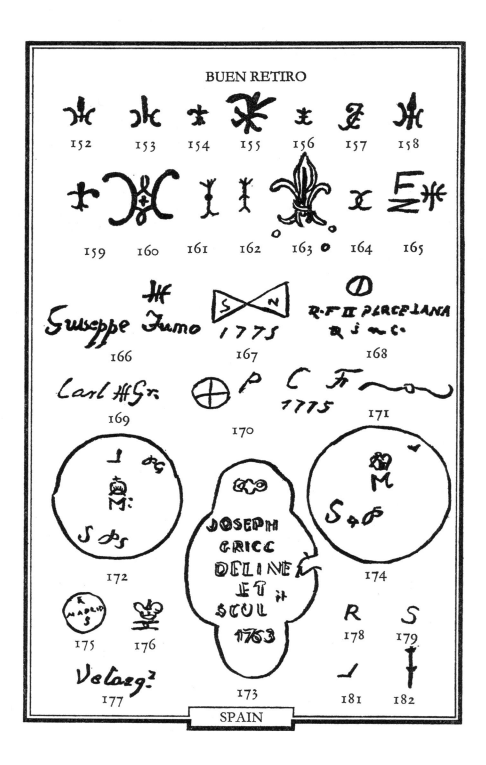

BUEN RETIRO

152   153   154   155   156   157   158

159   160   161   162   163   164   165

Guseppe Fumo   166   1775   167   R·F II PORCELANA R.S. en C.   168

Carl H Gr.   169   170   P C Fr. 1775   171

172   JOSEPH GRICC DELINE ET SCUL 1763   173   174

175   176   Velarg?   177   R 178   S 179   181   182

SPAIN

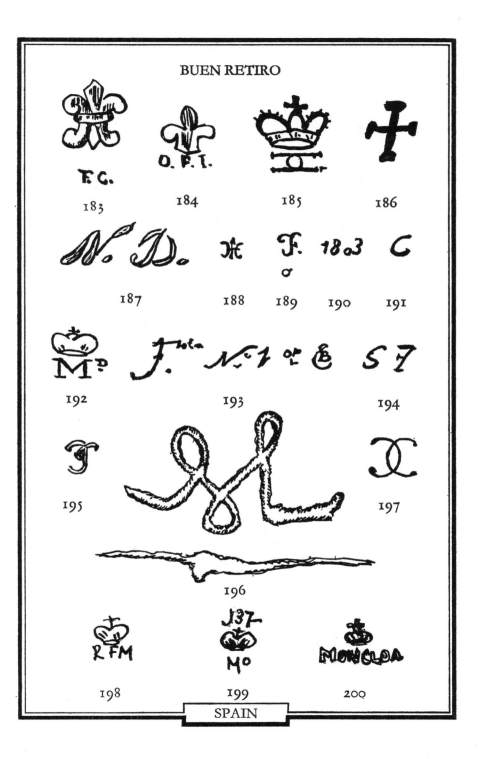

T. C.

183

O. P. T.

184

185

186

N. D.

187

188

F. 18∂3 C
σ

189 190 191

M.

192

J. ula N.º 1 e

193

5 7

194

F

195

X

197

196

R FM

198

J37
Mº

199

MONCLOA

200

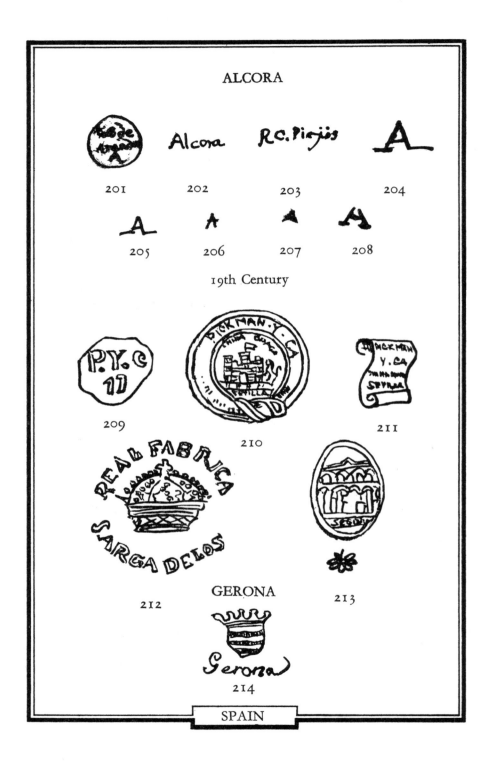

ALCORA

201 202 203 204

205 206 207 208

19th Century

209

210

211

212

213

GERONA

214

PORTUGAL

LISBON

A hard paste porcelain factory was founded in Lisbon at the end of the 18th century in 1773 by Bartolomeu Da Costa. Table services and tea-sets, as well as groups and statuettes in the Spanish and Italian manner, were produced.

VISTA ALEGRE

This factory was established in 1824 by José Ferreira Pinto Basto. The factory is still in operation. In the beginning Wedgwood produce was imitated, later pieces in Sèvres style were produced.

The painters, João Maria da Silva Fabre and Manuel de Morais and the modellers José Scorder and Anselmo Ferreira had worked there. The factory is still in operation.

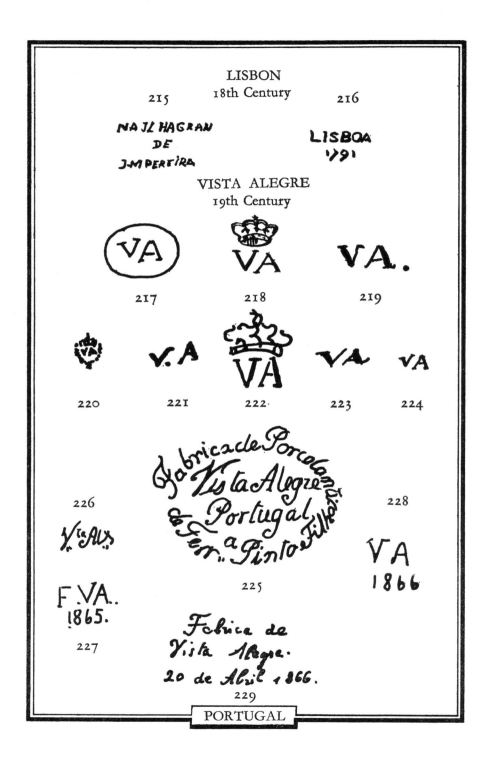

LISBON
18th Century

215

NA JL HAGRAN
DE
JM PEREIRA

216

LISBOA
'791

VISTA ALEGRE
19th Century

VA

217

VA

218

VA.

219

220

V.A

221

VA

222.

VA

223

VA

224

226

228

Fabrica de Porcelana
Vista Alegre
Portugal
a
Ferr.ª Pinto Filhos

VA
1866

225

V.ᵗᵉ Al.³

F.VA..
1865.

227

Fabrica de
Vista Alegre.
20 de Abril 1866.

229

PORTUGAL

28

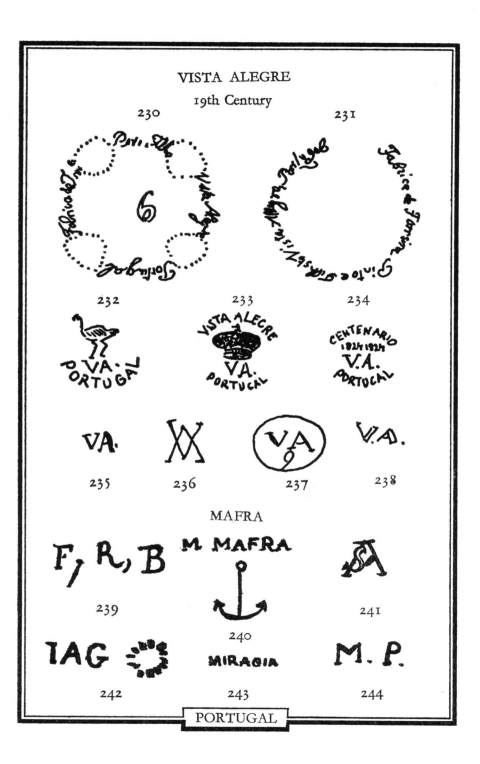

VISTA ALEGRE
19th Century

230   231

232   233   234

235   236   237   238

MAFRA

239   240   241

242   243   244

GERMANY

MEISSEN

The first man to produce hard paste porcelain in Europe was Johann Friedrich Böttger, who worked in close association with Ehrenfried Walter von Tschirnhausen. The last-named was a mathematician and physicist, who carried out a survey of the mineral deposits of Saxony by order of Augustus II. From 1699 onwards he experimented in an attempt to manufacture porcelain, but his efforts failed because he baked his hard paste mixture at insufficiently high temperatures.

Johann Friedrich Böttger was born at Schleisz in 1682, the son of a local banker. At sixteen years of age he was apprenticed to a Berlin apothecary to study medicine. He was attracted to the study of alchemy and tried to find the philosopher's stone. With its help he planned to turn base metal into gold, but was forced to leave Berlin precipitately because King Frederick I had ordered his imprisonment in a fortress for his activities in alchemy. He fled to Wittenberg, where he hoped to continue his studies, but was again threatened with prosecution and took refuge in Saxony. Here he was protected by Augustus II, who invited him to come to Dresden where a laboratory was placed at his disposal. A number of assistants were allotted to him, among whom was von Tschirnhausen.

In his search for gold Böttger melted down every mineral and all kinds of earths and in this way came to study ceramics. Von Tschirnhausen persuaded him to try his hand at the imitation of Delft pottery. For this purpose workers were imported from the Netherlands and a small factory was started, which was to become the famous Meissen factory. In 1706 the first pieces were produced by the Berlin potter Eggebrecht.

On the 28th March 1709 Schnorr brought to Böttger a kind of white earth which came from Aue and had been used for many years to powder wigs. This material was kaolin and had been known for a long time, but its use in the manufacture of porcelain had yet to be discovered. Experiments were made and on the 10th June the laboratory was moved to the Albrecht Castle. Here the first hard paste porcelain ever to be made in Europe was produced. From now on Böttger was kept under the strictest supervision as Augustus II feared that the secret might be discovered. The first porcelain produced by Böttger was of a reddish brown colour and very hard, it could be polished and sculpted. A number of ornamental pieces such as vases, pitchers, coffee- and tea-pots, cups, candlesticks, etc. were made. At first Chinese models were copied, but soon a new style developed under the influence of the art of the baroque silversmiths. Despite every precaution the secret of the new process soon leaked out. A number of scientists had come to Dresden and it was impossible to prevent all intercourse with the workmen employed in the factory. In 1718 the secret was known throughout Vienna.

The manufacture of white porcelain was begun in 1713. The paste was slightly yellowish in colour and the glaze sometimes had a greenish lustre. The models were the same as for the brown ware with moulded ornamentation. The painting on these early pieces was very primitive and executed in opaque colours. At a later date the colours were annealed. From this period dates a very beautiful opalescent violet. Still later pieces were richly decorated in gold and silver and with a black enamel paint. Figures and groups of this period are very rare and rather primitive.

No marks are found on these early pieces.

In 1720, Johann Gregorius Höroldt, the miniature painter, joined the new factory as manager. Under his leadership the products improved very much in quality and beauty of decoration. He at first copied Japanese models with so-called "Indian" flowers (Imari) and Chinese porcelain with decorations representing dragons, fantastic birds etc., on smooth surfaced vessels. In 1723 those gay paintings in gold or silver and later in brilliant and variegated colours, known as Chinoiseries began to appear. They are very vividly executed pictures of the carefree, fairylike existence of Eastern people according to the European conception. The monochrome pieces coloured yellow, red, violet and other colours with a space left free for Herold's decorative paintings belong to a slightly later date.

The first experiments with decoration in blue under glaze in imitation of oriental themes also seem to date from this period. During the period from 1730 to 1740 the miniature painter Höroldt and his pupils reached the zenith of their art. In wonderful friezes or medaillons, in intricate baroque cartouches with lattice and rocaille ornamentation, they painted scenes after Watteau, depicting gardens, seaports and rivers, hunting-scenes, cavalry-charges, battles and so on. Typical of this period is a lacy gilt pattern around the edges of plates, etc. with scattered flowers, while an opalescent violet was introduced in the painting of many pieces. In the period from 1720 to 1730 small services only were made, breakfast-, coffee- and tea-sets; large dinner services were not made until 1734.

From 1727 to 1733 the sculptor and modeller Kirchner worked at the Meissen factory. He modelled vases, clocks, candelabra and elaborate figure pieces for table decoration, such as wine-coolers and similar vessels and also animals and statuettes of the saints and apostles.

In 1731 the famous Court sculptor Kaendler was engaged as modeller. His creations, at first in the baroque style, but later in gay rococo, were revelations. In his first period he made life-sized pieces representing birds. The two artists, Höroldt and Kaendler, working in close collaboration, ushered in the golden period of the Meissen factory which reached the peak of its fame about 1750. Kaendler worked tirelessly till his death in 1775. His plastic art was of wonderful conception, full of life, grace and charm, a living source of inspiration for all European porcelain artists. His most famous works are the great service for Prince Sulkowski (1735–1738) executed in the baroque style of the goldsmiths of the period and the great Swan service for Count Brühl with wonderful rococo ornaments (1737–1741). From 1740 onwards he made figure pieces for table decoration and innumerable figures and groups of great charm and beauty. These groups include court ladies and gentlemen, the famous crinoline figures, loving shepherds and shepherdesses and all kinds of popular characters. The Gods, too, are represented among his works and there are many allegorical groups depicting arts and crafts, the months and the seasons. All these groups were

CAPODIMONTE. Sleeping fisherman and sweetheart. About 1750. Ht. 17 cm.
Victoria and Albert Museum, London

CAPODIMONTE. Cavalier and lady. About 1750. Ht. 14 cm.
Victoria and Albert Museum, London

DOCCIA. Cup with armorial and floral decoration. *Rijksmuseum, Amsterdam*

MEISSEN. Kuan-yin, after a Chinese model. About 1715. Böttger porcelain.
Staatliche Kunstsammlungen, Dresden

MEISSEN. The ape with the snuff-box.
Ht. 48 cm. *Rijksmuseum, Amsterdam*

MEISSEN. The ape with the snuff-box.
Ht. 47,7 cm. *Collection Dr. Erich Schneider,
Düsseldorf*

MEISSEN. The black ape. Ht. 42 cm.
Mark – *AR. Rijksmuseum, Amsterdam*

IV

originally designed as table decorations at festive banquets and were at first painted in brilliant colours under the influence of Höroldt; later they were executed in somewhat paler hues. Rococo groups are invariably mounted on a rocaille base. Kaendler's most famous assistants were the modeller Eberlein, who adhered to the baroque style, employed at Meissen 1735–1749, and that lover of the rococo Elias Meyer, employed at Meissen 1748–1761. About 1750 the factory was placed on a commercial footing and from that time onwards it produced services for domestic and every day use. These lacked originality and artistic merit, but all were executed in rococo style with decorations in relief. Höroldt remained at the factory, but created very few works of note. His painting during this period lacked the minuteness of detail of his earlier works. The Chinese and Indian subjects were replaced by German flowers and fruit. He frequently painted butterflies and insects but no longer created new designs. Foreign works were copied, especially engravings. The household ware produced was for the most part decorated in underglaze blue, usually with a pattern of China asters (Zwiebelmuster). Later such pieces were also decorated with German flowers.

The factory suffered greatly during the Seven Years War (1756–1763). The period from 1763–1774 is known as the point period, because during those years a point was added to the crossed swords mark used by the factory. This period marks the decline of painting and modelling at Meissen. The Far Eastern influence disappeared entirely and European influence, especially that of Sèvres, became noticeable. Characteristic of this period are the scale and bird patterns. In the year 1764 the sculptor Acier came to Meissen, where he remained till 1781. His works were executed in rococo style with a tendency towards the classical. They are often rather sentimental and show evidence of French influence. Typical of his work is the meticulous care in the representation of costumes, lace and other details. His best assistant was the sculptor Schönheit, who was engaged in 1745 and remained with the factory until 1794.

The next period (1774–1814) is named after Count Marcolini. He was the incarnation of the sober, academic, classical taste in art prevailing in his day. Under Marcolini's management the factory produced vases and other articles painted a deep blue with a space left free for miniature painting. Vienna and Sèvres models were copied. Typical of the period after 1780 are groups of white biscuit porcelain. The most important modeller of this time was Jüchtzer (1769–1812), who worked in the classical style, mostly from Grecian models. This period marks the end of the great school of modelling.

From 1814–1833 the products of the factory were executed in the Empire style with an excessive use of gold and colour. There was a very marked decline in taste and artistic value. During this period the modeller Rauch was working at Meissen and among his pieces was a statuette of Goethe. He was succeeded by Barre, who produced a large number of figures and groups, including a charming representation of the famous dancer Fanny Elsler.

The most prominent artist during the next period (1840–1860) was the sculptor Leuteritz who was strongly influenced by Kaendler and imitated his birds. Later he also made figures and groups.

From 1860 until 1890 the modellers Leuteritz, Hahnel, Ringler, Hirth and

Schott were working at Meissen. Hirth was the creator of the rather naïve and conventional groups of children. Schott modelled figurines in a pseudo-classical style. At the end of the 19th century the sculptor Andresen introduced the so-called Jugend style, Professor Sturm painted many vases and dishes in this manner. About 1920 Professor Scheurich modelled exquisite rococo figurines which are outstanding among ceramic products in Germany These fragile and subtle rococo figures seem to descend in a direct line from the creations of Bustelli, who was, in his way, a genius. Boerner modelled portraits and ultra-modern figurines and the modellers Esser and Langer depicted religious subjects and madonnas in an ultra-modern style.

MODELLERS

Johann Jacob Irminger, 1710–1726.
Kirchner, Johann Gottlieb, modeller 1727, chief 1731–1733.
Kaendler, Johann Joachim, 1731–1775.
Frietzsche, 1725
Lücke, Johann Chrisoph, 1728–29
Johann Friedrich Eberlein, 1735–1749.
Johann Gottlieb Ehder, 1739–1750.
Peter Reinicke, 1743–1768.
Friedrich Elias Meyer, 1762 in Berlin.
Carl Christoph Punct, 1761–1765.
Victor Acier, 1764–1779.
Walther, died 1763.
Johann David Elsasser, 1774–1807, arcanist.
Schönheit, Johann Carl, 1745–1794.
Christian Gottfried Juchtzer, 1769–1812.
Schiffner, Johann Gottlieb, about 1795.
Habenicht, Carl Gottfried, 1837–1849.
Ernst August Leuteritz, 1849–1886.
Emmerich Otfried Andresen, 1886–1902.
Erich Hösel, 1903.

MEISSEN PAINTERS

Auffenwerth, Johann, 1715–1728.
Beger, Joh. Gottfr. 1736–1786.
Petzoldt, Noah Ernst, 1721–1731.
Birkner, Gottlob Siegmund, 1726–1771.
Birnbaum, Johann Chr. August., 1743–1807.
Boehme, Carl. Wilhelm, 1736–1761.
Boehme, Joh. Tobias, 1729–1763.
Borrmann, Joh. Balthasar, 1742–61.
Brecheisen, Jos., 1765.
Birkner, Gottlob Siegmund, 1726–1771.
Busch, Chr. Daniel, 1741–45, 1765–1790.
Clauce, Johann Christoph, 1740–1752.
Clauce, Isaac Jacques, 1753.
Claus, flower-painter, 1786.

Kolmberger, Colmberg, Kolmberg, Peter, 1745–1779.
Dietrich, August Ferdinand, 1775–1786.
Dietrich, Joh. Christoph, 1728–1779.
Dietrich, Christoph Wilhelm Ernst, 1764–1770.
Dietze, Augustin, 1723–1740.
Donath, Ernst Friedrich, died 1826.
Eggebrecht, Carl Friedrich, 1741–1773.
Ehrlich, Carl Gottlob, 1763–1796.
Erbsmehl, Johann Gottlieb, 1722–1741.
Fehling, Karl Heinrich, 1743–1753.
Fleischer. Before 1746.
Foerster, Heinrich, 1753–1802.
Funke, Johann Georg, gilder, 1713–26.
Funke, until 1769.
Geissler, 1769.
Geissler, bluepainter, about 1775.
Gerlach, Johann Benjamin, 1728–1770.
Gotzsch, Johann Gottlieb, 1753–1786.
Grabs, Chr. Gottl., 1775.
Grahl, Carl Gottlieb, 1771–1782.
Grossmann, Christian Gotthelf, 1750–1766, 1774–1786.
Grünewald, Georg Wilh., 1775–1831.
Hahnemann, Johann Zacharias, 1763.
Hammer, bluepainter, 1775.
Hentzschel, Chr. Gottlob, 1739–1761.
Häuer (Hayer), Bonaventura Gottlieb, 1724–1782.
Haynemann, Chr. Adolf, 1762–1786.
Heerfurth, Chr., 1735–1786.
Heinrici, Johann Martin, 1741–1757, 1761–1786.
Heintze, Johann George, 1720–1749.
Hempel, bluepainter, 1775.
Henning, 1769.
Herrmann, J. Gott., 1727.
Herold, Christian Friedrich, 1725–1779.
Hitzig, till 1745.
Hoffman, Augustin, 1743–1751.
Hohorst, Peter, 1725.
Hottewitsch, Christian Gottlieb, 1801–1823.
Horn, Joh. Christoph, 1720–1760.
Höroldt, Johann Gregorius, 1720–1765.
Hunger, Christoph Conrad, 1717, 1727–1729.
Jahn, 1769.
Klinger, Johann Gottfried, 1726–1746.
Klipfel, Carl Jacob Christian, 1761–1763.
Knoch, Johann Leonard, 1725.
Kolmberger, bluepainter.
Köhler, David, 1706–1723. Inventor of a special underglaze-blue.
Krause, Johann Paul, 1727.

Kretzschmar, Johann David, 1731–1752.
Kühnel, Christian Friedr., 1740–1792.
Kühnel, Joh. Friedrich, 1784, last date.
Kühnel, Samuel Gottlieb, 1787, last date.
Lauch, 1725.
Lehman, Johann Gottlieb, 1725.
Lenz, Johann Friedrich, 1776–1812.
Leutner, Johann David, gilder, 1728–1741?
Lindemann, Chr. Ph. c. 1754, last date.
Lindner, Christian, birds, 1741–1806.
Lindner, bluepainter, 1775.
Löhnig, Joh. Georg, 1763–1806.
v. Löwenfinck, Christian Wilhelm, 1734–1741.
v. Löwenfinck, Adam Friedrich, 1727–1736.
v. Löwenfinck, Carl Heinrich, 1730–1735.
Matthaei, Chr. Ferd., 1775–1786.
Matthaei, Johann Gottlob, 1773–1795.
Mauksch, Joh. Carl, 1775–1821.
May, 1769.
Mayer, F. F., in Pressnitz (home decorator).
Mehlhorn, Johann Gottlieb, 1734–49.
Meerheim, David Conrad, 1711, arcanist.
Mehner, August, Johann, 1796–1832.
Moebius, sen. and jun., 1775.
Müller, 1769.
Nagel, Joh. Friedr., 1793–1825.
Nitsche, Chr., 1729.
Naumann, Chr. Gottlob, 1802–1860. c.
Otto, Johann Heinrich, animals, 1764–1775.
Pannasch, 1769.
Plesch, Chr. Wilh., 1736–1792?
Probshain, Johann Gottlob, 1746–1773.
Reinschberg, Johann Gottlob. c. 1743.
Richter, Christian Samuel Hieronymus, 1740–49.
Rögner, flowers, 1775–1786.
Richter, Chr. Samuel Hieronymus, died 1776.
Riedel, Gottlieb Friedrich, 1743–1756.
Rögner, 1775–1786.
Rudolph, bluepainter, 1775.
Schäffer, Johann Gottlob, 1731.
Schäffler, Johann Christoph, 1712.
Schatter, Dr. Johann Gottlieb, arcanist, 1737–1764.
Schaufuss, Heinrich Gotthelf, died 1838.
Schindler, Philipp Ernst, 1725–1765.
Schindler jun., Philipp Ernst, 1734–1750.
Schmidt, Johann Friedrich, 1742–1786.
Schneider, bluepainter, 1775.
Schönau, Johann Eleazar, 1773–1806. (Zeissig).

Schubert, Johann David, 1761–1822.
Schulz, August Traugott, 1754.
Schütze, Johann Carl, 1762.
Spittler, Johann Georg, 1729.
Stadler, Johann Ehrenfried, 1724.
Stechman, Johann David, 1712.
Stemmler, bluepainter, 1775.
Steinert, 1769.
Stöltzel, Samuel, arcanist, 1705–1719, 1720–1737.
Tannicen, Johann Samuel Friedrich (Tänich), 1747–1755.
Teichert, Johann Ferdinand, 1756–1789.
Thalwitzer, Johann Samuel, 1745.
Theil, 1775.
Thiele, Carl Christoph, 1740–1796.
Thiele, Carl Gottlieb, 1758–1811.
Thomas, 1769.
Tiebel, Johan Gottl. Friedrich, 1773–1796.
Töpfer, 1752.
Wagner, Johann Jacob, 1739–1797.
Wannes, Heinrich Christ, 1740–1752.
Walther, Christian Gotthold, 1738–1780.
Walther, Christian Gottlieb, 1776–1778.
Weller, David Friedrich, died 1789.
Wentzel, Johann Benj. jun., 1739–1778.
Wiedner, 1766.
Winkler, flowers, 1775.
Wolf, Heinrich August, 1758–1805.
Wolff, Johann Friedrich, 1724–1751.
Zschentsch, flowers, blue, 1786–1802.
Zschörner, 1769.
Zieger, Ferdinand August, 1781–1844.
Zimmermann, Johann Georg, 1729.

The porcelain factory of CARL THIEME in POTSCHAPPEL produced a number of perfect rococo imitations of Meissen, which were put on the market as real Meissen 18th century figurines.

From the middle of the 19th century HELENE WOLFSOHN in DRESDEN made a speciality of imitating AR Meissen porcelain. This firm had a large staff of painters who were specially trained to imitate this very valuable 18th century porcelain.

The firm of MEYERS and SON at DRESDEN was the greatest rival of Wolfsohn in the production of imitation Meissen porcelain. The firm used crossed swords with an M to mark its pieces.

DRESDEN

Franziska Hirsch used on her imitations of Meissen wares a mark similar to that of Samson.

BERLIN

MANUFACTURE DE PORCELAINE DE BERLIN

The first factory to be established in Berlin was founded in 1751 by Wilhelm Caspar Wegely, assisted by operatives from the factory at Höchst. He secured the services of the arcanist Reichardt and, in 1754, of the miniature painter Isaac Jaques Clauce. It was located in the Neue Friedrich Strasse. The paste used at this factory was a yellowish mass, very similar to that used at Meissen, and production mainly consisted of services in massive rococo style, very often unpainted, and vases, which were often copied from Sèvres or Meissen pieces, decorated with German flowers, Watteau pictures or painted dark red after the manner of the Höchst factory. The Berlin factory also produced a few figures of rather massive design, but sometimes not without charm. These were either unpainted or decorated in vivid colours.

The mark used was the letter W in underglaze blue together with numbers impressed in the clay. These are thought to indicate the type of paste used. This factory ceased operating in 1757.

AECHTE PORCELAINE MANUFACTURE

The second Berlin factory was established in 1761 by the merchant Johann Ernst Gotzkowsky. Soon after the end of Seven Years' War it was taken over in 1763 by king Frederick the Great, and became the "Königliche Porzellan Manufaktur", and was permitted to use the scepter as mark.

The services of Reichardt, Clauce, Friedrich Elias Meyer, Karl Wilhelm Böhme, Karl Jakob Christian Klipfel, Joachim Duwald, and 146 men working at the factory were retained.

The paste used during the early days of this factory was yellowish-grey in colour and from this material a large number of services, tea-sets and other pieces in the Meissen manner were produced by the modeller Friedrich Elias Meyer and several painters drawn from the Meissen factory. Typical products of this period are plain coffee-pots with a mask on the spout. The services produced at this time were handsomely decorated in relief.

In 1763, when the factory had fallen into debt, it was taken over by the King of Prussia as a State concern. The quality of the paste was improved and from 1770 onwards was very fine in texture, but of a cold, white shade. Beautiful vases were made, and services and other pieces were decorated with charming, original designs in relief, beautifully executed flower-paintings, and Watteau scenes. The Berlin factory is noted for its exceptionally fine flower-painting and for the modelling of its services. The most famous pieces produced during the first period of its existence as a State factory were the famous service for the royal palace at Potsdam (1765–1766) and the service for the palace at Breslau (1767–1768). This factory also made a speciality of pieces painted in one single colour, usually purple or red. From 1770 beautiful plain vases were produced with floral decoration in Sèvres style. After 1780 pieces were executed in the more formal classical style. After 1800 the Empire style was adopted with lavish use of gold and colour. Figures and groups were produced which, though of good quality, often lacked the charm and good taste of the products of Meissen and the South German factories.

The mark of the Gotzkowsky factory was the letter G, either in blue underglaze, or sometimes painted overglaze in blue, brown, black or gold.

The mark of the factory from 1763–1837 was a sceptre in underglaze blue. From 1837 to 1844 the letters K.P.M. were added. From 1844–1870 an eagle in various forms was employed, and in 1870 the sceptre mark was again introduced.

The chief modellers at the Berlin factory were Friedrich Elias Meyer (1761–1785) and his brother Christian (1766–1772) who made a service for the Empress Catherine of Russia (1770–1772). All the older figures, groups and table ornaments were made by these two craftsmen. Other noted modellers were Müller (1785–1789), Fr. Riese (1789–1834), who worked in the classical style from designs by Schadow and Genelli, and Wilhelm Riese (1834–1841).

The Lithophane process was a discovery of the Royal Porcelain Factory. This process involved the use of white biscuit plaques of varying thicknesses, which, when held against the light, formed pictures like those sometimes seen on Chinese porcelain. Cups were produced with their base decorated with portraits of famous people executed in this technique.

During the bombing raids on Berlin in World War II the Berlin factory in the Wegelystrasse in Moabit was totally destroyed.

BERLIN

PAINTERS AND MODELLERS

Bornemann, Johann Baptist Balthasar, 1761–1779.
Brecheisen, Joseph, 1748–1757.
Büttner, David Adam, 1762–1767.
Clauce (Gloss), Isaak Jacob, 1754–1757, 1761–1803.
Heinze, Johann George, 1749–
Horn, Johann August, 1762.
Klipfel, Karl Jacob Christian, 1763–1802.
Körner, Johann, modeller, 1769.
Lohse, Gottfried, 1762.
Meyer, Friedrich Elias, 1762–1785. Modeller.
Toscani, Carolus, 1762–1765.
Raschke, flower painter.

In 1905, Adolf Amberg modelled the table decorations for the wedding dinner of the Kronprinz Wilhelm and the princess Caecilia of Mecklenburg. The sculptor Hermann Hubatsch made the portraits of the queen Augusta Victoria and the dancer Ruth St. Denis. Both artists were expounders of the "Jugendstil". The well-known sculptor, professor Rudolf Marcuse, had also made some figurines for the factory.

After the destruction of the Berlin factory in 1943 a new one was established at Selb; the produce of the Selb factory was marked with a scepter in conjunction with the script S.

The factory is now rebuilt in Berlin.

HOECHST 1746–1796

This famous factory was founded by a group of Frankfurt merchants with the assistance of a porcelain painter from Meissen, Adam Friedrich von Löwenfinck. The paste used when the factory began producing was of a grey tint. The pieces turned out at the beginning were designed in rococo style and the earliest specimens were decorated with oriental flower designs, but before long the factory was producing pieces decorated with very fine German flower designs and multicoloured patterns after Meissen models. Also characteristic of this factory are landscapes painted in a single colour, usually crimson. The leading painter was Danhofer of Vienna, who worked at Höchst from 1749 onwards.

Among the many painters who have worked in Höchst are: Dieffenbach, Löwenfinck, F. K. Wohlfahrt, Heinrich Usinger, Zisler, Adam Ludwig, Philipp Gerhard Sommerlat, Joseph Angele, Johann Zeschinger, Joseph Johann Dissel, Johann Hackel, Ignaz Hess, Jakob Koch, Johann Carl Wagner and Johann Nikolaus Flach.

From 1758–1762 Gottlieb Christian Lücke, and from 1757–1758 Johann Friedrich Lück were employed as modellers.

The Höchst factory excelled in the production of figures, groups and portraits in relief. The earlier figures seem rather heavy, but from about 1754 some exceptionally fine rococo groups with very beautiful colouring were created.

Some ten years later Johann Peter Melchior began to make his graceful rather sentimental, but very life-like pieces depicting children and scenes from everday life. He also modelled groups representing Venus and Cupid and other mythological characters. These were very naturally depicted, devoid of any rococo influence and were painted in light harmonious colours. Melchior often designed the base of his pieces to represent moss-covered rocks. His works include a large number of portraits.

Melchior worked for the Höchst factory from 1764–1779. Two other notable modellers employed by the factory were Feylner (1749–1753) and Russinger (1754–1766).

The Höchst mark was a six-spoked wheel, with or without a crown, in underglaze blue. During the first period of the factory's existence this mark was applied on glaze in black, red, blue or gold. Sometimes it was impressed in the paste. In the second half on the 18th century the Höchst factory had a shop at the Hague.

There are numerous imitations of Höchst pieces. The old moulds of the Höchst factory came into the possession of the porcelain factory at Passau in 1850 and the management of this factory made use of the moulds in the production of imitations of many popular Höchst specimens. The pieces bore Höchst marks. An imitation patina was applied on the pieces to give them an antique appearance so that they could be sold as genuine pieces.

The woodcarved moulds used by Melchior were bought by the Heubach factory at Lichte in Schwarzburg-Rudolstadt.

FRANKENTHAL

This factory was established in 1755 by Paul Antoine Hannong, of Strasbourg, after he had been given two weeks in which to close down his porcelain works in France by order of Louis XV. The reason for this harsh decree was that the products of the Strasbourg factory offered serious competition to the soft paste porcelain of Vincennes. The pieces made during the first period of the Frankenthal factory were mostly similar to those made by Hannong at Strasbourg, and it seems likely that he had taken his old workers with him. In 1759 Paul Antoine was succeeded by his son Joseph Adam in the management of the factory, under whose leadership the products of Frankenthal speedily attained a perfection equal to the finest work of Meissen. Joseph Hannong himself worked as a modeller. J. W. Lanz was chief modeller from 1755–61. He excelled in the production of comedians, chinese, shepherds, groups, hunters and allegorical groups.

J. F. Lück worked as modeller from 1758–1764.

The modeller Carl Gottlieb Lück began working in the Frankenthal factory in 1757. His handiwork included figures representing courtiers, beggars, pedlars, labourers, shepherds and shepherdesses. He produced figurines and groups in chinese and rococo style. Konrad Link was employed as a modeller from 1762–1766, some very graceful allegorical and mythological groups and rococo figurines by this craftsman have come down to us.

In 1762 Joseph Hannong found himself in financial difficulties and sold the factory to the Elector Karl Theodor. Adam Bergdoll, formerly employed at the factory at Höchst became manager, while Link became chief modeller. In 1770 the factory secured the services of the Fürstenberg modeller, Simon Feylner, who soon became the soul of the factory. He invented a new blue known as "bleu céleste" which rivalled Sèvres. In 1777 the sculptor Adam Bauer was employed as modeller. He left in 1778. In 1779 the famous Höchst modeller Johann Peter Melchior was engaged, who specialised mainly in groups of children.

When French troops occupied Bavaria in 1795 the Frankenthal factory was leased to Peter van Reccum, who transferred it to Gruenstadt after the French left in 1800.

Towards the end of the 18th century many Hannong models from Strasbourg were produced by the factory with new bases and modern details. The flat Strasbourg base was replaced by a gilded rocaille base.

Painters as well as modellers put forth great efforts for the Frankenthal factory. Among them were Bernhard Magnus who painted battle scenes and landscapes, and S. Osterspey who painted Watteau scenes and Ovidian pastorals.

The hard paste used was of a warm yellowish tone in the early days of the factory, but towards 1780 it became greyish in colour. The products of Frankenthal were greatly influenced by Sèvres. Characteristic of the porcelain produced at this factory are the rich gilding and finely painted German flowers.

PAINTERS

Andrich, Rochus, 1780–82.
Apel, Michael, 1765–84.
Arnold, before 1772.

Arnold, Johann Samuel, 1780.
Bauer, Johannes, 1780.
Brandel, Johann Christian, 1767.
Braun, Johann, 1764, 1771.
Christfeld, Konrad, 1780.
Drach, Philipp, 1767, 1780.
Fretz, Johann Heinrich, 1756, 1782.
Gastel, Hiacinth, (?).
Glöckle (Klöckle), Michael, 1766–1799.
Handschuh, Andreas, 1768.
Handschuh, Karl Joseph, 1789–1799.
Hausmann, Karl, 1789–1799.
Henrici, Johann Martin, 1775.
Hermanni (Hermany), Georg Elias, 1775.
Herold, Philipp. 1777, 1780.
Hetterich, Georg, 1773–1799.
Hild, (?).
Höfel, Jakob, 1784.
Höflein (Höflen), Johann Jakob, 1761–1769.
Höflich, Gottfried, 1766.
Joch, (?), 1774.
Kaiser (Kayser), Bartholomäus, 1761–1799.
Kilian, (?), 1774.
Knüpfer, Christian, 1759.
Legrand, Anton, 1764, 1770.
Leyser (Leiser), Nikolaus, 1764–1774.
Magnus, Johann Bernhard, 1762–1798.
Marx, Sebastian, 1763–1789.
Mittmann, Nikolaus, 1756–1772.
Neuber, Chrysostomus, 1795.
Nierwein, (?), 1768, 1772.
Osterspei, Jakob, 1759–1782.
Öttner (Ettner), Andreas Philipp. 1759.
Quetscher, Michael, 1779.
Rachner, Johann Georg Konrad, 1766, 1780.
Riedel, Gottlieb Friedrich, 1757–1759.
Roth, (?), Johann Gottlieb, 1748.
Schneider, Johann Georg, 1767.
Steinkopf, Johann Friedrich, from 1759.
Stocksberger, Johann Adam, 1756.
Taennich (Tönnich), Johann Samuel, 1757.
Wannewitsch, Johann Georg, 1757.
Weber, Franz Joseph, ca. 1767, 1769, 1770.
Weißbrodt, Friedrich, Prof., 1767–1772.
Weißbrodt, Karl, 1770–1778.
Wingerstein, (?), 1764–1781.
Wohlfahrt, Friedrich Karl, 1766.

The original Frankenthal mark was an impressed shield with lozenges. A blue lion underglaze, sometimes with the letters P H impressed in the paste was used. Occasionally impressed letters alone were used as mark. In Joseph Hannong's time the mark was the Palatine lion with the monograms J H or J A H in blue underglaze.

When the Elector Palatine bought the factory, his monogram C T with the crown in blue underglaze replaced the lion and was used until 1795. After the factory was taken over by Peter van Reccum the Electoral initials and crown were replaced by his own initials. Very often initials, numbers and names are all found together on the Frankenthal pieces. They are easily identified with the aid of the list of painters.

In 1850 some of the Frankenthal moulds were sent to the Bardollo factory at Grünstadt, while others went to the museum at Speyer. The rest of the moulds were acquired by the Nymphenburg factory which used them again. The new figures produced were, however, marked with an additional Nymphenburg mark to prevent their being sold as genuine Frankenthal pieces.

LUDWIGSBURG

The first Ludwigsburg factory was established in 1736 by Joh. Ph. Weiszbrodt. The second factory was established by the merchants Zahn and Dörtenbach at Calw.

Weiszbrodt who had left the factory went to England. He was recalled in 1758, and received as porcelain painter of the official Ludwigsburg factory 600 florins annually.

LUDWIGSBURG 1758–1824

This factory, which was established by Duke Carl Eugen of Württemberg, was successfully managed by Ringler (1759–1804) who came from the Vienna works.

The paste used was of a yellowish-grey tint. The products of Ludwigsburg include delightful rococo table-ware and vases, decorated with a rocaille ornament in relief often completely covering the entire piece and heightened with purple. The pieces are beautifully painted in the prevailing style of the period and the colours, though rather dull, are very harmonious. Characteristic of this factory are very artistic and richly decorated rococo vases standing on three feet. Table ornaments in the manner of Meissen were also made. At a later date the more formal, classical style was adopted, to be followed, in course of time, by the empire style.

The art of modelling figures and groups was very highly developed at Ludwigsburg. At first these were made in rococo style on rocaille bases which were usually left white, though sometimes they were very beautifully painted. The painters employed at this factory included Riedel (1759–1779) who came from Meissen, Steinkopf (1758–1776), Danhofer from Höchst (from 1759 onwards) and Kirschner from about 1770–1784.

The leading modeller was W. Beyer (1762–1764). Lejeune, who modelled the famous series of musicians, worked at Ludwigsburg for ten years from 1768–1778. Feretti (1762–1772) designed some very fine mythological and allegorical groups in the classical style. The modeller Louis is credited with some excellent statuettes of animals. Models of the famous sculptors Joh.

Heinrich Dannecker and Philipp Jacob Scheffauer, both of whom were born in Stuttgart, were reproduced.

The Ludwigsburg mark from 1758 to 1793 was a double letter C in underglaze blue with or without a crown. During the ten years from 1793 to 1803 a letter L was employed, often without the crown, together with three antlers. From 1803 to 1816 the monogram F R with or without a crown, was used as mark. From 1816 onwards the mark consisted of the letters W R, sometimes crowned.

LUDWIGSBURG MODELLERS

Johann Carl Vogelmann, 1759–1764.
Johann Göz, 1759–1762.
Joseph Nees, 1759–1767.
G. F. Riedel, 1759–1779, chief painter.
Jean Jacques Louis, 1762–1772.
Johann Christoph Haselmeyer, 1760–1771.
Johann Christian Wilhelm Beyer, 1759–1767.
Joseph Weinmüller, 1765–1767.
Pierre François Lejeune, 1753–1778, premier sculpteur, professor of the "Académie des Arts".
Johann Heinrich Schmidt, 1766–1821.
Adam Bauer, 1770–1777.
Johann Valentin Sonnenschein, 1767–1775.
Johann Heinrich Dannecker, 1780–1790, and later.
Philipp Jakob Scheffauer, 1790–1800.

The old moulds of the Ludwigsburg factory were sent first to Regensburg. In 1850 the Amberg factory took them over and produced some very poor imitations of Ludwigsburg porcelain.

NYMPHENBURG

In the year 1747 the Elector Max Joseph III of Bavaria married Princess Maria Anna Sophia of Saxony. In the same year a small factory was started at Neudeck, with the experienced master potter Johann Baptist Niedermayer at its head. By 1754 it had become important enough to be included in the Electoral Mint and Mines Administration. In the following year the Italian sculptor and modeller Franz Bustelli joined this factory where he was to remain till his death in 1763. He was the creator of many famous figures – slim graceful ladies and gentlemen, who seem to dance through life; the actors of the Italian comedy, the lifelike craftsmen, the capricious, loving couples. He was also responsible for some admirable putti.

In 1761 the factory was moved to the castle of Nymphenburg with Count Haimhausen as the sole manager. Bustelli was succeeded by the Court modeller Dominicus Auliczek (born 1734) who, however, cannot be compared with his predecessor as an artist. He mostly imitated the work of foreign artists, such as, for example, the medaillon portraits of Schega. Among his best works are his hunting scenes.

Towards the close of the century new inspiration was introduced into the work of the factory with the engagement in 1797 of the Frankenthal modeller Johann Peter Melchior, who specialised in classical pieces and portraiture.

His pupil was Adam Clair, who had very little original talent and mostly copied his master. Melchior died at Nymphenburg on the 13th June 1825.

In 1810 the factory was reorganized by the Crown Prince Ludwig, who almost entirely abolished modelling as practised by Melchior, but cultivated the art of painting on porcelain. The best known painters of this period are Anton Auer and Christian Adler. During this period the factory was under the management of Joseph Claudius von Schwerin. The abandonment of modelling proved disastrous to the reputation of Nymphenburg, which gradually declined in importance until it was sold in 1862 to a private purchaser.

As a rule the Nymphenburg factory marked its products with the Bavarian shield with lozenges. However, there are some small variations in the mark, which are important for the purpose of dating pieces. It is possible to date the products of Nymphenburg more precisely than those of any other factory. The first mark used was a hexagram (not a pentagram as is usually stated) in blue underglaze together with some letters and ciphers which probably represent a chemical formula. This mark was used after the factory was moved to Nymphenburg Castle. These chemical or alchemical formulae are sometimes found without the hexagram, but only on small pieces on which the bigger mark could not be used. Together with the above mentioned marks a very small shield with lozenges having very sharp edges was impressed in the paste. Later, possibly from 1756, a somewhat larger shield was used and from its less well defined contours this latter one would appear to have been made of wood, like the stamps used by the Vienna factory. This stamp was always used with the hexagram. After 1761, when the factory was moved to Nymphenburg Castle, the impressed shield was used with no other marks. This mark is found on all pieces dating from 1761 to 1765, – the best period of Nymphenburg – particularly on pieces by Franz Bustelli. From 1766 up to the end of the 18th century another mark was used, again a shield with lozenges impressed in the paste, but somewhat smaller in size and with slightly different contours. During this period the factory sometimes used the old blue hexagram mark again. Towards the end of the century several other marks were used, one of which was a St. Andrew's cross with lozenges, while another was an oval shield with lozenges. These marks were used on only a few pieces. About 1780 a new shield with lozenges was introduced, this time in the shape of a target. This mark was used by Johann Peter Melchior and his pupil Adam Clair. From 1810–1850 the more conventional heraldic form was used, the lozenges, however, running from lower right to upper left. From about 1850 until the factory was sold by the Government, a small shield surmounted by a five-pointed star appeared on Nymphenburg pieces.

In 1888 it became the property of Kommerzienrat Albert Bäuml whose descendants are now operating this famous factory.

The first number of the weekly "Jugend" was published at Munich in january 1896. The "Jugendstil", a sophisticated style akin to the "Modern Style" in England and "Art Nouveau" in France originated in the same period, owes its name tot his weekly. The "Jugendstil" deeply influenced the applied arts and the produce of the Nymphenburg factory.

The following artists worked from 1900 at the famous factory: Louis Levallois, H. E. von Berlepsch and Adalbert Niemeyer. The modellers: Willi Zügel, Hans Behrens, August Göhring, Wilhelm Neuhäusser and Theodor Rainer. They made figures of birds and animals, decorated in colours underglaze. Joseph Wackerle, who was attached in 1902 to the Nymphenburg factory, was an expounder of the Jugendstil, but was ultimately the first to break its narrow bounds. Wackerle died in 1959.

After World War I the following artists worked for the factory: Josef Hillebrand, Prof. Wolfgang von Wersin and prof. Hermann Kaspar.

Resl Lechner, Johanna Runzli, Maria Delago, Louise Terletzki-Scherf, and the Sicilian sculptor Emilio Greco worked for the factory from the second half of the fifties.

ANSBACH

This factory was set up in the old pottery works at Ansbach by command of the Hohenzollern Margrave Christian Friedrich Karl Alexander of Brandenburg – in which principality the present Bavarian town of Ansbach was then situated – in 1758. A number of porcelain workers from Meissen were engaged to operate the new factory.

In 1763 the plant was moved to the Margrave's hunting lodge at Bruckberg near Ansbach. The manager at this time was Johann Friedrich Kaendler, a cousin of the famous modeller of Meissen, Johann Joachim Kaendler. He was the creator of the beautifully modelled groups and figurines of which the principal characteristic is the large, straight nose. Johann Melchior Schöllhammer was engaged as chief painter, assisted on landscapes by Johann Stenglein, who had worked in France and on flower painting by Kahl and Schreitmüller.

The famous modeller Laut succeeded Kaendler as manager of the factory. From his hand are the small figurines, mostly distinguished by rather puffy eyes which give them a comical expression; the modeller Scherber assisted Laut. After the principality of Ansbach was annexed to Prussia in 1791, an abortive effort was made to merge the Berlin and Ansbach factories.

Under the management of Schöllhammer the Ansbach works prospered for a short period following 1793. Then in 1806 the principality came under Bavarian rule and the factory was sold by auction the following year. Production ceased about 1860.

Little is known of the chronological sequence in which the various marks on Ansbach products were used. These were: a heraldic shield or an eagle in underglaze blue, both always used in conjunction with the letter A, also in underglaze blue; the letter A alone, and a coat of arms impressed in the paste. The mark A with the heraldic device of a brook with three fishes was used during the period 1758–1762, when the factory was situated in the town of Ansbach. When the plant was moved to the hunting lodge at Bruckberg the use of the town's coat of arms was probably discontinued. On the other hand it has been noted that all the figurines were marked with the coat of arms. It would appear that during 1782 and 1785 the A alone was used and it is probable that this mark was in use after the date of the removal to Bruckberg. The letter A does not stand for Ansbach as is generally thought, but refers to the Margrave Alexander (1757–1791) who encouraged the manufacture of porcelain. The official designation of the town of Ansbach during that period was Onolzbach.

The Brandenburg eagle in underglaze blue in conjunction with the letter A was probably used only during the first period. It was probably found to be too intricate when production increased. At any rate this mark was used during a short period only and is very rarely found. The fourth mark, a shield impressed in the paste, seems to have been used only on groups and figurines.

FÜRSTENBERG

This factory was established under the patronage of the Duke of Brunswick by porcelain craftsmen from Höchst. It began by producing services and other pieces in rococo style with decoration in relief in the style of Meissen, Berlin and other German factories.

The hard paste used in the early products of Fürstenberg (1747–1770) was of a greyish colour and the glaze was often faulty. In 1753 the arcanist J. Benckgraff from Höchst improved the paste. The painting, however, was very carefully executed. Some very fine vases, decorated with floral designs or scenes after Watteau, were produced during this period.

The best period of the Fürstenberg factory was from 1770–1790, when the paste used was very much improved. Some very charming flower paintings were produced during this period, often on vases copied from Sèvres or Wedgwood models. From 1769–1790 the works was managed by J. G. Kohls.

From 1795–1814 the factory was managed by a Frenchman named Gerverot who introduced the empire style. After his departure the activities of Fürstenberg were confined to very simple pieces. In 1859 the factory came into private ownership.

The leading painters employed by this factory were Zeschinger, who worked there from 1753 onwards, Oest and Brüning, who painted for Fürstenberg between 1797 and 1855 and J. F. Weitsch.

The modellers were Feylner (1753–1770), Rombrich (1758–1794), Luplau (1765-1776), the Frenchman Desoches (1769-1774) and Schubert (1778-1804). The factory never excelled in the production of groups and figures but its vases are justly famed. Desoches made interesting biscuit groups and Schubert was responsible for some charming equestrian statuettes.

The Fürstenberg mark – which is still in use – is a letter F in underglaze blue. The biscuit groups were marked with a jumping horse impressed in the paste.

The factory is still working, and now produces mostly tea-sets and table-services which are noted for their careful modelling.

FULDA

This factory was established by the Prince Bishop von Bibra and operated between 1765 and 1790.

It employed a very fine, white paste. The production of this factory consisted principally of tableware adorned with very tasteful and graceful designs of flowers and fruit, earlier pieces being in rococo style, while later ones were executed in the more formal style introduced towards the end of the 18th century. Johann Valentin Schaum and Wenzel Neu were attached to the factory, as well as G. L. Bartholome and J. G. Schumann.

Specimens of the plastic art of this factory are of great artistic value. Graceful figures were produced as well as very natural groups in rococo style on a white rounded base, resembling the best Frankenthal products.

The painting was particularly artistic and colourful. Figures produced at Fulda are very rare and valuable. The mark generally used was a double F in blue underglaze, usually with a crown, though this was sometimes omitted. Occasionally a plain cross in blue underglaze was employed.

VOLKSTEDT-RUDOLSTADT 1760

This factory was founded by Macheleid under the patronage of Prince Johann Friedrich von Schwarzburg-Rudolstadt and is still in existence. Between 1767 and 1800 it worked under the management of Nonne. It has been operated by a limited company since 1899.

The paste used in the early days was very grey, but the quality was gradually improved until a fine white material was evolved.

Up to 1800 production mainly comprised ordinary tableware and other articles in common use. These were of massive design and decorated in rococo style. In addition this factory produced a few services of superior quality, artistically decorated and beautifully, though sparingly, painted in delicate colours. In some instances a single colour only was employed, usually purple or red. Very beautiful vases in formal style were produced as well as figures in a somewhat heavy rococo style. Groups and portrait-busts were also made, but these are of no artistic value. A speciality of this factory was a multicoloured plaque, bearing a portrait-bust in relief with rococo-decoration.

The original factory mark was a two-pronged pitchfork in blue underglaze. From about 1767 two crossed pitchforks were used and this mark, like the Meissen sword mark, is greatly sought after. From 1787 a single fork was used and, from 1804 onwards, the letter R in blue under glaze.

Figures produced at Volkstedt-Rudolstadt usually bear no marks.

The factory's style is now Staatliche Thüringer Porzellan Manufactur Vorm. Älteste Volkstedter G.M.B.H.

KLOSTER VEILSDORF

This factory was originally built by Prince Friedrich Wilhelm Eugen von Hildburghausen, who employed the arcanist Meyer, at Veilsdorf in 1760. It was the property of the Greiner family from 1797 until 1832 and has been operated by a company since 1884.

A charming collection of Commedia dell' Arte figures was modelled, these were copied from drawings by Johann Jacob Schübler.

At first a greyish paste was employed, but later the quality was very much improved and a very fine material of a warm white tint was evolved.

Very attractive and tasteful table ware was produced at Veilsdorf, decorated in rococo style and painted with figures, floral designs and landscapes. Some very fine vases, often painted with designs of fruit, were produced and many pieces bear monochrome paintings in purple, among which the most famous are the romantic tableaux. Oriental motifs were also used in decoration.

48

From 1780 until well into the next century services were made in classical style.

The Veilsdorf craftsmen developed the art of modelling to a very high degree. Their rustic scenes were greatly in demand and the decoration with flowers in the German manner is characteristic of their work.

The factory mark was a monogram of the letters C V in underglaze blue in varying forms. Pieces bearing the early mark – a coat of arms between the letters C V in underglaze blue – are very rare. From 1797 a three-leaved clover in underglaze blue was also employed. The figures and groups bear rarely marks.

WALLENDORF

This factory is still in existence. It was founded in 1763 by Hammann, and remained in possession of this family until 1863. At present it is operated by a limited company. In the early days china of poor quality was produced in rococo style. In the later period a more formal style was adopted, and a few carefully decorated services of superior quality were made.

Subsequently the mass production of blue china was introduced. Landscape painting executed in purple and later in brown and black was the usual decoration employed by this factory. At the end of the 18th century, black and blue porcelain was made with multicoloured paintings in the spaces left blank. Brown glaze was often employed. Coffee cups without handles were made for export to the Levant.

A number of figures of little artistic merit were made. The best of these were rustic figures, painted in delicate colours or left white, and usually bearing no marks.

The factory mark was the letter W in blue under glaze. In the early days this closely resembled the Meissen sword mark, but from 1780 onwards a smaller Wallendorf mark, no longer tending to imitate the Meissen mark, was adopted.

KASSEL

This factory was established by the Landgrave of Hesse and was operated from 1766 to 1788. China of plain design for every day use, including coffee- and teapots painted in many colours, were made, but the main production consisted of ordinary ware decorated in underglaze blue. Some unpainted figures including groups and animals, were made during a short period only, but these are of no importance. I. G. Pahland worked for the factory.

The factory mark was usually a lion or sometimes the letters H. C. (Hesse-Cassel).

PFALZ–ZWEIBRÜCKEN, GUTENBRUNN 1767–1775

This factory was established in 1767 by Dr. Stahl under protectorate of the duke Christian IV. Services and figures were produced.

NASSAU–SAARBRÜCKEN, OTTWEILER

This factory was established in 1765 by Pellevé of Sincény, the merchant Wagner and Isaac Wille. For a short time the famous modeller Paul Louis

Cyfflé worked for the factory. The establishment was patronized by duke Wilhelm Heinrich von Nassau. It was operated until c. 1777. The produce was very artistic.

GERA

This factory was established in 1779 under the protection of Prince Henry Reuss but was sold to the family Greiner in 1780. It subsequently changed hands many times but still exists to-day. During the first twenty years of the factory's existence the paste used was grey in colour and not very pure and the glaze was greenish. Inferior china was made in formal style as well as a good deal of blue porcelain. Better quality china from this factory is rare. During the early 19th century presentation cups were made.
The factory mark was the letter G in blue under glaze.

SCHNEY

Established in 1780, this factory is still in existence. The production consisted of ordinary table ware, usually blue, and coffee cups for the Levant.
The mark was the letter S in blue under glaze or the word "Schney" impressed in the paste. Later a cross over the letter S in blue under glaze was introduced.

RAUENSTEIN

This factory was established in the old castle of Rauenstein in 1783 by permission of the Duke of Saxe-Meiningen. The founders were the brothers Greiner. The factory is now operated by a limited company.
At first a grey paste was used and production consisted of interior china and coffee cups for export to the Levant. Services of better quality, decorated in the classical style, were produced.
The factory mark was the letter R with or without a star, in blue under glaze. In the 19th century the letters R-n were used in blue under glaze or in purple on glaze.

WÜRZBURG

On 7th November 1775 the Prince Bishop of Würzburg, Adam Friedrich von Seinsheim, granted a concession to Johann Kaspar Geyger, Ecclesiastical Councillor, for the erection of a factory for the manufacture of porcelain and faience. Despite the fact that early books on porcelain have recorded the Würzburg mark as being a mitre, no specimens bearing this mark have ever been found. In fact, Geyger died five years after receiving the concession. Some figurines were made, and a violet four-dotted pattern was favoured. A few pieces, dating from 1775 to 1780, decorated with views of Würzburg, have, however, been collected in that town. These bear the mark WB in black over glaze which, by analogy with other faience factory marks (e.g. NB for Nürnberg, KB for Künnersberg), may well be interpreted as Würzburg.

RATISBON (REGENSBURG)

Towards the end of the 18th century Dominicus Auliczek, a son of the Nymphenburg modeller, started a factory at Ratisbon which operated until 1860. This factory was admirably equipped but produced only cheap ware.

During the 18th century several painters were employed in Ratisbon on the decoration of coffee cups, most of which were produced by the Wallendorf factory for export, mainly to the Danubian countries.

An interesting specimen of the work of one of these men, who may have been a goldsmith by trade, has been preserved. It bears the mark B R G R.

GOTHA

The Gotha factory, established by W. von Rotberg in 1757, is still in existence. In 1802 it was sold to Crown Prince Augustus of Gotha and in 1805 it was leased and later sold outright to E. Henneberg.

This factory used a cream coloured paste with translucent glaze. Very beautiful china was produced at Gotha, including exceptionally fine breakfast services in rococo style and, later, in a graceful classical style.

The figure painting on these pieces was particularly well executed and they were often decorated with gold and floral designs. From 1790 onwards landscapes painted in sepia were carried out and cups were adorned with black silhouette designs framed in gold.

The factory mark was an R in blue under glaze. From 1790 the letters R G under glaze were employed and in 1805 the mark was again changed to "Gotha" in black or red over glaze, occasionally varied by G under glaze in black, red or yellow.

KELSTERBACH AM MAIN

Established by the Landgrave of Hessen-Darmstadt, and managed by the arcanist Christian Daniel Busch.

This factory, which operated from 1758–1768, used a paste of a yellowish tint. Production was small and included very good table china decorated with flowers and designs in relief, and lifelike figurepieces, usually unpainted and executed in the manner of Meissen or, more often, of Frankenthal and Nymphenburg.

The first modeller of the factory was Johann Carl Vogelmann, he was succeeded in 1766 by P. A. Seefried from the Nymphenburg factory who copied there the figurines of Bustelli.

In 1768 the factory was closed and was reopened under the management of J. J. Lay in 1789. The produce was a close imitation of Höchst and Meissen models; production ceased in 1802. J. M. Höckel has also worked here.

The factory mark consisted of the letters H D with a crown either under glaze or impressed in the paste. The letters H D were also used without the crown in blue under glaze.

BRANDENBURG

One of the chief assistants of Böttger of Meissen left that factory in 1713 and offered his services to the King of Prussia who had built a small factory near the town of Brandenburg. The inferior china produced here became known by the name of Brandenburg china and was exhibited at the Leipzig Fair from 1717 to 1723.

GROSSBREITENBACH

This factory, which still exists, was established by Major von Hopfgarten in 1779, who sold it to Greiner in 1782, when it became a branch of the Limbach factory. The production closely resembled that of Limbach and as the same marks were used it is not possible to distinguish between the products of the two factories.

LIMBACH

This factory still exists. It was founded in 1762 by Greiner and is now operated by a limited company. The paste used in the early days was yellow and the quality did not improve until the beginning of the 19th century, when both paste and glaze became very fine and white. Production consisted mostly of common table ware, decorated in blue or purple. About 1780 very beautifully decorated vases were produced, and pieces turned out during the first half of the 19th century were very carefully painted and gilded. The factory was very successful with the production of figures, usually representing rustic characters or the middle class types met in small towns. They were painted in many colours.

The factory mark consisted of a monogram of the letters LB or two crossed L's, usually in purple or red on glaze, but occasionally in black. On blue porcelain the crossed L was employed with a star in blue under glaze, closely resembling the Meissen Marcolini mark. From 1787 a three-leaved clover was used in blue under glaze and later in gold, black, purple or green on glaze.

ILMENAU 1777

This factory still exists. It was founded by von Gräbner under the patronage of Duke Carl August of Weimar. In 1782 it came under the management of that prince, who purchased it in 1786, and leased it first to Greiner, and later to Nonne. In 1808 it came into private hands, and since 1871 has been operated by a limited company.

In the early days of this factory the paste and glaze used were of poor quality. Common table ware, mostly tea and coffee-sets, was produced in a formal style. From the beginning of the 19th century the quality of paste and glaze was much improved. A number of presentation cups were made, decorated with views of Thuringia. Records show that figures have been made, but none are known to exist. Small portrait busts were made from 1800 onwards. Several factory marks were employed. A letter I in blue under glaze was used after 1792; before that date a single J or two J's crossed were used and, during a short period, a three-leaved clover in blue under glaze. The single J was used during the 19th century.

BLANKENHAIN

This factory was established in 1790. It produced ordinary china, usually patterned in blue.

The factory mark, still in use, is a striped shield bearing the word "Weimar" in blue under glaze.

TETTAU

This factory, which was established in 1794 produced ordinary china decorated with simple designs. Some services of finer quality were also made. The Tettau mark is a T in blue or purple over glaze.

EISENBERG

This factory, established in 1796, is still in existence. Plain table ware and blue china were produced, and also some beautifully painted services of finer quality.

The mark originally used was the letter E; subsequently the mark was changed to the letters SPM in blue under glaze.

ROSENTHAL

The Rosenthal porcelain factory was established in 1879 by Philip Rosenthal at Selb. During its first period the factory chiefly decorated porcelain for other plants. In 1891 the Rosenthal factory began to produce on a larger scale, mostly services and coffee- and tea-sets. From 1897 the works rapidly expanded.

Rosenthal established factories at Kronach, Marktredwitz and Waldenburg. Rosenthal porcelain is carefully modelled and decorated. The porcelain tea- and coffeesets competed successfully with the best German factories. After World War I modellers and sculptors of note were attached to the factory, among them the sculptor Scheurich, who designed some very beautiful figurines. Rosenthal also made modern porcelain jewelry, such as necklaces and bracelets.

Marks in greyish green printed above glaze.

SCHWARZBURGER WERKSTÄTTEN FÜR PORZELLANKUNST

Works were established at Unterweisbach, Schwarzburg-Rudolstadt and Volkstedt. The factory was founded at the end of last century. It produced very artistic tableservices, coffee and teasets. Many well known sculptors have worked for this plant among whom Ernst Barlach. Groups and figures as well as animal statues and birds were produced. The mark is an impressed fox, sometimes in black or blue under glaze.

PÖSZNECK

This factory, founded in 1799, is still in existence. It produces plain china, porcelain of better quality and blue china.

The factory mark is a shield with an arm holding a sword, painted under or on glaze, or impressed in the soft paste.

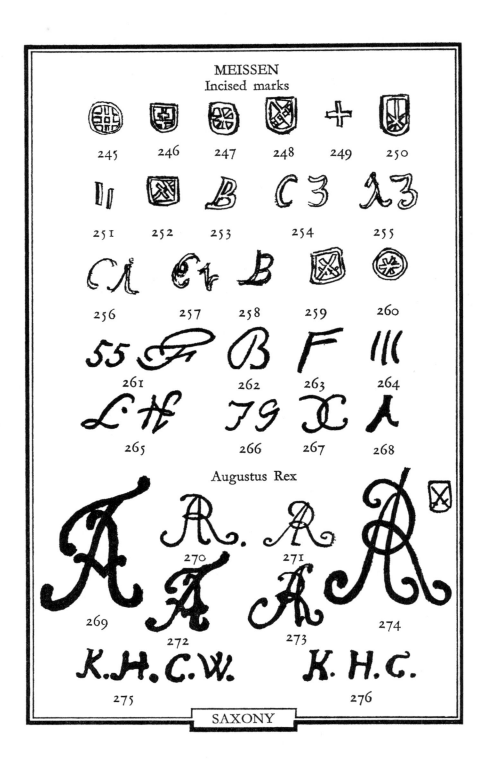

MEISSEN
Incised marks

245 246 247 248 249 250

251 252 253 254 255

256 257 258 259 260

261 262 263 264

265 266 267 268

Augustus Rex

269 270 271 272 273 274

275 276

SAXONY

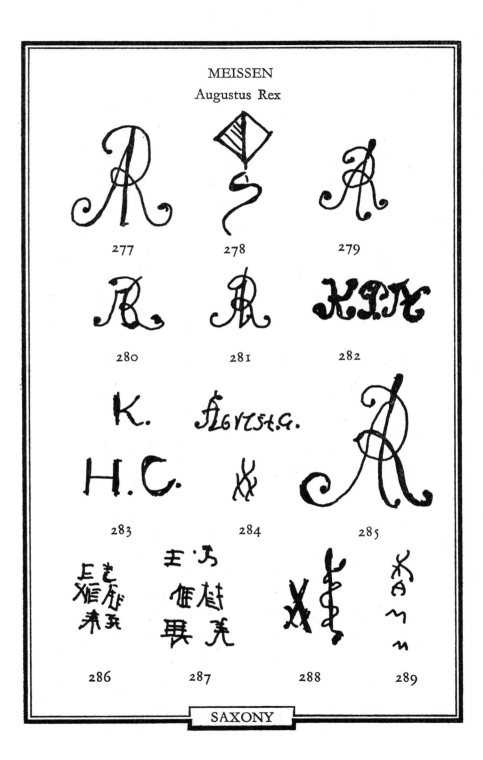

MEISSEN

Augustus Rex

277   278   279

280   281   282

283   284   285

286   287   288   289

SAXONY

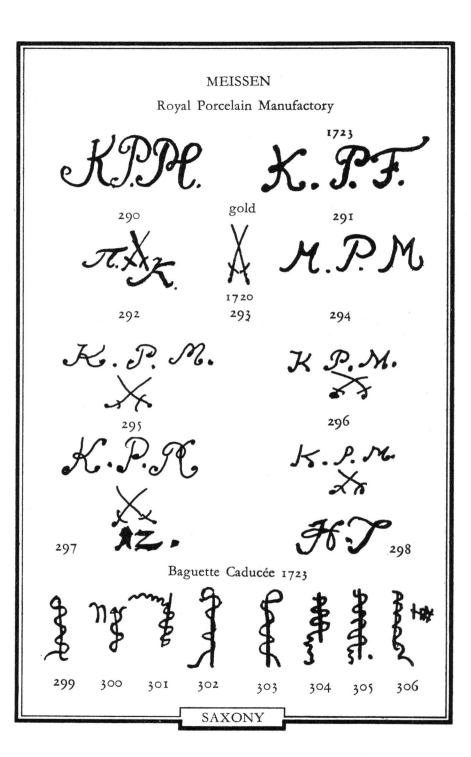

MEISSEN
Royal Porcelain Manufactory

290   gold   1723   291

292   293   294

1720

295   296

297   298

Baguette Caducée 1723

299   300   301   302   303   304   305   306

SAXONY

MEISSEN

Imitations of Chinese marks 1723

307 308 309 310 311

312 313 314 315 316

318 319 320

317 321 322 323 324

Swords marks 1725–1730

325 326 327 328 329

330 331 332

SAXONY

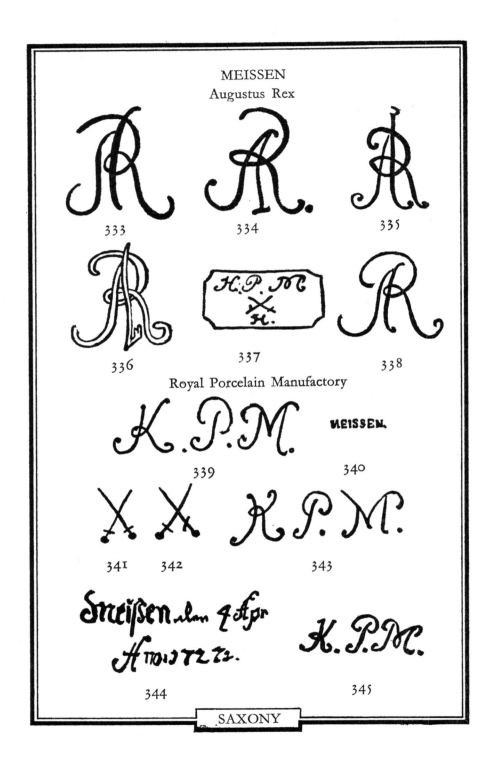

MEISSEN
Augustus Rex

333   334   335

336   337   338

Royal Porcelain Manufactory

339   340

341   342   343

344   345

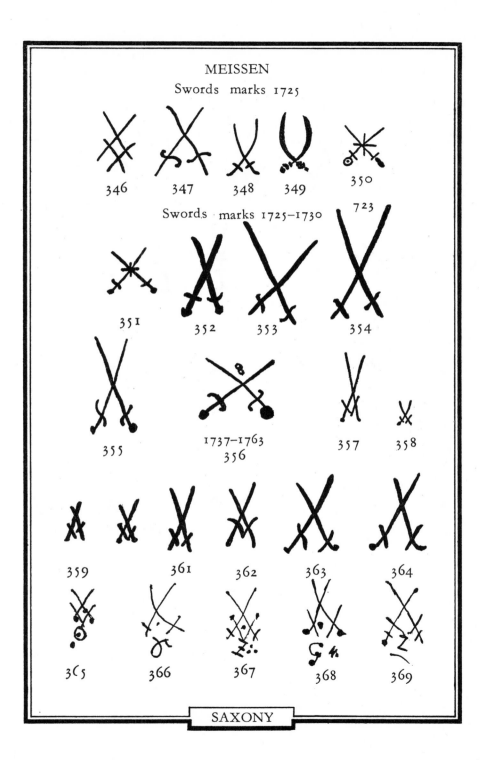

MEISSEN
Swords marks 1725

346   347   348   349   350

Swords marks 1725–1730

723

351   352   353   354

355   1737–1763 356   357   358

359   361   362   363   364

365   366   367   368   369

SAXONY

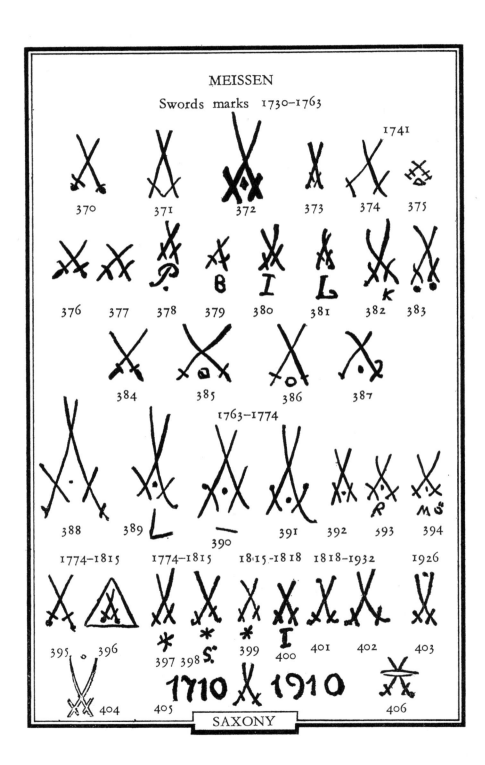

MEISSEN

Swords marks 1730–1763

370   371   372   373   374   1741   375

376   377   378   379   380   381   382   383

384   385   386   387

1763–1774

388   389   390   391   392   593   394

1774–1815   1774–1815   1815–1818   1818–1932   1926

395   396   397 398   399   400   401   402   403

404   405   1710   1910   406

SAXONY

407

408

409

Rosina Dorothea
Beßlerin Anno 1747

410

411

412

413

414

415

416

417

418

419

420

421

422

423

424

425

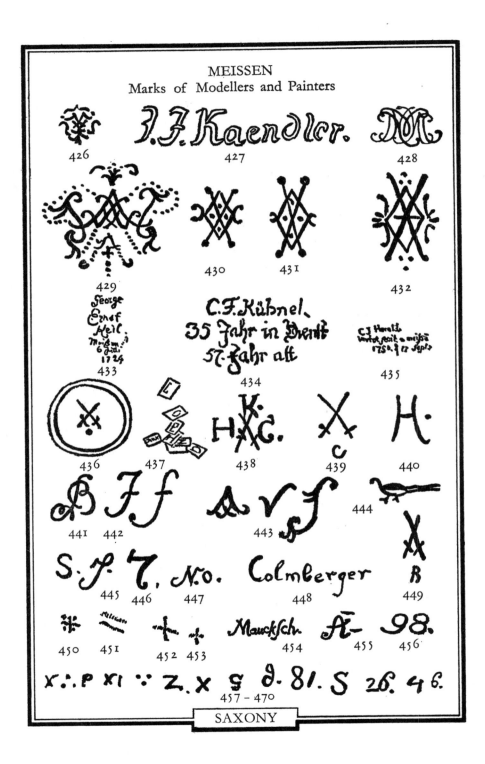

MEISSEN
Marks of Modellers and Painters

426   427   J.J.Kaendler.   428

429   430   431   432

433   George Ernst Heil. Meissen 6 Jul. 1724

434   C.F.Kühnel. 35 Jahr in Dienst 57 Jahr alt

435   C.J Herold malt seit a mißä 1750. ß 17 Sept?

436   437   438   H.X.G.   K.   439   X C   440   H.

441   442   B F f   443   a v f   444

445   S.   446   J.   447   7.   No.   448   Colmberger   449   R

450   451   Pelican   452   453   454   Mauckfch.   455   Æ   456   98.

457 – 470   X.·. P XI ·.· Z. X g ꝺ. 81. S 26. 4 6.

SAXONY

62

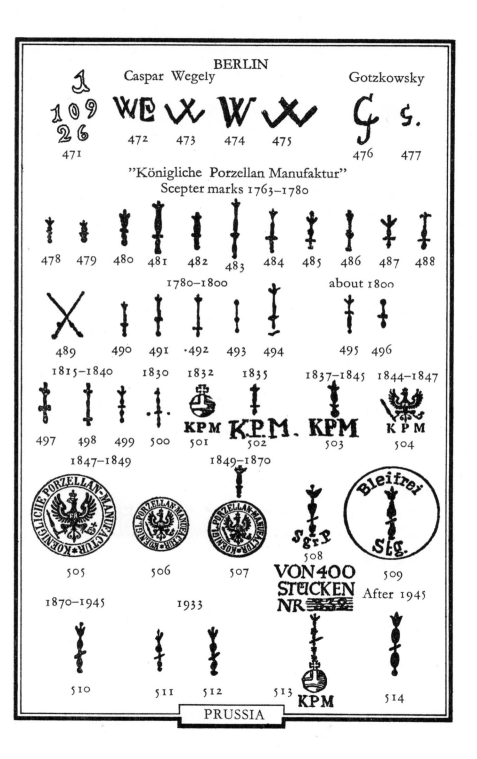

BERLIN

Caspar Wegely

471 472 473 474 475

Gotzkowsky

476 477

"Königliche Porzellan Manufaktur"
Scepter marks 1763–1780

478 479 480 481 482 483 484 485 486 487 488

1780–1800   about 1800

489 490 491 ·492 493 494   495 496

1815–1840   1830   1832   1835   1837–1845   1844–1847

497 498 499 500 KPM 501 K.P.M. 502 KPM 503 KPM 504

1847–1849   1849–1870

KOENIGLICHE PORZELLAN MANUFACTUR FR
505

KOENIGL. PORZELLAN MANUFACTUR
506

KOENIGL. PORZELLAN MANUFACTUR
507

SgrP
508

VON 400
STÜCKEN
NR

Bleifrei Stg.
509

1870–1945   1933   After 1945

510   511   512   513 KPM   514

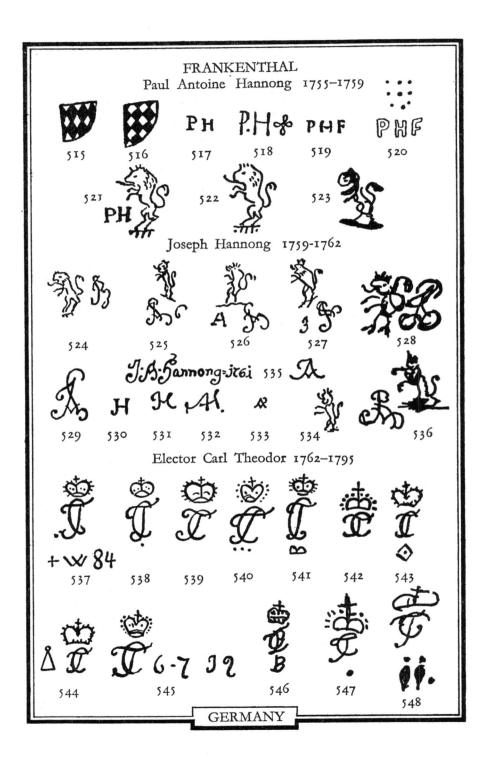

FRANKENTHAL
Paul Antoine Hannong 1755–1759

515 516 517 518 519 520

521 522 523

Joseph Hannong 1759-1762

524 525 526 527 528

J·A·Hannong=1761 535

529 530 531 532 533 534 536

Elector Carl Theodor 1762–1795

537 538 539 540 541 542 543

+w 84

544 545 546 547

548

MEISSEN. Columbine and Pantaloon, part of a clock-case. Model by J. J. Kändler.
Rijksmuseum, Amsterdam

MEISSEN. Harlequin and Columbine, model by J. J. Kändler. Ht. 20,7 cm.
Rijksmuseum, Amsterdam

V

MEISSEN. Little girl, biscuit. About 1776. Mark – *incised crossed swords in triangle and script G and 7*. Ht. 10,2 cm. *Private Collection*

MEISSEN. The little wood-cutter, biscuit. About 1776. Mark – *incised crossed swords and script G and 4*. Ht. 10,7 cm. *Private Collection*

MEISSEN. Magdalena, from the painting by P. Battoni. Model by C. G. Jüchtzer, biscuit. Ht. 13.8 cm. Ht., with base, 27 cm. About 1772. Mark – *incised H*. *Collection M. Penkala*

BERLIN. WEGELY. Lion. About 1753. Ht. 14.4 cm. Mark – *incised numerals* 1, 109, 26. *Collection M. Penkala*

Lioness. About 1753. Ht. 11.2 cm. *Collection M. Penkala*

BERLIN. Inkstand. Model by Friedrich Elias Meyer. About 1764. Marks – early *scepter*. *Collection M. Penkala*

FÜRSTENBERG. Bust of the Duke Carl von Braunschweig. Ht. 21,5.
Private Collection

FÜRSTENBERG. Equestrian figure of the Duke Carl von Braunschweig. Model by Joh. Christoph Rombrich. Ht. 30 cm. Lth. of base 24 cm., width 18 cm.
Collection M. Penkala

X

FRANKENTHAL
Elector Carl Theodor 1762–1795
Marks of Painters and Modellers

549 550 551

552 553 554 555 556 557 558 559 560 561

562 563 564 565 566 567 568

Niebergall Clair A.C Jacob Legrand 1786

569 570 571 572

Schächter J. Schoch H Sch 2

573 574 575

576 577 578 579 580 581 582 583

Hi Joch. pinxit. Gastel ·K H:K:Pin: Ma

584 585 586 587 588 589

B.M.P Magnus pi Michael Kloeckle Pinx. 1783

590 591 592

HM G:HM: HM: GLÖCKEL Raner pinx.

593 594 595 596 597

mi MI N. O. Os J·O Osterspey pinxtj T₃

598 599 600 601.a b c 602 603

Wi Winterstein pinx. 1784 I. Michael quelcher 1779 Web

604 605 606 607

van Reccum 1795–1800

608 609 610 611 612

GERMANY

65

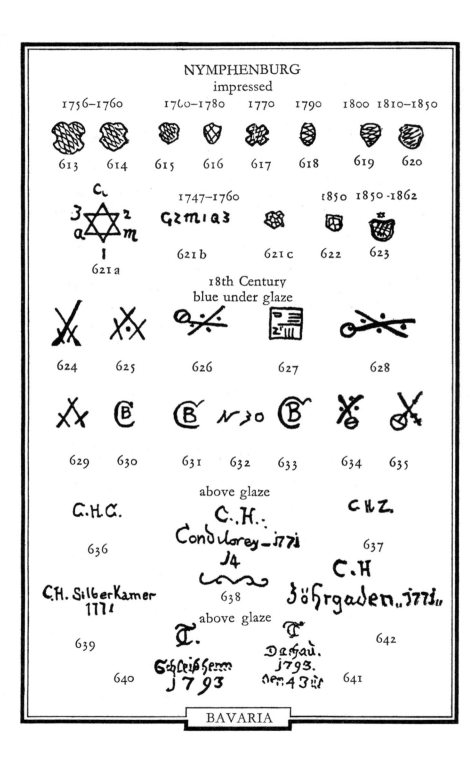

NYMPHENBURG
impressed

1756–1760   1760–1780   1770   1790   1800 1810–1850

613   614   615   616   617   618   619   620

1747–1760   1850 1850 -1862

621a

G Z m I Q Z

621b   621c   622   623

18th Century
blue under glaze

624   625   626   627   628

629   630   631   632   633   634   635

above glaze

C.H.G.

636

C.H.
Condulorey – 1771
J4

C.H.Z.

637

C.H. SilberKamer
1771

639

638

C.H
Zöhrgaden . 1771 .

642

above glaze

640

Schleißherm
J793

Damau.
J793.
Den.43 uhr

641

NYMPHENBURG
Marks of Modellers 18th Century

F·B
642

Franz Antony Bustelli
643

MR
644

PF
645

647

Leich
648

Püttscher
649

I: Peter

Melchior

fecit 1799
650

Georg Dilli's
nach dem Leben
von
Joh Peter Melchior
1800
651

Workmen's marks 18th century

X
652

V J
653

A
654

ID
655

D5
656

H
657

IH
658

M T F ⁑ ℞ ⊦B Ⓢ Ⓟ ⊖ ✿ ⊗ 9 ⊙ ⊗ ⊃ ♂ ♀
659 — 674

Marks of Painters

675

C· Pulcher
17 62
676

Zachenberger
Pictor
677

Reis
678

Ќ
679

F I
680

F
681

S
682

Z
683

J:
684

S:
685

:I
686

:L:
687

L
688

St.
689

E
690

H.
691

M.ga.
692

C P
693

694

BAVARIA

67

NYMPHENBURG

Marks of Painters

⅂F j76ʒ .IAH.	i·A·H· j76ʃ	iᴧH j778	w J:Haag
695	696	697	698

w J:Haag	Heinrich Haag. J:Haag	J⸗Haag
699	700	701

IᴧH j778 D10 8⅚	t·A·H j778 D. 17. 8⅚	K 704 Klein 705 Klein 77 706	707 708
702	703		

F: W: 1795 apriſſ 709	Amber a.1774 710 Amberg 1774 711	M: Willand ja 713
	Joseph Schinotterer Fecit 712 F Willand Jne 714	

Marks of Painters 19th Century
715 - 725

a m. R Nir Auer punx:1806   N Heinzmann 1830

C Adler 1832 A:A. Auer pinx: Böhngen p:

Auer pin:

Marks of Modellers 19th Century
726 — 738

Danner f

A C A AM Hohenluchner 2 Leo

Kt Kein Cf: 5 C nlp. WB Fstl:

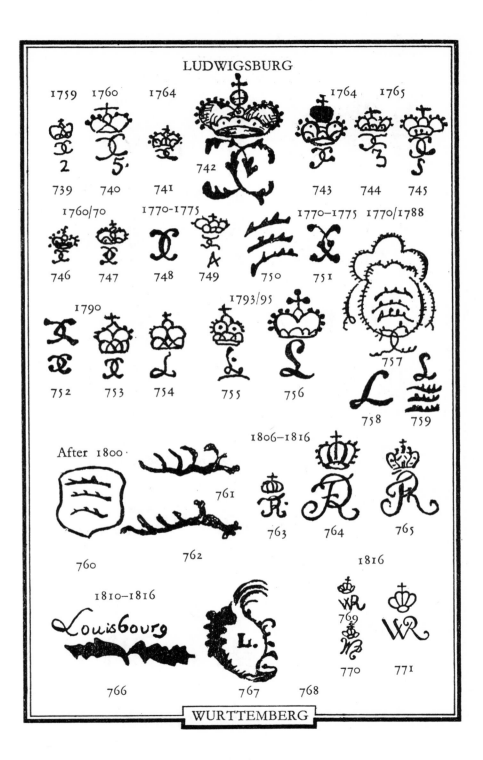

LUDWIGSBURG

1759   1760   1764   1764   1765

742

739   740   741   743   744   745

1760/70   1770–1775   1770–1775   1770/1788

746   747   748   749   750   751

1790   1793/95

757

752   753   754   755   756

758   759

After 1800   1806–1816

761

763   764   765

760   762   1816

1810–1816

Louisbourg

766   767   768   769   770   771

WURTTEMBERG

LUDWIGSBURG
Marks of Painters and Modellers

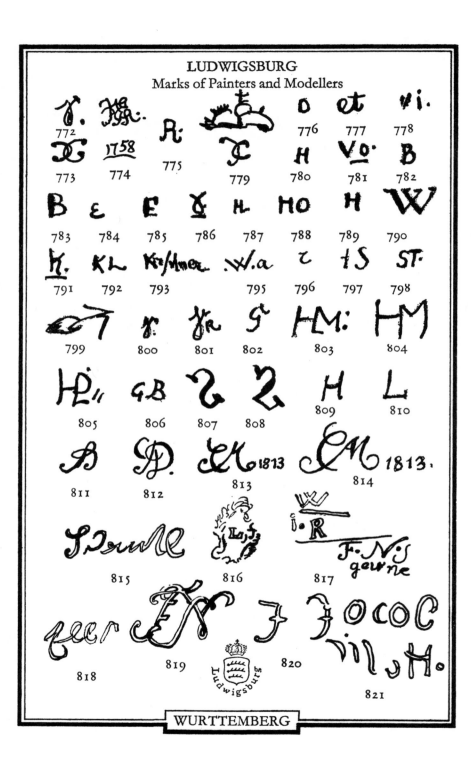

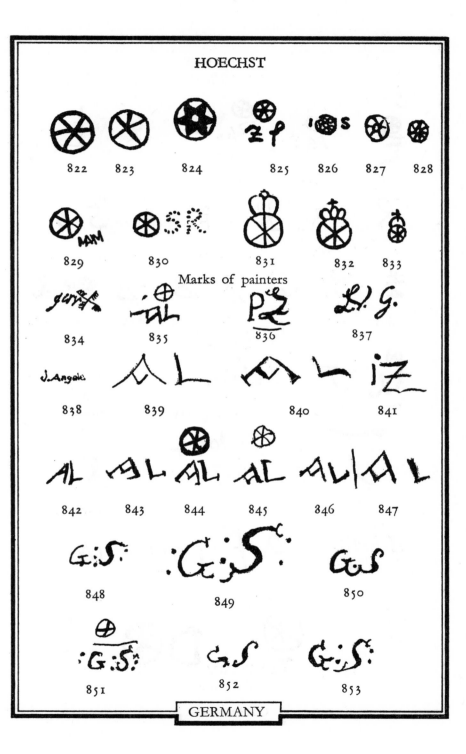

HOECHST

822   823   824   825   826   827   828

829   830   831   832   833

Marks of painters

834   835   836   837

838   839   840   841

842   843   844   845   846   847

848   849   850

851   852   853

GERMANY

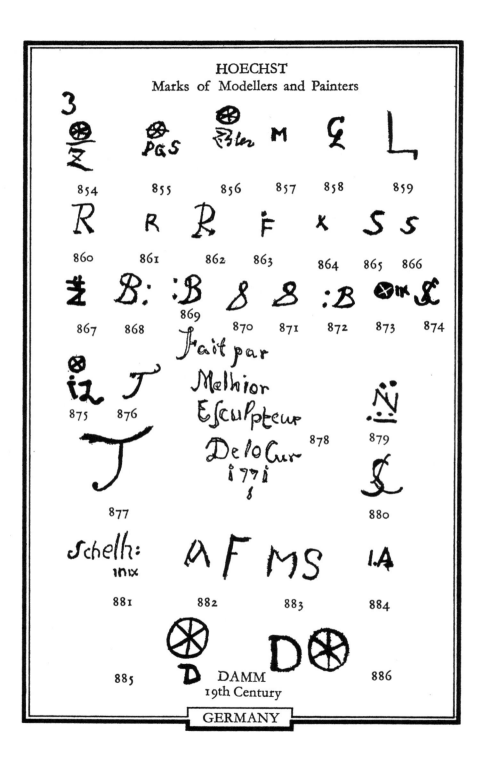

HOECHST
Marks of Modellers and Painters

GERMANY

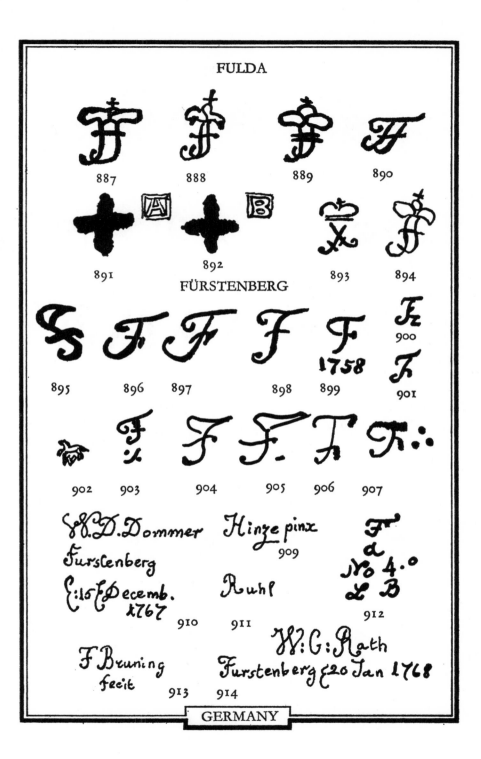

FULDA

887 888 889 890

891 892 893 894

FÜRSTENBERG

895 896 897 898 899 900 901

902 903 904 905 906 907

S.D.Dommer

Furstenberg

C:15 Decemb. 1767

910

Hinze pinx
909

Ruhl

911

F
d
N° 4.0
L B

912

F.Bruning
fecit

913

W:C:Rath

Furstenberg ç 20 Jan 1768

914

GERMANY

73

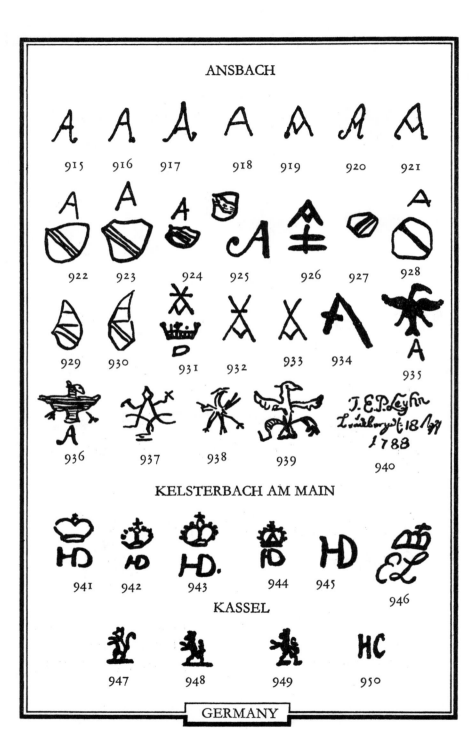

ANSBACH

915 916 917 918 919 920 921

922 923 924 925 926 927 928

929 930 931 932 933 934 935

936 937 938 939 940

KELSTERBACH AM MAIN

941 942 943 944 945 946

KASSEL

947 948 949 950

GERMANY

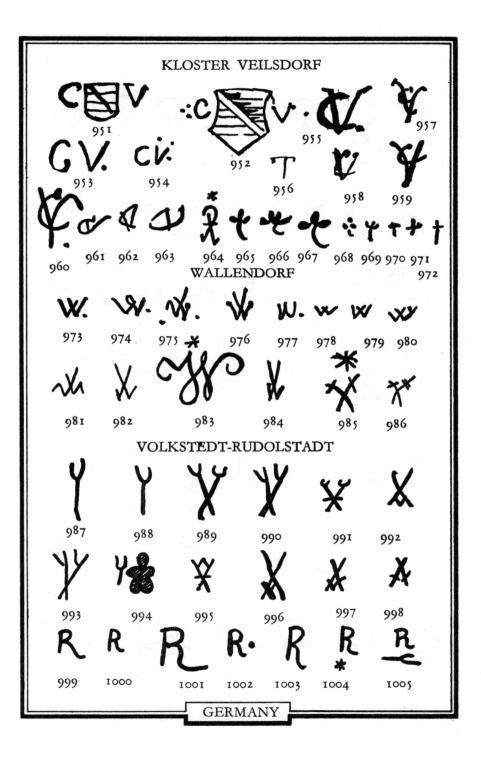

KLOSTER VEILSDORF

951 952 953 954 955 956 957 958 959
960 961 962 963 964 965 966 967 968 969 970 971 972

WALLENDORF

973 974 975 976 977 978 979 980
981 982 983 984 985 986

VOLKSTEDT-RUDOLSTADT

987 988 989 990 991 992
993 994 995 996 997 998
999 1000 1001 1002 1003 1004 1005

GERMANY

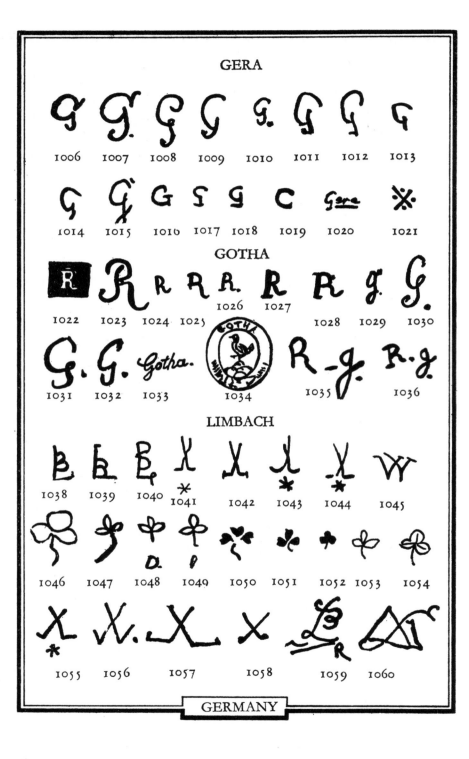

GERA

1006 1007 1008 1009 1010 1011 1012 1013

1014 1015 1016 1017 1018 1019 1020 1021

GOTHA

1022 1023 1024 1025 1026 1027 1028 1029 1030

1031 1032 1033 1034 1035 1036

LIMBACH

1038 1039 1040 1041 1042 1043 1044 1045

1046 1047 1048 1049 1050 1051 1052 1053 1054

1055 1056 1057 1058 1059 1060

GERMANY

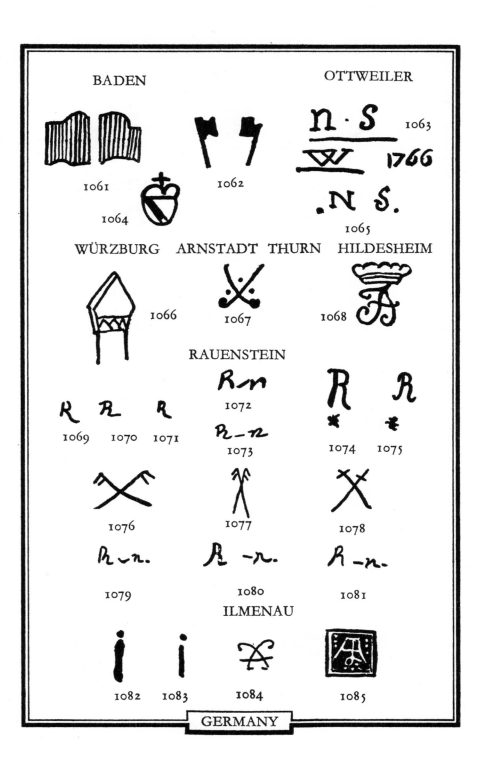

BADEN

OTTWEILER

1061

1062

1063

1766

1064

1065

WÜRZBURG   ARNSTADT THURN   HILDESHEIM

1066

1067

1068

RAUENSTEIN

1072

1069   1070   1071

1073

1074   1075

1076

1077

1078

1079

1080

1081

ILMENAU

1082   1083

1084

1085

GERMANY

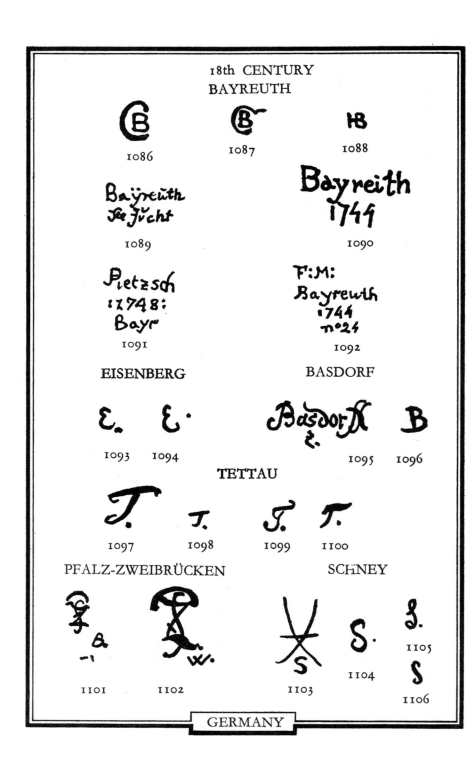

18th CENTURY
BAYREUTH

1086

1087

1088

Bayreuth
See Fucht

1089

Bayreith
1744

1090

Pietzsch
:1748:
Bayr

1091

F:M:
Bayreuth
1744
n°24

1092

EISENBERG

1093   1094

BASDORF

Basdorf

1095   1096

TETTAU

1097   1098   1099   1100

PFALZ-ZWEIBRÜCKEN

1101   1102

SCHNEY

1103   1104

1105

1106

GERMANY

78

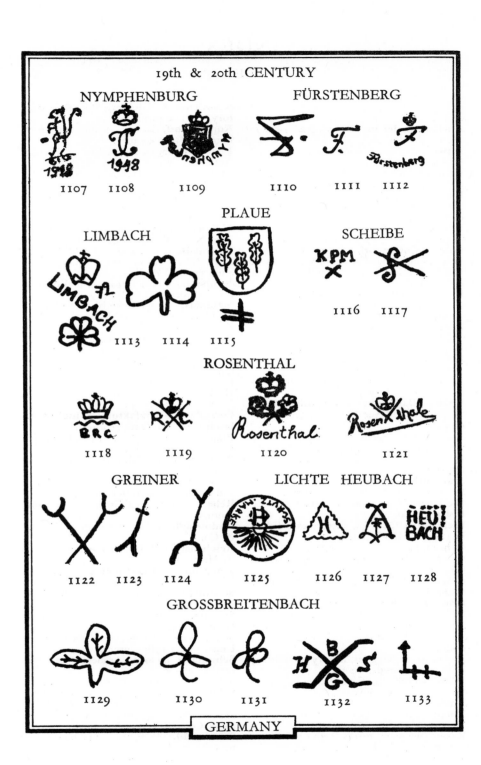

19th & 20th CENTURY

NYMPHENBURG   FÜRSTENBERG

1107   1108   1109   1110   1111   1112

PLAUE

LIMBACH   SCHEIBE

1113   1114   1115   1116   1117

ROSENTHAL

1118   1119   1120   1121

GREINER   LICHTE HEUBACH

1122   1123   1124   1125   1126   1127   1128

GROSSBREITENBACH

1129   1130   1131   1132   1133

GERMANY

INDEX

GERMAN FACTORIES OF THE 19TH AND 20TH CENTURY

Schaller & Co (19th century).

Sitzendorf, factory established in 1845 by The brothers Vogt

Suhl, factory established by Schlegelmilch (19th eentury).

Sophienau, factory established by J. Schachtel (19th century).

Tiefenfurt, factory established by P. Donath (19th century).

Tillowitz, factory established by Count von Frankenberg (19th century).

Tischenreuth, factory established in the 19th century.

Unterködiitz, factory established by Möller & Dippe (19th century).

Unterweissbach, factory established by Voigt & Höland (19th century).

Volkstedt, Eckert and Co. (19th/20th century).

Volkstedter Porzellan Fabrik (19th/20th century).

Volkstedt, Ackermann and Fritze, (19th/20th century). (König, Ackermann and Fritze). M. 1193, 4, 5.

Volkstedt, Ens factory (19th century).

Volkstedt, Dressel, Kister & Co. (19th/20th century).

Volkstedter Porzellan Manufaktur Seedorf (19th/20th century).

Waldenburg, factory established by K. Krister (19th/20th century).

Wallendorf, Heubach, Kämpfe and Sonntag (19th century).

Weiden, factory established by A. Bauscher (19th and 20th century).

Weingarten, factory established by Baumgarten (19th century).

19th & 20th CENTURY
HELENE WOLFSOHN in DRESDEN

Dresden

1134

1135

1136

WALDENBURG

K. P. H.

1137

1138

1139

1140

1141

MEYERS and SON at DRESDEN

1142

1143

1144

1145

1146

GRÄFENRODA   WEINGARTEN   TEICHERT

1147

1148

1149

1150   1151   1152

VOLKSTEDT Dressel, Kister & Co.

1153

1154

1155

1156

REHAU   VEILSDORF

1157   1158

GERMANY

19th & 20th CENTURY
VOLKSTEDT, ECKERT

1159   1160   1161   1162   1163   1164   1165

1166   1167   1168   1169   1170

VOLKSTEDTER PORZELLANFABRIK

1171   1172   1173   1174

CARL THIEME POTSCHAPPEL

1175   1176   1177   1178   1179   1180   1181

SCHORNDORF

1182   1183   1184   1185

GERMANY

SCHNEY   TEICHERT, MEISSEN   BURGAU

1186   1187   1188   1189   1190

VOLKSTEDT-RUDOLSTADT

ENS

1191   1192   1193   1194   1195

BLANKENHAIN   ILMENAU

1196   1197   1198   1199

ILMENAU   BOHNE

1200   1201   1202   1203   1204

HÜTTENSTEINACH   SITZENDORF

1205   1206   1207   1208

SUHL   OBERKASSEL

1209   1210   1211

GERMANY

19th & 20th CENTURY
LETTIN

1212   1213   1214   1215   1216

NEUHAUS
NONNE & ROESCH

RUDOLSTADT   GEHREN

N & R

1218

CORTENDORF

1890

1220

1217   1219

ELGERSBURG   WEIDEN

1221

SCHEDEWITZ

1223

1222

OBERBOHNDORF

PÖSSNECK   SCHÖNWALD

  J.NM

1224   1225   1226

FRAUREUTH   UNTERWEISBACH
Roemer & Födisch

1227   1228

GERMANY

85

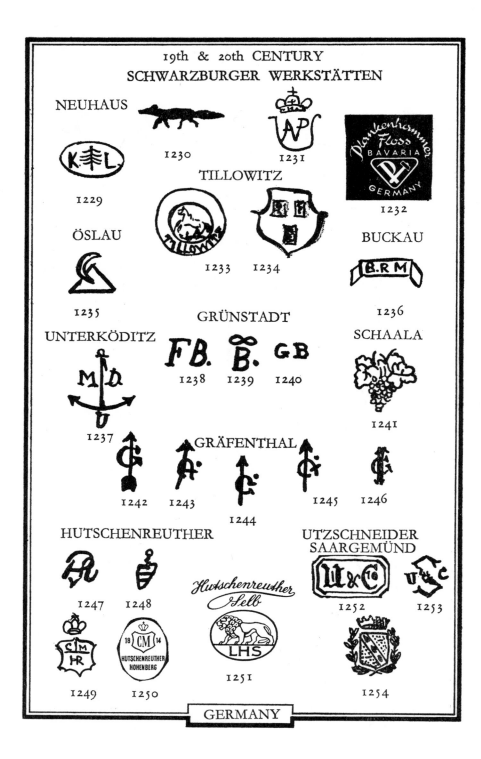

19th & 20th CENTURY
SCHWARZBURGER WERKSTÄTTEN

NEUHAUS

1230

1231

1229

TILLOWITZ

1232

ÖSLAU

1233   1234

BUCKAU

1235

1236

UNTERKÖDITZ

GRÜNSTADT

SCHAALA

1237

1238   1239   1240

1241

GRÄFENTHAL

1242   1243

1245   1246

1244

HUTSCHENREUTHER

UTZSCHNEIDER
SAARGEMÜND

1247   1248

1252

1253

1249   1250

1251

1254

GERMANY

19th & 20th CENTURY

FREIWALDAU   TIEFENFURTH-DONATH

1255

1256

1257

1258

1259

1260

EICHHORN   OBERKOTZAU   STANOWITZ   SOPHIENAU

1261

1262

 St·PM
1263

 JS
1264

NEU-HALDENSLEBEN   ALT-HALDENSLEBEN
NATHUSIUS

1265

1266

BERLIN
MOABIT

1270

N
1271

1272

1273

1267

1268

 F.A.S
1269

KOPPELSDORF-MARSEILLE

1274

1275

1276

TIEFENFURTH   SCHWARZENBACH   KÖNIGSZELT

B.M.P.
1277

1278

A.R.
1279

GERMANY

87

ARZBERG

1280

SCHÖNWALD

1281

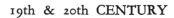

HUTSCHENREUTHER

ARZBERG

BAVARIA · GERMANY

S.P.M.
WALKÜRE·BAYREUTH
BAVARIA

1282

1283

1284

K & A

PORZELLAN

1285

Edelstein

BAVARIA

1286

TETTAU

1287

1288

1289

GEROLD PORZELLAN
BAVARIA

1290

1291

1292

Royal
KM
PORZELLAN
BAVARIA
GERMANY

1293

GERMANY

88

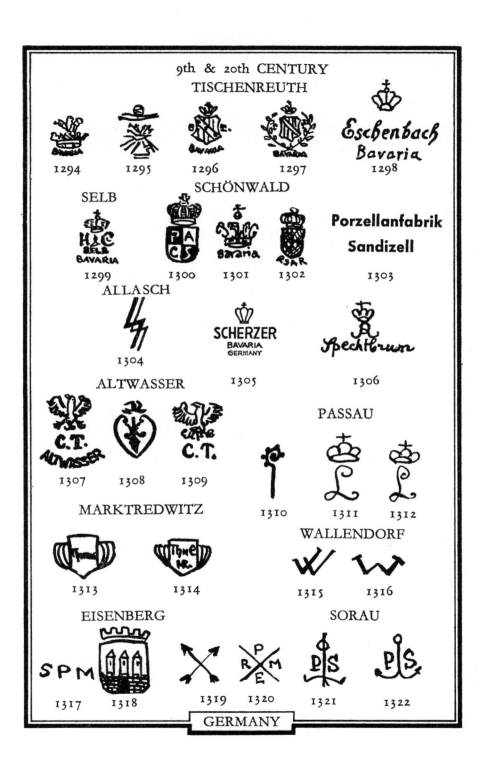

9th & 20th CENTURY

TISCHENREUTH

1294   1295   1296   1297

Eschenbach
Bavaria
1298

SELB

SCHÖNWALD

1299   1300   1301   1302

Porzellanfabrik

Sandizell

1303

ALLASCH

1304

SCHERZER
BAVARIA
GERMANY

1305

1306

ALTWASSER

1307   1308   1309

PASSAU

1310   1311   1312

MARKTREDWITZ

1313   1314

WALLENDORF

1315   1316

EISENBERG

1317   1318

SORAU

1319   1320   1321   1322

GERMANY

AUSTRIA

VIENNA

This factory was founded by a Dutchman, Claude Innocent du Pasquier, or Du Paquier, who engaged a craftsman from the Meissen factory by the name of Samuel Stölzel and the arcanist Hunger. In order to secure his services Du Paquier had gone secretly to Meissen, where he contrived to make Stölzel's acquaintance in a coffeehouse. Du Paquier obtained a concession for twenty-five years from the Emperor Charles VI.

The factory, which was established in 1718, was located in the house of Count Kufstein and at first employed ten men, the number being later increased to twenty. However the enterprise proved a failure and Du Paquier offered it to the Government. Maria Theresia took it under her protection and appointed Du Paquier as manager.

The paste used in the early period of the factory was of a yellow tint and the forms and decorations were primitive. Typical of the early pieces were handles in the form of animals or elongated figures. Grips on dish covers were also in the form of figures. The pieces were executed in the Meissen style, but the paintings were often inaccurately copied and the colours lacked the lucent quality which characterised Meissen products. The miniature painter Höroldt who was later employed at Meissen, worked at Vienna until 1719.

From 1720 to 1740 the pieces produced at Vienna were decorated with colourful Chinese scenes – these appear on the very early specimens of this period –, Japanese flowers (Imari), multicoloured patterns of leaves, flowers and fruitbaskets, Chinese pagodas and landscapes with figures, often in cartouches. The same motifs were also executed in black relieved with gold. German floral patterns, mythological subjects, scenes of battle and romantic tableaux appeared as early as 1725. The factory was also engaged in the decoration of oriental porcelain.

From 1730 onwards pieces were executed in typical Vienna baroque with trellis patterns. Painters on the staff at that early date included Gabriel (1725–1745), Anreiter (1724–1747), Danhofer (1730–1737) and the most important of all, Jacob Helchis. Many pieces were decorated at home by painters not actually on the staff of the factory. During this period no figures or groups were made. These early pieces were not marked.

In 1744 the factory was taken over by the State. Marks were introduced and a whiter paste of better quality was brought into use. The rococo influence is noticeable in the form and decoration of pieces produced during this period. Patterns in relief in the Meissen tradition were adopted, often executed by workers formerly employed by the Saxon factory, notably the painter Klinger (employed at Vienna 1748–1781), the noted figure painter Schindler (1750–1793), and Hitzig (1745–1751). The curious design of gold lace and purple which appears on some rocaille relief ornaments produced at Vienna dates from this period. It might be assumed that the famous Nymphenburg modeller Bustelli had for a short time worked at Vienna. Two objects of the former Lanna collection bear a striking likeness to similar Nymphenburg pieces: a dog figurine and a fount.

From about 1760 Sèvres influence became noticeable. From 1770 onwards particularly fine "fond" porcelain was manufactured, very often in a beautiful deep blue, decorated with a network design in gold.

About 1750 figures and groups in the Meissen manner were first introduced, these being modelled by J. J. Niedermayer who was employed at the factory from 1747 to 1784. His creations, usually depicting mythological subjects, were executed in the classical style. Graceful and charming rococo groups were modelled by F. Caradea. The figures were very often left unpainted or were decorated with the minimum of colour.

From 1784 to 1805 the factory, under the management of Sorgenthal, reached the peak of its fame. Services were made in a beautiful but severe classical style, very richly decorated with classical subjects, inspired mostly by Greek, Roman and Egyptian models. Very fine decorations in relief in different shades of gold were introduced. The pieces were very beautifully painted with copies in miniature of world-famous pictures. The most noted painters of this period were Leithner and Perl, the last-named specialising in gold ornamentation. Leopold Dannhauser modelled hunting groups.

The sculptor A. Grassi, a pupil of Beyer, who joined the factory in 1778, designed many fine figures and groups. The pieces were at first executed in colour, but later in white biscuit porcelain.

From 1805 onwards pieces designed with decorations of other materials, such as wood, bronze, marble etc. were attempted. The blue mark was no longer used, a development which coincided with the first visible signs of a decline in the factory. The decline continued during the ensuing years (1825–1864), when the artistic quality of the pieces and decorations deteriorated. In 1864 the factory was closed.

The mark used was a beehive, which from 1744 to 1749 was impressed in the moist clay, with rare exceptions when it was painted on glaze in red or black. This same mark was continued in several forms in underglaze blue until 1827. From that date until the factory was closed this mark was again impressed in the paste. From 1783 onwards, in addition to the factory mark, pieces were dated and numbers and letters were used to denote the modellers and painters who had worked on the pieces.

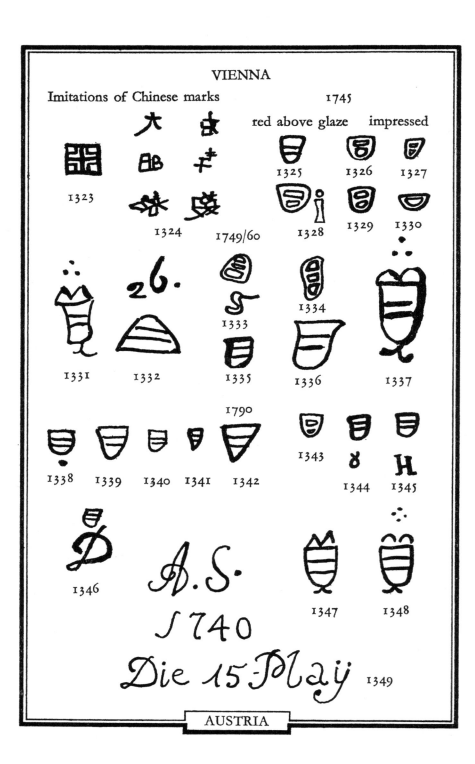

VIENNA

Imitations of Chinese marks

1745

red above glaze   impressed

1323

1324   1749/60

1325   1326   1327

1328   1329   1330

1331   1332   1333   1334   1335   1336   1337

1790

1338   1339   1340   1341   1342   1343   1344   1345

1346

A.S.
1740
Die 15 May   1349

1347   1348

AUSTRIA

VIENNA
Marks of Painters

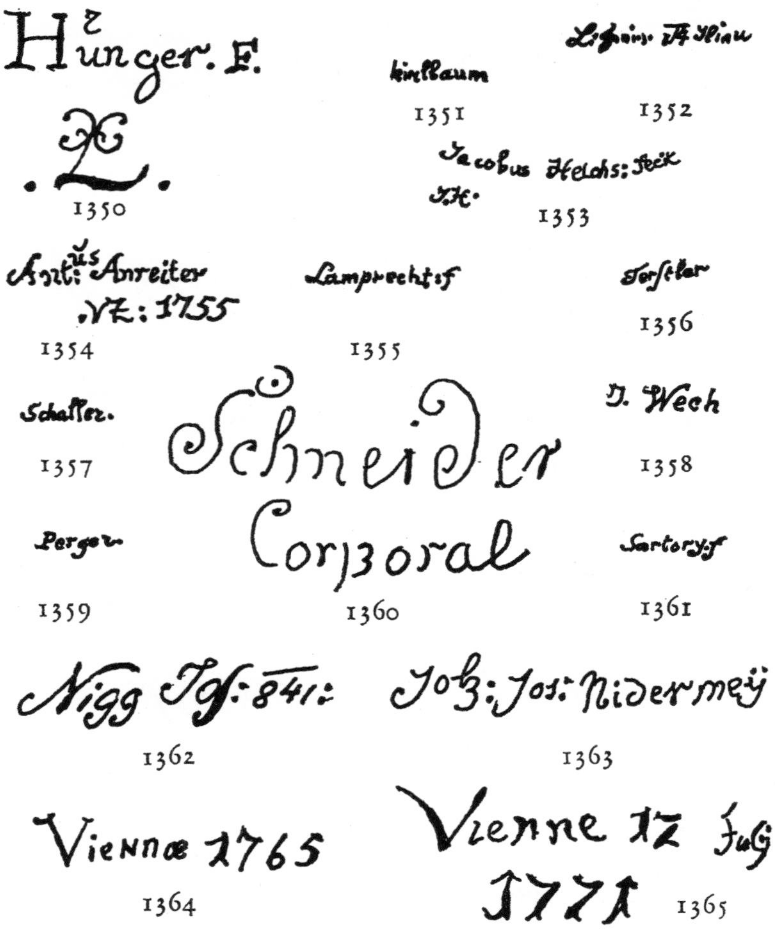
Hunger. F.
Lamprecht f
Schneider
Corporal
Vienne 1765

1350 1351 1352 1353 1354 1355 1356 1357 1358 1359 1360 1361 1362 1363 1364 1365

Marks of Modellers

86
88
19
902
806
E
M

1366 – 1372

AUSTRIA

VIENNA

Marks of Painters

Bottengruber
f. Vienna 1730

1373

W
A 1726

1374

Bottengruber Sso:
f. Vienne 1730.

1375

1376

1377

Carolus Ferdinandus de
Wolfsbourg et Wallsdorf
Eques Silesia pinxit Viennae Aust. 1731.

1378

19th CENTURY

1379

AUGARTEN
20th CENTURY

Wien

1380

AUGARTEN

1381

AUSTRIA

BOHEMIA

SCHLAGGENWALD

Established in 1792, this factory is still operating. A fine white paste is used. In the early days of the factory, production was confined to plain tableware. Richly decorated services of superior quality were produced at a later date. Presentation cups, vases in empire style, figures and groups were also manufactured, but none of particular merit.

The factory mark is the letter S in blue under glaze or in red over glaze. From 1830 this letter was impressed in the paste.

A shield with the letters L & H was also used as mark.

KLÖSTERLE-ON-EGER

Established in 1793, this factory was owned till recently by the Counts Thun. In addition to ordinary table china, services of finer quality were also made, as well as presentation cups in empire style. Decorated figures were made, but these have no artistic merit.

The mark used was the letter K with antlers, in blue under glaze or in red, green or purple over glaze. On later pieces the antlers were omitted. Another mark used by the factory consisted of the letters TK impressed in the moist paste.

PRAGUE

This factory, established in 1793, produced plain china as well as services of better quality; some figures of no artistic significance were also made. The mark, originally the letter P impressed in the paste, was later changed to the word PRAG.

GIESZHÜBEL

This factory, which is still in operation, was established in 1802.

The paste used is of fine quality. Plain china and elegantly decorated services of superior quality as well as presentation cups were made here. No figures or groups were produced.

The mark originally used was the letter G with an arrow, in blue under glaze. From 1815 onwards a mark consisting of the letters BK impressed in the moist paste was used.

DALLWITZ

Founded in 1802, this factory is still in existence. It produces china of ordinary and superior quality, as well as presentation cups. The factory mark consists of the letters D or DD or the word "Dallwitz".

PIRKENHAMMER

Established in 1803, this factory still exists. Fine white paste is used in the production of ordinary table ware and very finely decorated and painted china, presentation cups, vases and coffee pots in empire style and old Vienna style.

The oldest factory mark is the monogram HK in blue under glaze or in red and gold over glaze. From 1810–1847 the mark used consisted of the letters F&M.

TANNOWA

This factory was established in 1813, and produced ordinary table ware. The mark is a T in blue under glaze, or the word "Tannowa" impressed in the moist paste.

ALTROHLAU

This factory was established in 1813 and is still in existence. Ordinary and better quality table ware is produced.

The mark used is the letter H or the word "Altrohlau" impressed in the paste.

ELBOGEN

This factory was founded in 1815 and is still in operation. Fine white paste was used. Products included presentation cups, vases both plain and of finer quality, multicoloured figures and services.

The mark is a sword arm in blue under glaze; from 1833 this was impressed with the addition of the word "Haidinger".

FRANKENTHAL. Pastoral group, biscuit. Model by Adam Bauer. About 1776. Ht. 14.8 cm. *Collection M. Penkala*

NYMPHENBURG. The Sneering Soldier. Model by Franz Anton Bustelli. About 1757-62 Mark – *impressed shield*. Ht. 21.3 cm. *Bayerisches Nationalmuseum, München*   XI

Höchst. Flora. Mark – impressed *B2* and *G.S.* (Phil. Gerh. Sommerlat) in iron red. About 1750–53. Ht. 31 cm. *Collection M. Penkala*

Flora. Mark – impressed *B2* and *AL* (Adam Ludwig) in crimson. About 1750–53 Ht. 30.6 cm. *Collection M. Penkala*

FULDA. Sultan and Sultana. About 1770. *Rijksmuseum, Amsterdam*

VIENNA. Bowl and dish. Du Paquier period. About 1735. Ht. of the bow 27 cm., D. of the dish, 30,5 cm. *Rijksmuseum, Amsterdam*

VIENNA. Coffee-pot from a solitaire given by Maria Theresia to the painter Liotard. About 1778. Ht. 16,5 cm. *Rijksmuseum, Amsterdam*

18th CENTURY
KLÖSTERLE

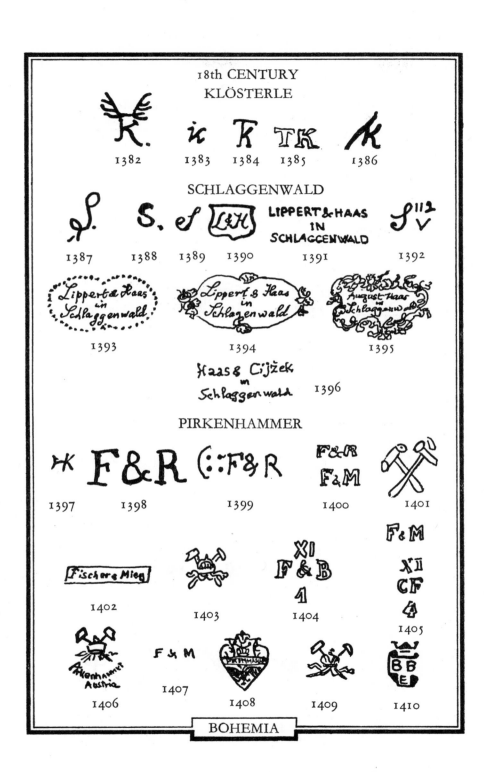

1382   1383   1384   1385   1386

SCHLAGGENWALD

1387   1388   1389   1390   1391   1392

1393   1394   1395

1396

PIRKENHAMMER

1397   1398   1399   1400   1401

1402   1403   1404   1405

1406   1407   1408   1409   1410

BOHEMIA

PRAGUE

1411 1412 1413 1414 1415 1416

1417 1418 1419 1420 1421

1422 1423 1424

1425 1426 1427

1428 1429 1430

TANNOVA LADOWITZ LUBAU BUDAU

1431 1432 1433 1434

ALTROHLAU DALLWITZ

1435 1436 1437 1438 1439 1440

FISCHERN BRÜX

HEGEWALD

1441 1442 1443 1444

BOHEMIA

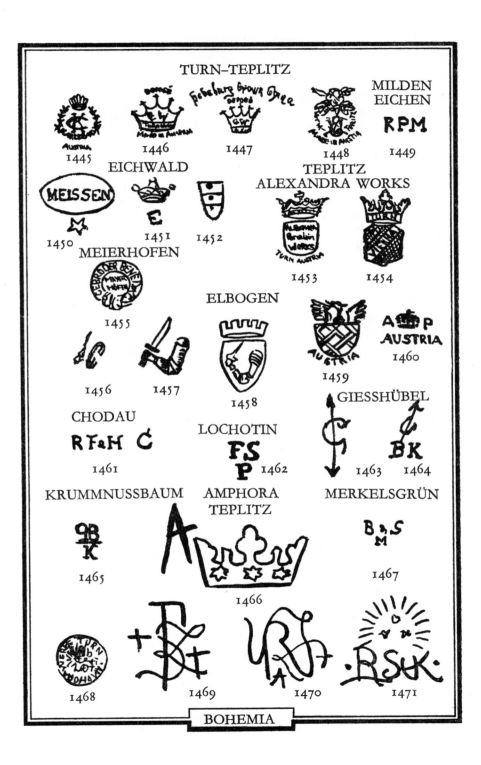

TURN–TEPLITZ

MILDEN EICHEN

RPM

1445 1446 1447 1448 1449

EICHWALD

TEPLITZ
ALEXANDRA WORKS

MEISSEN

1450 1451 1452 1453 1454

MEIERHOFEN

1455

ELBOGEN

1456 1457 1458 1459

A P
AUSTRIA

1460

CHODAU

RF&H Ć

1461

LOCHOTIN

FS
P 1462

GIESSHÜBEL

BK

1463 1464

KRUMMNUSSBAUM

1465

AMPHORA
TEPLITZ

1466

MERKELSGRÜN

B S
M

1467

1468 1469 1470 1471

BOHEMIA

99

HUNGARY

Towards the close of the 18th century Bathyány founded a small porcelain factory which he was obliged to close by Imperial decree. The kilns of this factory had to be destroyed.

The REGÉC FACTORY was founded in 1830 at Telkibánya by Ferdinand Bretzenheim. The produce was of good quality.

The HEREND FACTORY, now operated by the Hungarian State, was established by Mór Fischer in 1839. The high artistic quality and the sophisticated decoration of the produce have made it very popular. In 1939 porcelain church windows in lithophane technique were given by the factory to the Herend Church. Lithophane technique was discovered towards the end of the 18th century in Berlin at the Royal Porcelain Factory. The process involved the use of white biscuit plaques of varying thickness, which when held against the light formed pictures. Since 1945 the factory's output consists of tableware and tea-sets decorated in the classic Herend style; and figurines and groups modelled by János Horvay, Adolf Huszar, Miklós Iszo, Zsigmond Kisfaludy, Strobl, Miklós Ligeti, Elek Lux, János Pásztor, Istvan Lorine, Ede Telos, Györy Vastagh and Sándor Keleti.

ZSOLNAY FACTORY was founded in 1853 at Pecs, this factory very soon produced superior porcelain ware. The decoration consists of Hungarian folkore motifs. The factory is still in operation. The painters were Henrik Darilek, Geza Nikelsky, Tádé Sihorszky, László Matyasovszky, Zsolnay and János Bodor.
Gyula Pompar, Sándor Apári Abt. Lajos Szomer and András Sinko were employed as modellers.

TIVADAR HÜTTL FACTORY.
Established in Budapest in 1852, this factory produced delicately decorated table services and tea-sets. Pál Horthy was chief decorator.
The Ignac and Emil Fischer factory of Budapest produced artistic table services and tea-sets.
László Pálinkás has worked there as decorator.

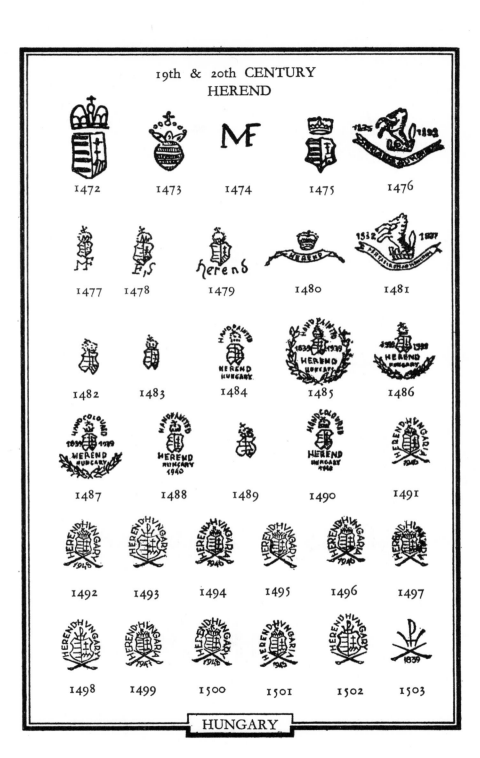

1472   1473   1474   1475   1476

1477   1478   1479   1480   1481

1482   1483   1484   1485   1486

1487   1488   1489   1490   1491

1492   1493   1494   1495   1496   1497

1498   1499   1500   1501   1502   1503

HUNGARY

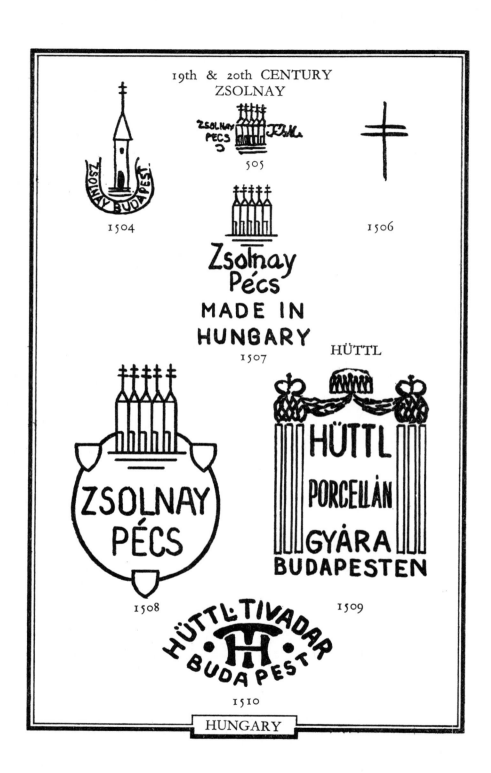

19th & 20th CENTURY
ZSOLNAY

505

1504

1506

Zsolnay
Pécs
MADE IN
HUNGARY
1507

HÜTTL

ZSOLNAY
PÉCS
1508

HÜTTL
PORCELLÁN
GYÁRA
BUDAPESTEN
1509

1510

HUNGARY

FRANCE

ROUEN 1673–1696.

This factory was established by Louis Poterat. Soft paste was used. Rouen products – mostly pieces decorated in blue – are very rare. Marks are in underglaze blue. The paste is very translucent and of greenish hue.

SAINT-CLOUD

This factory was founded by Pierre Chicanneau under the patronage of the Duke Philippe d'Orléans. After Chicanneau's death in 1702 his wife Barbe Coudret or Coudray operated the factory, then she remarried Henri Charles Trou. Later the factory passed into the hands of Trou.

Fine, ivory white soft paste was used for the pieces produced here, which were decorated in Japanese style; white pieces were also produced with decorations in relief in imitation of Fukien ware, and pieces with encrusted elaborate gildings in the glaze. Pieces produced at St.-Cloud were marked: From 1677-1696-S.T.C. From 1696–1724, a sun; from 1724–1766 — St.C.T., in underglaze blue, or incised or impressed under glaze. The widow of one of Chicanneau's sons, Marie Moreau, established in 1722 a factory in the Rue de la Ville l'Evêque in Paris. After her death this factory belonged to Henri Trou. He was succeeded in 1746 by his son, who operated the works until 1766.

PAINTERS

1692, Bellegneule, François, painter.
1712, Chicaneau, François, painter.
1693, Miete, Jacques; Fillet, Guilaume; Picard, Jacques; Vallet, Claude, workmen.
1695, Dechar or Dechan, Nicolas, painter, Maugras, Jacques, Guay, Jean, turner.
    Picard, Joseph, painter.
    Borgnet, François, painter.
1698, Vinant, François, painter.
    Chesneau, François, painter.
1701, Pottier, Guillaume, enameller.
1703, Fillien, Claude, painter.
1718, Picard, Henry, painter.
1757, Bolvry, Henry, painter.
1743, Laronde, Antoine, painter.
1738, Goujon, Louis Jacques, modeller.
1740, Le Picard, Jacques Henry, painter.
    Massüe, Louis Pierre, painter.
    Neppel., Jean Louis, painter.
1750, Pain, Jean, painter.
    Jobert, Nicolas, painter.
1753, Mouchart, Frédéric, painter.
1754, Cuvillier, Antoine, painter.
1756, Provost, Henri Marin, painter.
1757, Simogé, Claude, painter.

1758, Haye, Jacques de la, painter.
1759, La Ville, Pierre, painter.
1760, Baize, Jacques de, painter.
   Mérian, Louis, painter.
1766, Michel, Jean, painter.
   Robinot, Pierre, painter.

CHANTILLY

This was a soft paste porcelain factory, founded by Sicaire Cirou in 1725 under the patronage of Prince Louis-Henri de Condé, a collector of oriental porcelain. Cirou, who ignored the composition of porcelain glaze, covered the pieces with tin glaze. The paste was yellowish, greenish-white. Different motifs of decoration were favoured: "à la branche fleurie", "à la chimère", "dessin coréen à la haye", Japanese scenes. Copies of blanc de Chine figures were also made.

The decoration was copied from Japanese and Chinese models. White pieces with decorations in relief in imitation of blanc de Chine were produced. After the death of Cirou in 1751 the factory passed into the hands of Buquet de Montvallier and Roussière (from 1751–1754). Buquet de Montvallier, from 1754–1760. From 1760–1766, the works belonged to Pierre Peyrard. Louis François Gravant bought Chantilly in 1766, from 1779–1781 his wife operated the factory. Anthéaume de Surval owned it until 1792, when he sold it to the Englishman Christophe Potter who closed the works in 1800. The Mayor of Chantilly, Pigorry, reopened the factory after the revolution in 1803 and after this date, hard paste porcelain was manufactured. The products were decorated with German flowers or imitations of Sèvres designs. The factory was finally closed in 1830. The marks were a hunting horn in red, blue or gold on glaze.

PAINTERS AND MODELLERS

1731, Dubois, Gilles.
1734, Grémy, Antoine, born in Delft.
1736, Goujon, Louis, modeller.
1737, Bulidon, Henri, modeller.
1745, Robin, Jean.
1745, Dudos, demoiselle.
1748, Robin, Edmond.
1752, Butteux.
1752, Louis Fournier, modeller, later in Copenhagen.
1753, Anteaume, Jean-Jacques.
1754, Toussoc, Jacques.
   Parpette, Philippe.
1756, Gobin, Etienne.
1761, Drand, Jean-François.
1765, Mathieu, Jacques.
1793, Zwinger, Joseph, from Vienna, painter.

In the first quarter of th 19th century Michel-Isaac Aron operated a hard paste factory at Chantilly. The produce was mediocre. The factory was closed in 1870.

The marks imitated the Chantilly hunting horn, but the name Chantilly was also used without the hunting horn.

MENNECY-VILLEROY

This factory was established on the estate of the Duke de Villeroy in 1735. The founder was François Barbin, who worked there till 1762. He was succeeded by Symphorien Jacques and Joseph Julien in 1765. Graceful figures in Meissen style and biscuit groups were produced.

In 1773 the factory was moved to Bourg-la-Reine. Very beautiful milkwhite porcelain was produced, decorated with Japanese Imari designs and sprigs of flowers.

MODELLERS

      1753, Gauron, Nicholas François.
      1760, Charton, Jean Nicolas.
      1766, Gottlep Berger (Chrétien) from Saxony.
      1767, Mô, Christophe, and Jean Baptiste.
      1759–1772, Fournier, Simon.

PAINTERS

      1737, Dubray, Jean-Baptiste.
      1738, Barbin, Etienne François.
      1753, Neppele, Louis.
      1753, Boucher, Etienne Nicolas.
      1763–1768 Bousch or Pouch, André.
      1761, Sonnere, Jean.
      1764, Seigne, François.
      1764, Haroux, Jean Baptiste.
      1766, Bertrand, Etienne.
      1766, Barre, Jacques.

BOURG-LA-REINE 1773–1804

This factory produced soft-paste porcelain. The characteristic marks are in under-glaze blue or impressed. A small factory it at present operating at Bourg-la-Reine.

VINCENNES

This factory, operating from 1738 to 1756, was the cradle of the great factory of Sèvres. It was situated in the neighbourhood of the Château de Vincennes. The soft paste porcelain manufactured was decorated in Chinese style, with festoons and birds (pheasants and long-billed waterfowl). In a later period scenes after Boucher were executed in a single colour or in polychrome and imitations of Saxon porcelain were attempted. Bouquets of porcelain flowers were a speciality.

Biscuit porcelain was invented at this factory. The two brothers, Gilles and Robert Dubois, who had worked at Chantilly, were employed at Vincennes, when the factory first operated. Subsequently the King took the factory under his patronage, granted a monopoly and exempted its employees from military service. In 1745 the factory was considerably enlarged and placed under the management of the famous jeweller Duplessis and the chemist Hellot. The latter, in 1752, introduced the beautiful turquoise ground colour, which, like the cobalt "bleu de Vincennes", was much sought after. The Marquise de Pompadour took a great interest in the factory.

The factory mark was a double L and the fleur de lys.

SÈVRES

The famous Sèvres factory originated at Vincennes. After the important development of the production of soft-paste porcelain at Vincennes, King Louis XV granted a concession to manufacture porcelain to Eloi Brichard on August 19th 1753. The production of the new factory which was moved to Sèvres in 1756 was from this date distinctly marked. Porcelain from the Vincennes factory was marked in a similar manner to the early products of Sèvres. The Sèvres factory was housed in a spacious, specially designed building.

In 1760 the King of France became sole proprietor and appointed Boileau de Picardie as director. The factory thereafter bore the name of "Manufacture de Porcelaine de France".

In 1761 the secret of making hard paste porcelain was obtained from Pierre Antoine Hannong in return for an annuity of 3000 livres. Boileau was succeeded in 1773 by Parent, who remained in office till 1779, when Régnier took over the direction of the factory. Régnier was later imprisoned during the French Revolution in 1793, when three members of the Convention together administered the factory, assisted by Chanou. The latter was subsequently replaced by a triumvirate consisting of Salmon, Ettlinger and Mayer. These three were succeeded in 1800 by Brogniart, who founded a museum of ceramics, with the assistance of Napoleon, and greatly improved the manufacture of hard paste porcelain.

The name "Vieux Sèvres", is applied to all "pâte tendre" and hard paste porcelain manufactured from the date of the foundation of the factory until the French revolution. The various styles originated at Sèvres are P o m p a-d o u r o r R o c a i l l e (1753-1763), Louis XV (1763-1786) and Louis XVI (1786-1793). In 1778 a magnificent service valued at 318.188 livres was made for the Empress Catherine II. It consisted of 744 pieces, incrusted with porcelain gems and cameos. When a fire broke out in Czarskoye Selo, 160 pieces were stolen. These were bought by a Mr. Webb who later resold them to the Emperor Nicholas I.

Another remarkable service was a dessert service made for Louis XVI which was afterwards purchased by King George IV. It was executed in "bleu du Roi" and painted by Legay, Asselin, Philippine and Dodin.

There are thousands of imitations of "Vieux Sèvres" in existence. Some are modern, others are redecorated pieces produced at Saint Amand, Mennecy and Tournay in the eighteenth century, the original marks of which were destroyed by acids. After the introduction of hard paste, the factory disposed of the entire stock of soft paste china, which was very considerable, to three dealers, Perès, Jarman and Irland, at a very low price. These pieces were afterwards decorated by many former painters from the Sèvres works. Some of them were so beautifully executed that a service was presented to Louis XVIII as a family relic. Some doubt having arisen over the genuineness of the service, it was sent to the factory for inspection. The ornamentation and gildings betrayed their recent decoration and the painters' monograms proved fictitious. Soft paste specimens decorated with chrome green were painted after 1804. The use of this colour, which is richer in tone than the green employed in the 18th century, is a sure sign that the specimen is no real "vieux Sèvres".

Modern imitations of "vieux Sèvres" in hard paste porcelain are easily recognized. Genuine soft paste porcelain shows holes in the underside caused by the supports during the firing process.

The pieces manufactured during the first few years after the foundation of the factory were modelled in very restrained rococo style in imitation of Meissen. Brilliant decoration was executed in soft colours. Magnificent vases with painted flowers and plastic flower decorations were produced. About 1750 a deep blue known as "bleu du Roi" was used as the ground colour and this was often covered with golden network decorations. Shortly afterwards another blue, turquoise, was introduced as "couleur de fond", followed still later by Pompadour rose, apple green, violet and slate grey. Pieces with yellow fond colour are rare. Space was left free for colourful decorations, framed in dull gold. The first period is noted for paintings of flowers and birds. Later Watteau scenes were favoured. Services were often decorated with floral designs including German flowers. Very original was the "Oeil de perdrix" – "partridge eye" – pattern. Sèvres porcelain was also painted in one colour, usually blue or purple. About the year 1770 pieces were painted a deep blue with pearl-like enamel decorations in relief and gold leaf. About this time the classical style was introduced. With the introduction of the empire style the special character of Sèvres porcelain was lost. The plastic art in soft paste porcelain was of a high order. Groups and figures, in white biscuit of a warm tone, were finely modelled and very graceful. Among the modellers were: Jean-Baptiste Fernex, Blondeau, Suzanne, Le Riche, Duru, Liance, Huet, Tristan and Perrotin.

In the early period these were designed by Boucher. The most important modeller of this period was Falconet (1757–1766) who was succeeded by Bachelier and Boizot. Pieces produced by these craftsmen were modelled on classical marble sculptures. Table decorations in the manner of Meissen were very popular and later, busts in biscuit were made. After 1770 figures were almost exclusively executed in hard paste porcelain, left unglazed and unpainted. Towards the end of the 18th century white figures in relief on blue ground, were executed in biscuit porcelain in imitation of Wedgwood ware. Augustin Pajou has made many models for the factory.

Albert Ernest Carrier de Belleuse, painter and sculptor, born in 1824, fled owing to political persecutions in 1850 to England, where he worked from 1850 to 1855 as modeller to the Minton factory at Stoke-on-Trent. He was from 1876 to 1887 artistic director at the Sèvres factory, where he extended his protection to many young artists, among whom was Auguste Rodin, who for a time worked for the factory, attached as a modeller. His grandson, Pierre Carrier de Belleuse, made many drawings of dancers.

Gregoire Calvet modelled graceful figurines after these designs for the Sèvres factory, among them a corps de ballet biscuit table decoration in 1908.

Agathon Léonard (Léonard Agathon van Weydeveldt) made in 1900 for the Exposition Universelle a beautiful table decoration consisting of seven dancers ("Le jeu de l'echarpe") in biscuit. The size of the figures varies from 48,5 to 45,5 cm.

The success of these figures led to the production of Agathon Léonard figures by other factories.

The factory mark from 1740 onwards was the double letter L painted on glaze and afterwards baked in. From 1745 to 1752 a point was inserted between the L's. From 1753 until the French revolution a letter was inserted, this being an A for the year 1753 and so on (see table). During the period 1793-1800 the monogram R.F. and the name "Sèvres" were used as marks and from 1800 to 1802 the word "Sèvres" only. From this date onwards the mark was stamped on in red.

From 1803 to 1804 the mark was "MN Sèvres" and from 1804-1809 "M. Imp. de Sèvres". From this date only hard paste porcelain was manufactured. During the period from 1810-1814 the mark consisted of the French eagle with a circular inscription. After that date the mark changed with every change of King or Government. During the period 1818-1834 the year was given in addition to the factory mark. Up to 1834 this was abbreviated, but after that year it was shown in full.

The few pieces of hard paste porcelain produced from 1770-1793 were marked with a crown over the initials in blue and the letter of the year. Every painter signed with his own mark.

In 1943 on the orders of the occupation authorities a piece of china was produced at the Manufacture Nationale de Sèvres. Shaped like a medium-sized saucer it was classified as "le cendrier Charlemagne" in the records of the manufacture. 80 copies were made. The saucer is decorated with a replica of the medieval statue of Charlemagne in the Louvre. A latin inscription states: The Empire of Charles the Great divided by his grandsons in the year 843 was defended by Adolf Hitler with all the peoples of Europe in the year 1943. The piece is marked with the mark of the Manufacture Nationale de Sèvres with the date 1943 and the German Iron Cross.

CHRONOLOGICAL TABLE OF YEARLETTERS EMPLOYED IN THE ROYAL MANUFACTORY AT SÈVRES.

A	Vincennes 1753	L	1764	X	1775	FF	1783
B	Vincennes 1754	M	1765	Y	1776	GG	1784
C	Vincennes 1755	N	1766	Z	1777	HH	1785
D	Sèvres 1756	O	1767			II	1786
E	1757	P	1768			JJ	1787
F	1758	Q	1769			KK	1788
G	1759	R	1770	AA	1778	LL	1789
H	1760	S	1771	BB	1779	MM	1790
I	1761	T	1772	CC	1780	NN	1791
J	1762	U	1773	DD	1781	OO	1792
K	1763	V	1774	EE	1782	PP	1793

MARKS OF PAINTERS AND GILDERS
OF THE SÈVRES MANUFACTORY
1753–1800

1	Aloncle, birds, animals	1758–1781
2	Antheaume, landscapes and animals	1752–1758
3	Armand, birds, flowers	1746–1785
4	Asselin, portraits, miniatures	1764–1803
5	Aubert Sr., flowers	1754–1758
6	Bailly Jr., flowers	1745–1793
7	Bardet, flowers	1751–1800
8	Barré, German flowers	1780–1791
9	Barrat, flowers, bouquets	1769–1791
10	Baudoin, decorations, borders	1750–1800
11	Becquet, flowers	1748–1765
12	Bertrand, German flowers	1750–1800
13	Bienfait, gilder	1755–1758
14	Binet, flowers	1751–1775
15	Binet, Madame, (Sophie Chanou), flowers	1750–1800
16	Boucher, flowers etc.	1757–1793
17	Bouchet, landscapes	1757–1793
18	Bouillat, flowers, landscapes	1800–1811
19	Boulanger, German flowers	1779–1785
20	Boulanger, Jr., pastorals	1700–1781
21	Bulidon, German flowers	
22	Bunel, Mme. (Manon Buteux) flowers	1763
23	Buteux Sr., flowers	1759–1786
24	Buteux (elder son) flowers	1760–1766
25	Buteux (younger son) pastorals, children	1773–1790
26	Capelle, borders	1749
27	Cardin, German flowers	1749–1786
28	Carrier (Carrié) flowers	1752–1757
29	Castel, landscapes. hunting scenes	1771–1797
30	Caton, pastorals, children, portraits	1747–1793
31	Catrice, flowers	1757–1774
32	Chabry, miniatures	1763–1787
33	Chanou, Mme. (Julie Durosey) flowers	1779–1800
34	Chapuis Sr., flowers, birds	1756–1793
35	Chapuis Jr., German flowers	1800
36	Chauvaux Sr. gilder	1752–1793
37	Chauvaux Jr., German flowers, gilder	1773–1783
38	Chevalier, flowers, bouquets	1755–1757
39	Choisy, de, flowers, arabesques	1770–1812
40	Chulot, attributes, flowers, arabesques	1755–1793
41	Commelin, German flowers, garlands etc.	1765–1793
42	Cornaille, flowers, German flowers	1755–1800
43	Couturier, gilder	1762–1785
44	Dieu, chinoiseries, Chinese flowers, gilder	1780–1811
45	Dodin, figures, portraits	1754–1803

142 Belet, L., decorator................................. 1879–1904
143 Bienville, H., decorator 1877–1904
144 Blanchard, L. E., gilder 1849–1867
145 Blanchard, A., modeller, decorator................... 1902–1904
146 Boquet, decorator................................... 1902–1904
147 Boitel, gilder 1800
148 Bonnier, A., decorator.............................. 1850
149 Bonnenuit, decorator 1858–1904
150 Boullemier, gilder 1830
151 Boullemier, gilder 1807
152 Brecy, Paul, decorator.............................. 1880–1904
153 Brunel, R., painter................................. 1863
154, 155 Bulot, Eugène, flowers, birds.................. 1862–1883
156 Buteux, flowers 1800
157 Cabau, flowers..................................... 1847–1884
158 Capronnier, gilder................................. 1814
159 Catteau, painter 1902–1904
160 Celos, decorations pâte sur pâte.................... 1865–1894
161 Charpentier, decorator 1850
162 Charin, Fanny, figures, portraits................... 1800
163 Constant, gilder................................... 1804–1815
164 Constantin, figures 1813–1845
165 Courcy, du, figures................................. 1860–1886
166 Coursaget..
167, 168 Dammouze, figures and ornaments............... 1878–1880
169 David, decorations, gildings....................... 1850–1882
170 Davignon, D. F., landscapes, died.................. 1812
171 Gault, De, figures and grisaille.................... 1808–1817
172 Fosse, De la, figures 1805–1815
173 Derichweiler, decorator 1858–1888
174 Desperais, ornaments 1794–1812
175 Deutsch, gilder 1805–1817
176 Develly, C., landscapes and figures................. 1813–1848
177, 178 Dericq, figures 1880–1904
179 Didier, ornaments.................................. 1819–1849
180 Drouet, E., figures, decorations.................... 1879–1904
181 Drouet, Gilbert, flowers............................ 1800
182 Ducluzeau, Mme., portraits......................... 1807–1849
183 Durosey, chief gilder.............................. 1802
184 Aubonne, d'., decorator............................ 1904
185 Escallier, Marie, flowers........................... 1874–1888
186 Faraguet, Mme., figures............................ 1856–1870
187 Ficounet, Chas., flowers............................ 1864–1888
188 Fontaine, J. J., flowers............................ 1827–1852
189, 190, 191 Fournier, A., decorator 1878–1904
192 Fragonard, figures, genre........................... 1847–1869
193 Froment, figures 1853–1884
194 Ganeau, gilder..................................... 1800

MODELLERS AND SCULPTORS
OF THE SÈVRES MANUFACTORY
1900–1946

DIRECTORS OF THE SÈVRES MANUFACTORY
1900–1946

VINCENNES II

This factory, which operated from 1765 to 1788 was founded by Pierre Antoine Hannong, son of the famous Strasbourg porcelain maker. Hard paste porcelain was produced. The marks were applied in blue under glaze and in red and gold on glaze.

STRASBOURG

The Hannong family played a very important part in the history of ceramics in the eighteenth century. The first Hannong, Charles François, started an industry at Strasbourg in the rue du Foulon, where clay pipes and stoves were manufactured. The products were decorated in relief and glazed.

In 1721 Hannong went into partnership with a man named Wachenfeld, who had been employed in the Meissen porcelain works. Together they opened a faience and porcelain factory.

Three years later, in 1724, a second factory was established at Hagenau.

Hannong died in 1739, but he had transferred his factories to his two sons, Paul Antoine and Balthasar in 1732.

During the second period of this factory (1745–1750), hard paste porcelain was produced, which, owing to an excess of feldspar, resembled glass. The pieces were decorated in red and pale gold.

Paul Antoine Hannong soon became sole proprietor of both factories, and by 1753 his works at Hagenau and Strasbourg had become important enough to overshadow completely Vincennes.

By order of King Louis XV of France, Paul Antoine was forced to demolish his own kilns and dismantle his factory within a fortnight, notwithstanding the protests of his protector, the Duc de Noailles. Paul Antoine was, however, compelled to obey the King's order and went to Frankenthal. He retained possession of his faience factory at Strasbourg and left the factory at Hagenau under the management of his two sons, Pierre Antoine and Joseph. The porcelain factory was dismantled in 1754.

Joseph-Adam reopened the porcelain factory in 1766, but, although the output was considerable, it was a profitless business. He was compelled to close the works in 1781.

Pierre-Antoine sold the secret of producing German hard paste porcelain to the Sèvres factory. He made several attempts to found porcelain factories but without lasting success. His brother Joseph fled to Munich, where he died, ruined by French tax collectors and beset by his creditors.

STRASBOURG, A. G. STUTZ uses the double L in imitation of the 18th century Sèvres mark in conjunction with an S on his hard paste porcelain produce.

NIDERVILLER

This faience factory was established in 1754 by Baron Beyerle, who took into partnership the Count de Custine. The factory was afterwards sold to Lanfrey. It was in operation until 1827.

Very beautiful tea-sets, table ware and services were made.

The hard paste used was very white. Pieces were often decorated in the manner of Sèvres. Lemire (1759–1806) and Saly have worked there.

The factory also produced some exquisitely modelled figures and groups. Clodion, the famous French sculptor, worked here from 1795–1798.

The chief mark used during the Custine period is a crossed double C, in blue under glaze. Sometimes a crown was added to the mark. After the factory had been sold to Lanfrey the letter N was used as a mark, in blue under glaze, or the name Niderviller or Niderville impressed in the moist clay.

LILLE

In 1711 a soft paste porcelain factory was established here by Barthelémy Dorez and Pierre Pélissier. The pieces were decorated with Chinese designs. In 1784 hard paste porcelain was made by Leperre Durot. In 1786 the French Dauphin became the patron of the factory and a dolphin was chosen as mark. Very fine and beautifully decorated porcelain was produced. There is a modern factory at Lille which also uses a dolphin to mark its pieces. The original factory was closed in 1800.

LA SEYNIE

In 1774 the Marquis de la Seynie established a porcelain factory at Saint Yrieix. The pieces were marked L S. The hard paste was usually white. Designs in imitation of Sèvres were used. In 1805 Closterman of Limoges bought the factory.

LIMOGES

This hard paste porcelain factory was founded by Massié in 1771 in association with the brothers Grellet, who sold it to the French Government in 1784, when it became a branch of the Sèvres factory. The marks used were red.

In 1840 David Havilland of New York established a factory at Limoges, the products of which were specially made for export. The mark of the factory was HAVILLAND. This factory makes very good services and artistic figurines.

PIERRE THARAUD – LIMOGES

In 1817 Pierre Tharaud established a factory in the former building of the Grellet Factory, after selling the enterprise to Barbe and Ponset in 1819, he founded later a manufactury at the Place Tourny under the patronage of King Charles X.

POUYAT

Two factories were established by Pouyat: The manufactury of the "Place des Carmes" in 1842, and the factory of Saint Léonard in 1849.

ARON AND VALIN, talented modellers established a factory in 1833 in the "Faubourg Montjovis".

J. B. Ruaud operated from 1833 an important plant.

FRANÇOIS ALLUAUD established in 1797 a workshop which his son, who took over the enterprise in 1801, developed into a flourishing factory.

ETIENNE BAIGNOL, who had merely been a director of the "Manufacture de la Seynie" established in 1797 a factory in the monastery "Des Grands Augustins" where he employed Closterman, a former chemist of the "Manufacture Royale". The products of this factory are marked: Baignol, Fabricant à St. Yrieix.

35 factories were operated at Limoges in 1882.

LA TOUR d'AIGUES

This factory, established in 1752, produced soft paste porcelain until 1773, when the manufacture of hard paste porcelain was introduced. The products were translucent and decorated in enamel colours with flowers and birds.

MARSEILLE

The factory was founded in 1766 by Joseph-Gaspard Robert. A hard paste porcelain was made which was not very translucent. The glaze, of a greyish tint, was often unevenly applied. The pieces were sometimes very handsomely decorated with flowers. Very beautiful vases were produced. The factory was closed in 1793. The marks of this factory were sometimes applied in gold.

MONTREUIL-SOUS-BOIS

This factory manufacturing hard paste porcelain was established by Tinet in 1815. Various types of decoration were used, including imitations of Chinese and Japanese patterns.

BRANCAS DE LAURAGUAIS

This factory was established in Paris in 1764 by Count Brancas de Lauraguais, who was a chemist and had been making porcelain since 1742 at his castle at Lassay, using kaolin found near Alençon. His paste was greyish in tint. He made statuettes, medaillons and several pieces bearing Chinese decorations. Lauraguais porcelain is very rare. The factory was closed in 1768. The pieces produced here were marked with the initials or the name of the Count under glaze.

LUNÉVILLE

This factory, founded in 1730, produced some very beautiful services, of soft paste porcelain and exquisite figures by Cufflé. (See European Pottery.)

SAINT-CLÉMENT 1750

This factory produced soft paste porcelain of the same type as that made at Lunéville.

CHOISY-LE-ROI

This factory was founded by Clément in 1785. Hard paste porcelain was produced and the factory expanded considerably during the 19th century.

BORDEAUX

This factory was founded by Verneuil in 1784 and produced a hard paste porcelain of good quality resembling the products of Limoges and Paris. Various patterns were used and services and Masonic cups were made. It belonged to Johnson in 1836 and in 1845 it was bought by Viellard.

BOISETTE-PRÈS-MÉLUN

A pottery was established at Boisette-près-Mélun in 1733 and in 1777 the brothers Vermont were making hard paste porcelain here. Very white paste was used and the products were ornamented with flower decorations. Biscuit figures were also made. The letter B was used as mark.

CAEN

This factory was established in 1797 by Desmarés, Mallet & Thierry. Hard paste porcelain, both white and decorated in colour, was made in imitation of Sèvres. A red mark was used. In the middle of the last century a factory owned by Le François was also established in Caen.

CHATILLON

A hard paste factory established here by Roussel & Cie in 1775, subsequently came into the hands of Lortz & Rouget. The pieces produced were decorated in blue and gold in imitation of Paris porcelain.

ETIOLLES

Monnier established this factory in 1768, which produced soft paste porcelain in imitation of St. Cloud. In 1770 the manufacture of hard paste porcelain was begun. Pieces produced here are very rare. The marks were incised.

FONTAINEBLEAU

Benjamin Jacob and Aaron Schmoll founded this factory in 1795. They imitated Sèvres pieces and made statuettes in the manner of Meissen.

JACOB PETIT–BELLEVILLE

Jacob and Mardochée Petit established a porcelain factory in Belleville in 1830. In the same year they bought the factory of Jacob & Schmoll at Fontainebleau and subsequently transferred it to Avon in 1851. They sold it to Jaquemin in 1862. The products of this factory were at first greatly prized, but later activity was mostly confined to copying Meissen models in a very naïve style.

VALENCIENNES

This hard paste porcelain factory was established by Fauquez & Lamoninary in 1785 and was closed in 1795. In 1800 it was re-opened and flourished till 1810, producing imitations of Lille and Paris porcelain. Verboekhoven executed some very remarkable biscuit groups here.
Marks were blue under glaze and red over glaze.

ARRAS 1782–1786.

This factory was founded by the Demoiselles Deleneur, under the protection of M. Colonne, Intendant de Flandre. The porcelain produced here was equal to that of Sèvres both in quality and decoration. The mark used was the letters A R in blue under glaze. Arras pieces are very rare.

SAINT-AMAND-LES-EAUX

This factory, which was founded in 1771, produced soft paste porcelain in imitation of Sèvres. Many St. Amand pieces were bought by painters who redecorated them with Sèvres designs and then sold them as genuine "Vieux Sèvres", the St. Amand marks having been previously destroyed by acids. The marks used were red. This factory flourished during the 19th century.

CRÉPY-EN-VALOIS 1762–1770.

This factory was founded by P. Bourgeois and Louis François Gaignepain, a potter who had worked at Mennecy-Villeroy. Products of this factory are very rare. Very good soft paste porcelain was produced, including such objects as snuff-boxes and vases in imitation of Sèvres. The marks were incised.

ORLÉANS 1757–1811

Gérault d'Araubert established a soft paste porcelain factory here in 1757 and switched over in 1764 to hard paste. The soft paste china was decorated in blue with camaïeu bouquets. The hard paste products were decorated with polychrome patterns. The pieces were marked in underglaze blue. During the time of Bênoit Le Brun (1808–1811) pieces produced at this factory were marked with his initials in blue and gold.

VAUX-PRÈS-MELUN

This factory was established by Hannong in 1770 and operated during a very short period only.

BAYEUX (CALVADOS)

This factory producing hard paste porcelain was founded in 1810.

LURCY-LÉVY (ALLIER)

This hard paste porcelain factory was founded by the Marquis de Sinety in 1783 in his Château of Lévy. The Marquis was assisted by a chemist named Hasenfratz. In the sixth year of the Republic, Déruelle was appointed as director and in 1815 his place was taken by Burguin. In 1855 the factory was transferred to La Couleuvre. The mark was a letter B impressed in the paste.

PARIS-FAUBOURG ST. ANTOINE

A hard paste porcelain factory was established here by Pierre Antoine Hannong in 1773 after his failure at Vincennes.

PARIS-FAUBOURG ST. DENIS

A hard paste porcelain factory was established here by Hannong for the Comte d'Artois in 1769. Artistically decorated pieces in Sèvres style were produced and were marked in blue. This factory later came into the hands of Schmidt & Cie., and Benjamin Schoelcher.

PARIS-RUE DE LA ROQUETTE

A factory was established here by Souroux in 1773. Hard paste porcelain was produced and was marked in underglaze blue.

PARIS-FAUBURG ST. ANTOINE – RUE DE LA ROQUETTE

This was a hard paste porcelain factory established by Vincent Dubois. Marks were in blue.

PARIS-RUE THIROUX

This hard paste porcelain factory was established by Leboeuf in 1778 under the patronage of Marie Antoinette. Beautifully finished pieces in Sèvres style or decorated with German flowers, were produced here. The Thiroux porcelain was known as "la porcelaine de la Reine". Marks were in red and gold.

PARIS-PASSY

This factory produced soft paste porcelain in imitation of Rouen and St. Cloud.

PARIS-BARRIÈRE DE REUILLY

This factory situated at Barrière de Reuilly worked from 1779–1785, producing hard paste porcelain with polychrome decorations. Marks were in red or gold.

PARIS-RUE DE BONDY

This factory was established in 1780 under the patronage of the Duc d'Angoulême by Dihl and Guerhard. Services and vases of excellent quality in Sèvres style were produced as well as very good figures and groups in biscuit-ware. The factory competed succesfully with Sèvres. In 1825 it was transferred to the Boulevard St. Martin.

PARIS-RUE CLICHY

There was a hard paste porcelain factory here of which no details are known.

PARIS-RUE DE CRUSSOL

A hard paste porcelain factory was founded here in 1789 by Potter, who called his products "Prince of Wales China". Marks were in red and blue.

PARIS-MANUFACTURE DU PETIT CAROUSSEL

This factory was founded by Charles Barthélemy Guy, who owned a porcelain decorating workshop in 1775. In 1797 he bought the factory in the rue Thiroux from Le Boeuf.

PARIS-RUE PONT-AUX-CHOUX

This factory, producing hard paste porcelain, was established in 1787 in the rue Pont-aux-Choux by Lamarre de Villers under the patronage of the Duc d'Orléans. It was transferred to the rue Amelot in 1786. Pieces produced here were gilded and decorated with flowers and birds.

PARIS-CLIGNANCOURT

Pierre Deruelle established this factory in 1775 under the patronage of the Comte de Provence. Both soft and hard paste porcelain were produced. Table services were made in Sèvres style. The marks were in blue and red.

PARIS-FAUBOURG ST. ANTOINE – RUE DE REUILLY

This was a hard paste porcelain factory established by Lassia in 1774. Marks were in gold.

PARIS-RUE FONTAINE AU ROI "DE LA COURTILLE"

This was a hard paste porcelain factory founded by Locré de Roissy in 1773. In 1787 it was taken over by Russinger. Numerous vases, services and very artistic figures were produced. Porcelain produced here was known as German porcelain. Marks were in blue, red and gold. Laurentius Russinger was a native of Höchst and was attached from 1759–1767 to the famous Höchst factory. The group "Venus and Cupid", "Amynthas and Sylvia", the "Bergère endormie" are ascribed to him by Röder.

1768. Russinger arrives' to Paris to work at the Sceaux factory with Chapelle.
1777. Russinger is director of the factory "Fontaine au Roi."
1787. Russinger purchases the factory "Fontaine au Roi."
An V. Russinger takes into partnership François Pouyat.
An VIII. Russinger leaves the manufacture.
Pouyat acquires the factory in 1810.
1816. The sons of Pouyat take into partnership Guillaume Le Bourgeois.
1823. Pierre Saurède, is proprietor of the factory.

In 1825 Jean-Marie Clauss transferred the factory from rue de la Courtille to the rue Pierre Levée.

The Clauss produced during three generations porcelain decorated in "Compagnie des Indes" style, Louis XVI motifs and Napoleon III roses.

The Production of Porcelaine de Paris is very much extended since 1880. Pieces in the style of Locré, Empire, Pate tendre Sèvres, Compagnie des Indes, Lowestoft, Chantilly, famille rose, verte, jaune, noire, Capodimonte, Buen Retiro. Groups, figurines, and a vast collection of beautiful birds of all kinds are manufactured. The mark of the factory has been always used on all pieces and marks of other factories have never adorned them, but the original mark can be easily transformed by fakers into a Meissen mark, or if wiped out, the piece can be mistaken for the produce of one of the very expensive factories.

Porcelaine de Paris came under the full control of Achille Bloch in 1880. Robert Bloch, started with his father and brother in 1913. His brother was killed in World War I, and his father died in 1926.

During World War II Bloch got out of France just ahead of the Germans (who took over his business) and lived in the United States for the duration. Michel Bloch served in the American Army. After the war they returned to France and undertook the restoration of their enterprise.

PARIS-RUE DE LA PAIX

This factory was founded by Feuillet. Characteristic marks are in red and blue with a crown in gold and either the initial F or the signature of Feuillet. Feuillet worked as a painter in his own decorating workshop in 1820.

PARIS-RUE DU PARADIS

This factory was founded by Gille in 1845. It produced a large number of very good biscuit groups, sometimes decorated in colour by the modeller Charles Baury. The mark in relief under the base represents the initials of the founder and is followed by the letters L G impressed.

PARIS-RUE BÉRANGER 7 – SAMSON

This factory is one of the most important among the modern porcelain factories in Paris. It produces excellent imitations of old Chinese, Japanese, and all the old European porcelains.

No mystery whatever is hidden in this famous works. In 1845 Edme Samson acquired the hard paste factory of Tinet established at Montreuil-sous-Bois by Tinet, who imitated all kinds of porcelain, including Chinese and Japanese pieces. According to the law of the 22 Germinal of the year 11 (1803) the "contrefaçons de noms et marques" as well as the "concurrence deloyale" were forbidden and the imitators had to mark their produces with their own marks. Edme Samson eluded the law by marking his produce both with the mark of the original of the copy and his own. The original mark was usually underglaze, his own on glaze.

After the death of Edme Samson in 1891, the factory passed into the hands of his son Emile, who operated the works until 1913, when the works was inherited by Léon Samson, who had successfully managed it until 1928. Pierre Samson, who took over the factory in 1928, sold it in 1964 to G. C.

Richardière, who has given a new élan to this famous establishment. The early Samsons are now gradually ripening into collector pieces. The factory has copied during 117 years Meissen, Höchst, Frankenthal, Nymphenburg, Sèvres, Chantilly, Mennecy, St. Cloud, Sceaux, Tournay, Chelsea, Worcester, Capodimonte, Buen Retiro, Persian and Hispano Moresque ware, Palissy, Moustiers, Alcora Strasbourg and Delft. All of them with beautiful original marks. Compagnie des Indes, famille rose, verte, jaune and noire were not omitted. Different biscuit figures were manufactured from moulds taken over from Sèvres. The factory has never used soft paste. The imitations of German hardpaste pieces are especially successful because the quality of the paste very much resembles the German originals.

The copies of the French and English pieces are not so deceptive as those made in the second half of the 19th century at Coalport.

SCEAUX

This factory was established under the patronage of the Duchess de Maine in 1748 by an architect, de Bey, and was very succesfully managed by Jacques Chapelle. He was assisted by the painter Joseph Jullien and the modeller Symphorien Jacques. After the death of the Duchess de Maine in 1753, the Duke de Penthièvre, Grand Admiral de France, became the new patron of the factory.

The soft paste porcelain produce of Sceaux was artistically decorated with birds, flowers and cupids. Jacques Chapelle retired in 1768, and the factory subsequently came into the hands of Jullien and Jacques. The factory was sold to Richard Glot in 1772, and was closed in 1795

The marks of the factory were the letters SX impressed in the moist clay, an anchor, the letters SP, and the name Sceaux, impressed or in blue, black or gold.

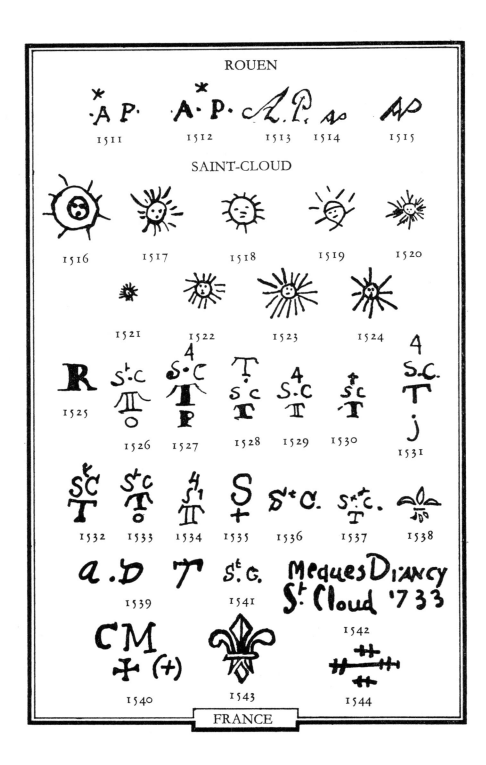

ROUEN

SAINT-CLOUD

FRANCE

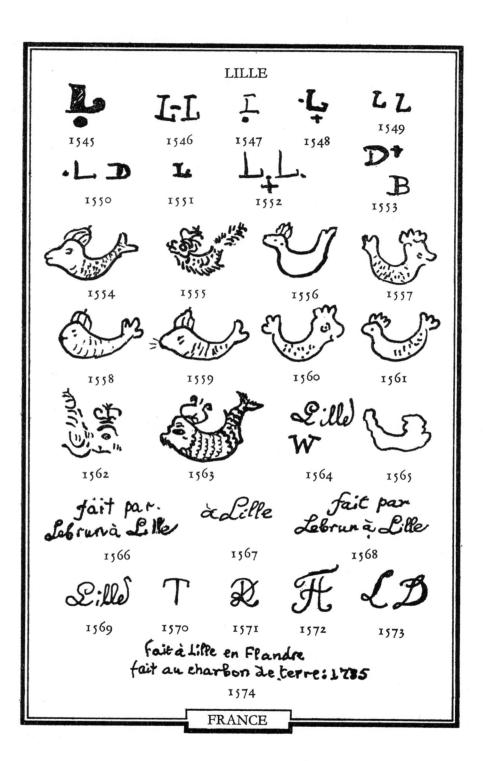

LILLE

FRANCE

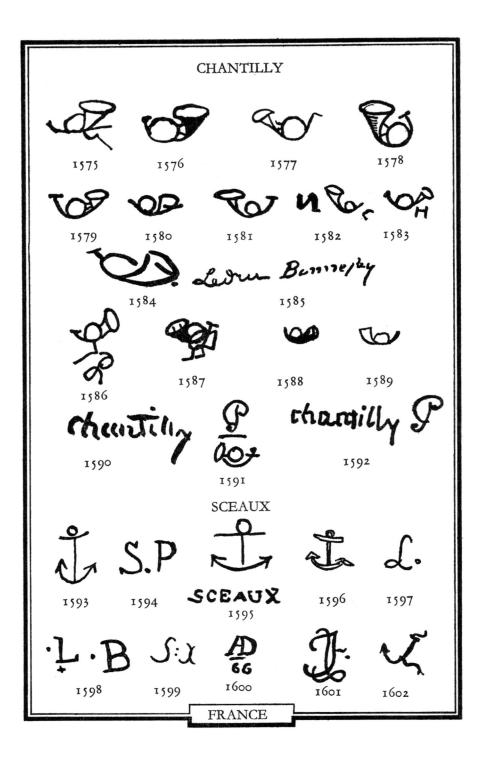

CHANTILLY

1575 1576 1577 1578

1579 1580 1581 1582 1583

1584 1585

1586 1587 1588 1589

1590 1591 1592

SCEAUX

1593 1594 1595 1596 1597

1598 1599 1600 1601 1602

FRANCE

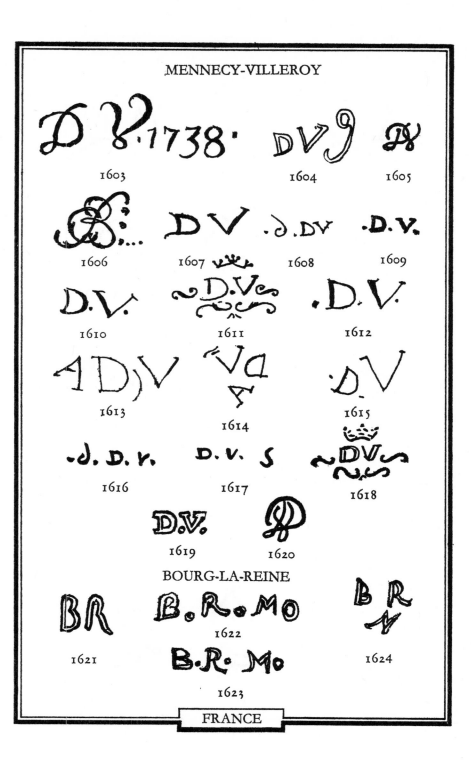

MENNECY-VILLEROY

1603 · 1738 ·   1604   1605

1606   1607   1608   1609

1610   1611   1612

1613   1614   1615

1616   1617   1618

1619   1620

BOURG-LA-REINE

1621   1622   1624

1623

FRANCE

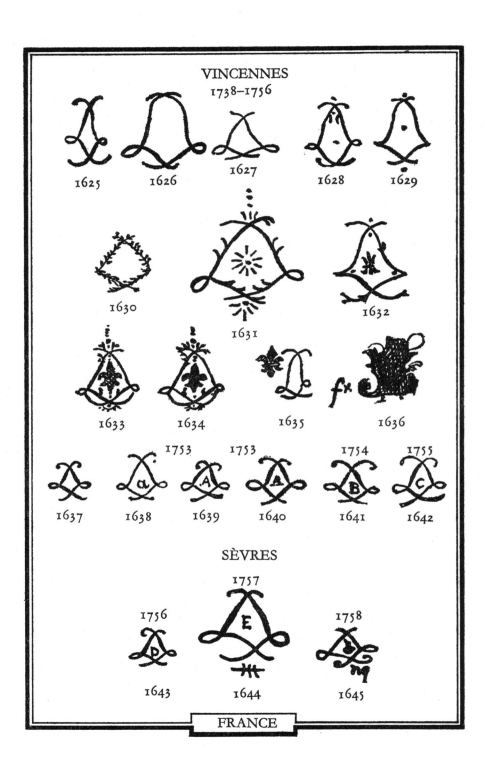

VINCENNES

1738–1756

SÈVRES

FRANCE

VIENNA. Solitaire, Sorgenthal period. Marks – *beehive* in blue under glaze. About 1785   XV
Collection J. Morpurgo, Amsterdam

XVI   SAINT-CLOUD. "Chinaman". About 1720. Ht. 22,7 cm. *Pâte – tendre*. *Victoria and Albert Museum*

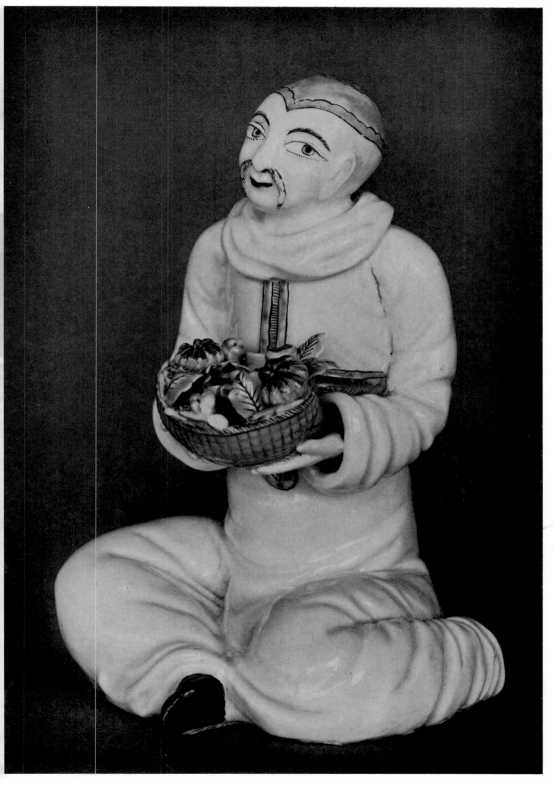

CHANTILLY. Jug, Imari decoration.
About 1738
Rijksmuseum, Amsterdam

CHANTILLY. Four-lobed vase
decorated with moulded prunus
sprigs. About 1730.
Bayerisches Nationalmuseum, Munich

XVIII

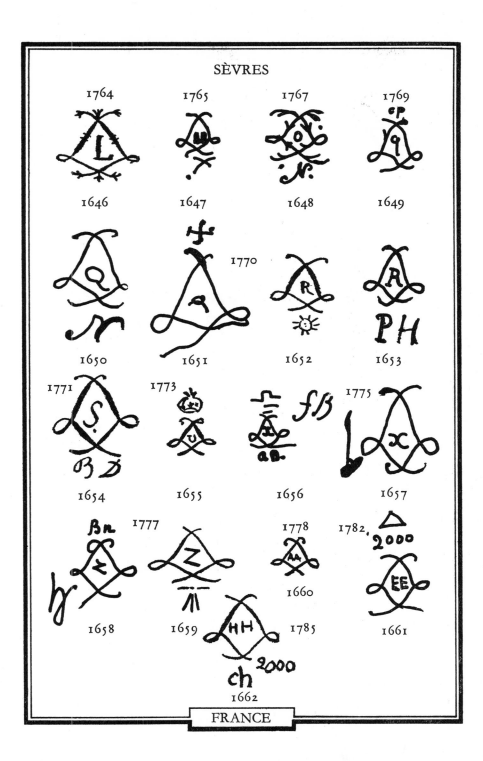

1764   1765   1767   1769

1646   1647   1648   1649

1770

1650   1651   1652   1653

1771   1773   1775

1654   1655   1656   1657

1777   1778   1782

1658   1659   1660   1785   1661

1662

FRANCE

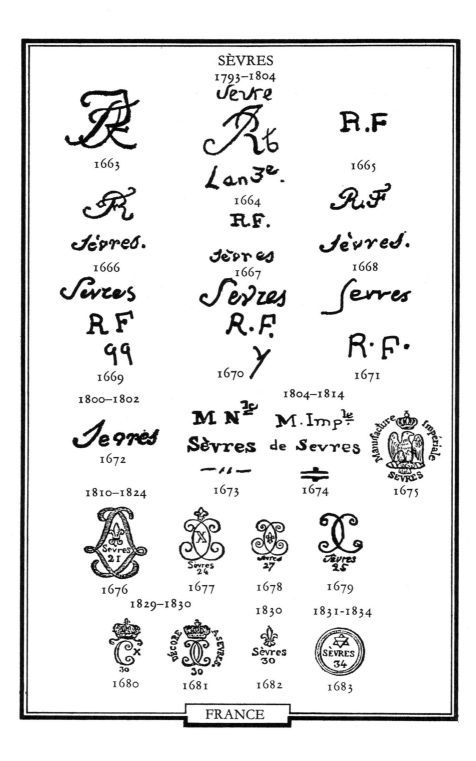

SÈVRES
1793–1804

1663

1664

1665

1666

1667

1668

1669

1670

1671

1800–1802

1672

1804–1814

1673

1674

1675

1810–1824

1676

1677

1678

1679

1829–1830

1680

1681

1830

1682

1831–1834

1683

FRANCE

SÈVRES

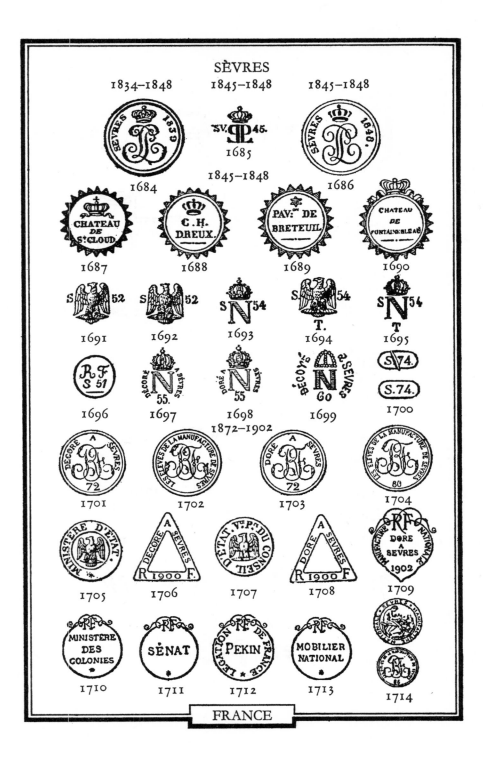

1834–1848   1845–1848   1845–1848

1685

1684   1845–1848   1686

1687   1688   1689   1690

1691   1692   1693   1694   1695

1696   1697   1698   1699   1700

1872–1902

1701   1702   1703   1704

1705   1706   1707   1708   1709

1710   1711   1712   1713   1714

FRANCE

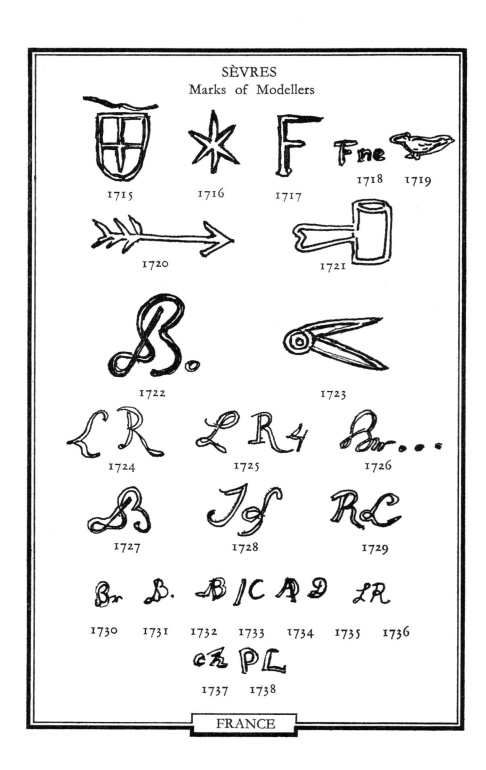

SÈVRES
Marks of Modellers

1715   1716   1717   1718   1719

1720   1721

1722   1723

1724   1725   1726

1727   1728   1729

1730   1731   1732   1733   1734   1735   1736

1737   1738

FRANCE

SÈVRES
Marks of Painters

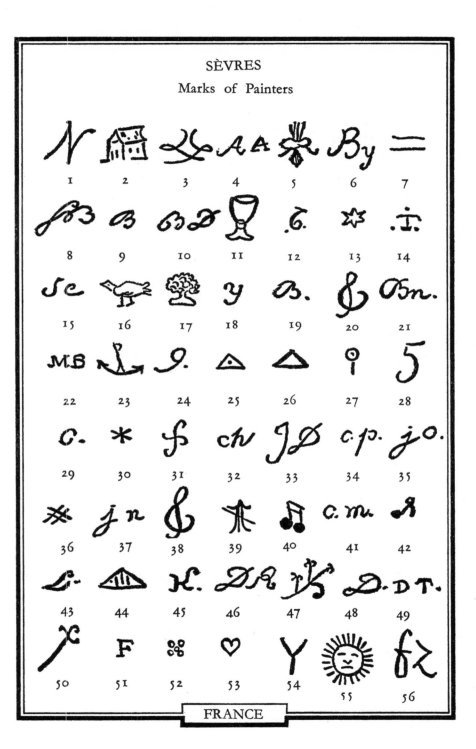

SÈVRES
Marks of Painters

FRANCE

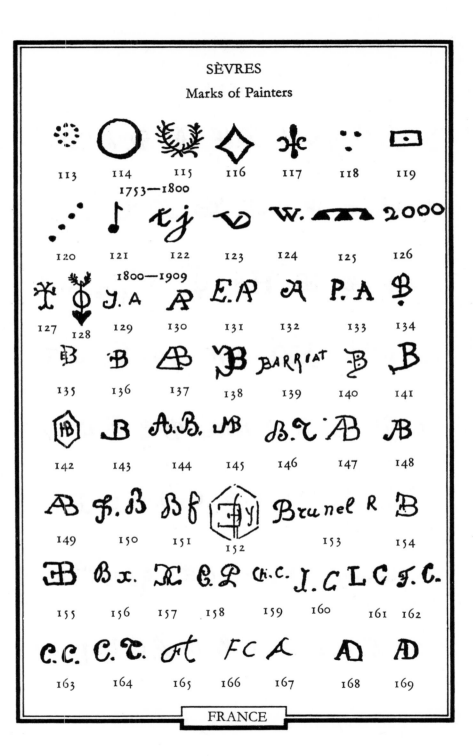

SÈVRES

Marks of Painters

113   114   115   116   117   118   119

1753—1800

120   121   122   123   124   125   126

1800—1909

127   128   129   130   131   132   133   134

135   136   137   138   139   140   141

142   143   144   145   146   147   148

149   150   151   152   153   154

155   156   157   158   159   160   161   162

163   164   165   166   167   168   169

FRANCE

SÈVRES
Marks of Painters

170   171   172   173   174   175

176   177   178   179   180   181   182

183   184   185   186   187   188   189

190   191   192   193   194   195   196

197   198   199   200   201   202

203   204   205   206   207   208   209

210   211   212   213   214

215   216   217   218   219   220   221   222   223

FRANCE

SÈVRES
Marks of Painters

FRANCE

SÈVRES
20th Century

1739
SÈVRES
MANUFACTURE
NATIONALE
FRANCE
m

 1740

Marks of Painters

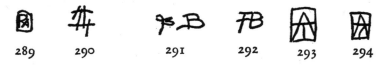

289   290   291   292   293   294

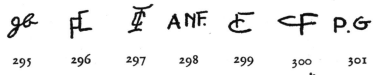

295   296   297   298   299   300   301

302   303   304   305   306   307   308   309

310   311   312   313   314   315   316

Marks of Modellers

317   318   319   320   321   322

323   324   325   326   327   328

FRANCE

C·D· 1741
C D 1742
c.d. 1743
C·D 1744
c) 1745
c.D. 1746

c·D· 1747
c d 1748
CD 1749
C·D 1750
c) 1751
c.d 1752

1755

CD 1753
C d 1754

c d 1756
c d 1757

C D ... DT 1758

1759

Limoges

c d 1760

porcelaine royalle de Limoges CD 1761

porcelaine de Limoges c d 1762

Manufacteur Roiyalle de Limoges 1763

POUYAT.LIMOGES HAVILAND
19th Century

BAIGNOL Fabricant. à St Yrieix 1764

J.P L 1765

Haviland France 1766
19th and 20th

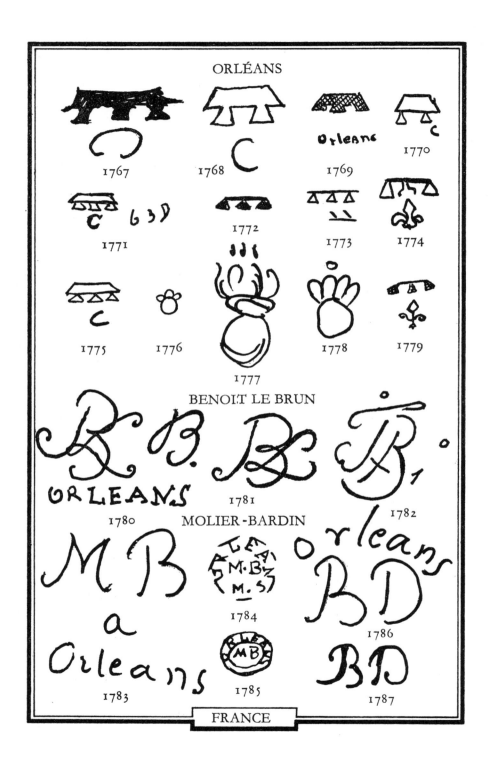

ORLÉANS

1767 1768 1769 1770

1771 1772 1773 1774

1775 1776 1777 1778 1779

BENOIT LE BRUN

ORLEANS
1780 1781 1782

MOLIER-BARDIN

1783 1784 1785 1786 1787

FRANCE

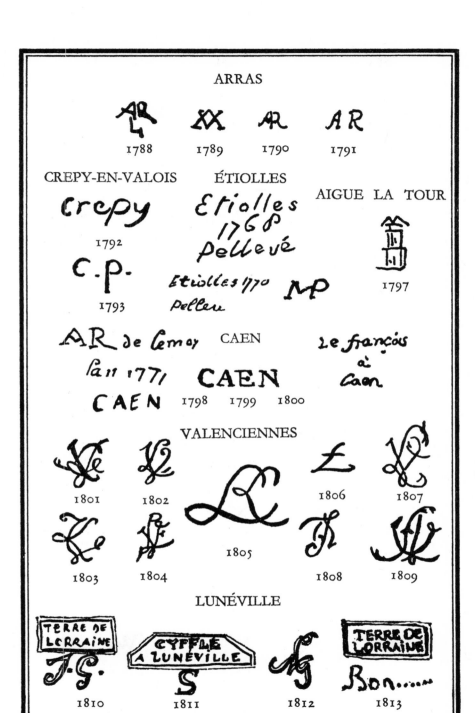

ARRAS

1788 · 1789 · 1790 · 1791

CREPY-EN-VALOIS · ÉTIOLLES

Crepy
1792

C. P.
1793

AIGUE LA TOUR

Etiolles
1768
Pellevé

Etiolles 1770
Pellev

1797

AR de Lemoy · CAEN

l'an 1771

CAEN

CAEN
1798 · 1799 · 1800

Le françois
à
Caen

VALENCIENNES

1801 · 1802 · 1806 · 1807

1805

1803 · 1804 · 1808 · 1809

LUNÉVILLE

TERRE DE LORRAINE
J. G.
1810

CYFFLÉ A LUNÉVILLE
S
1811

1812

TERRE DE LORRAINE
Bon......
1813

FRANCE

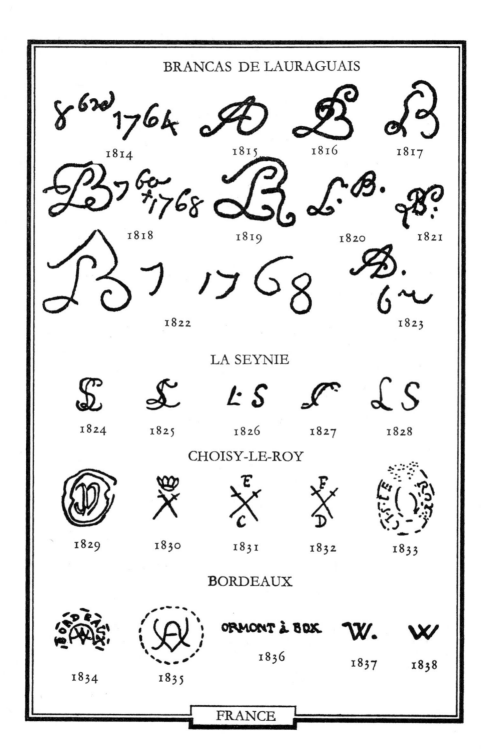

BRANCAS DE LAURAGUAIS

1814 1815 1816 1817

1818 1819 1820 1821

1822 1823

LA SEYNIE

1824 1825 1826 1827 1828

CHOISY-LE-ROY

1829 1830 1831 1832 1833

BORDEAUX

1834 1835 1836 1837 1838

FRANCE

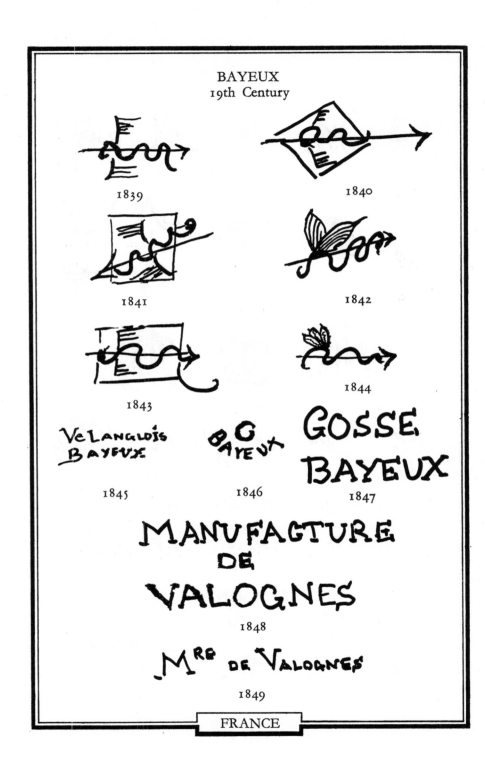

BAYEUX
19th Century

1839

1840

1841

1842

1843

1844

1845

1846

1847

1848

1849

FRANCE

143

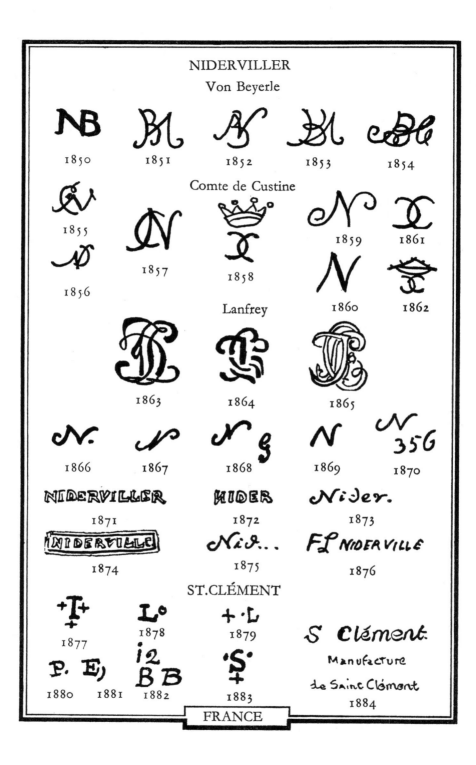

NIDERVILLER
Von Beyerle

1850	1851	1852	1853	1854

Comte de Custine

1855			1859	1861
1856	1857	1858	1860	1862

Lanfrey

1863	1864	1865

1866	1867	1868	1869	1870

NIDERVILLER	HIDER	Nider.
1871	1872	1873
NIDERVILLE	Nid...	FL NIDERVILLE
1874	1875	1876

ST. CLÉMENT

1877	L° 1878	+·L 1879	S Clément.
P. E) 1880	1881	i2 B B 1882	Manufacture de Saint Clément 1884
		·S· 1883	

FRANCE

STRASBOURG
Paul-Antoine Hannong

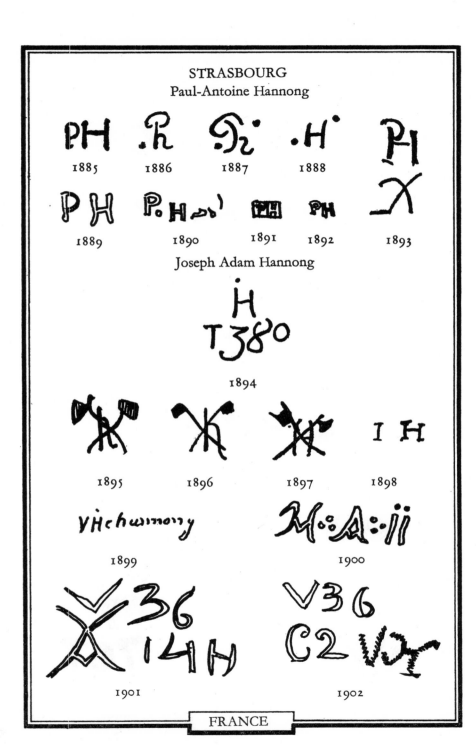

1885 1886 1887 1888

1889 1890 1891 1892 1893

Joseph Adam Hannong

1894

1895 1896 1897 1898

1899 1900

1901 1902

STRASBOURG
Joseph Adam Hannong

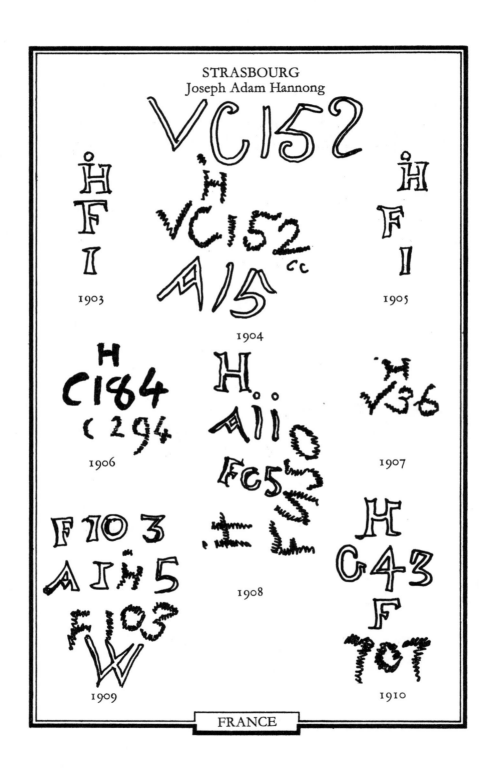

FRANCE

STRASBOURG
Joseph Adam Hannong

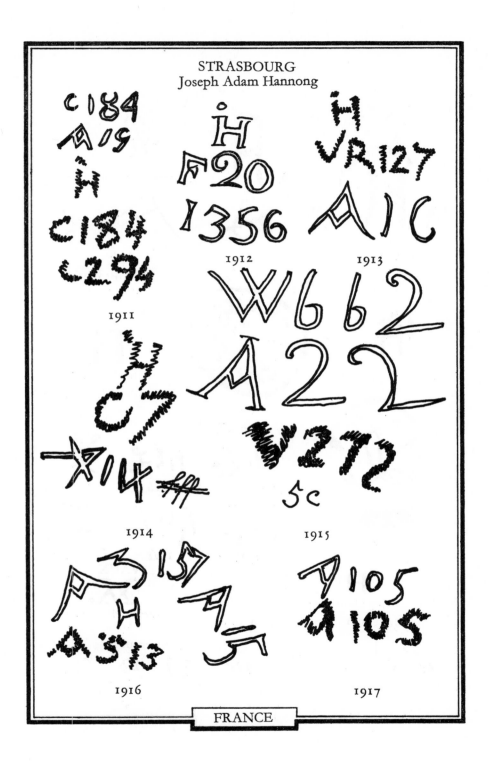

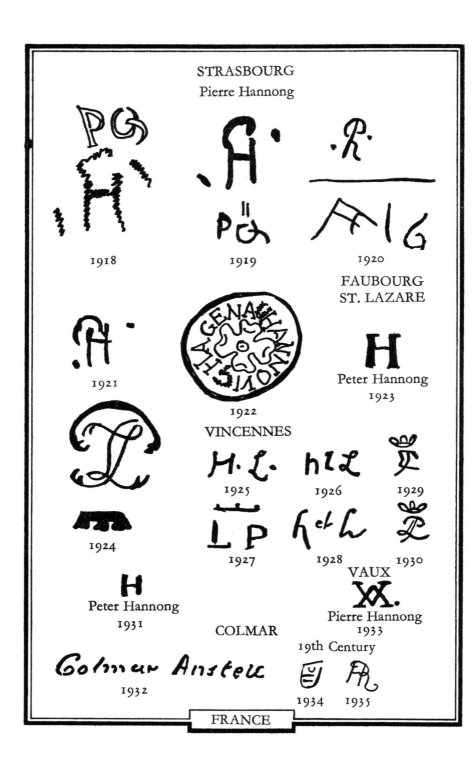

STRASBOURG

Pierre Hannong

1918

1919

1920

FAUBOURG
ST. LAZARE

1921

1922

Peter Hannong
1923

VINCENNES

1924

1925

1926

1929

1927

1928

1930

Peter Hannong
1931

VAUX

Pierre Hannong
1933

COLMAR

19th Century

1932

1934   1935

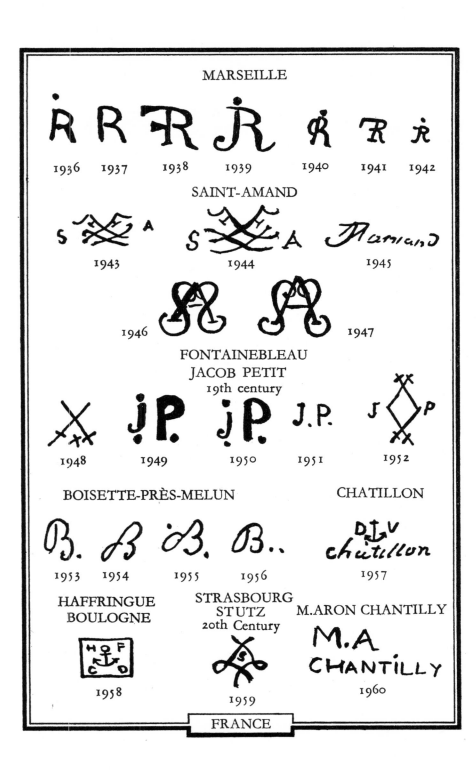

MARSEILLE

1936 1937 1938 1939 1940 1941 1942

SAINT-AMAND

1943 1944 1945

1946 1947

FONTAINEBLEAU
JACOB PETIT
19th century

1948 1949 1950 1951 1952

BOISETTE-PRÈS-MELUN

CHATILLON

1953 1954 1955 1956 1957

HAFFRINGUE
BOULOGNE

STRASBOURG
STUTZ
20th Century

M.ARON CHANTILLY

1958 1959 1960

FRANCE

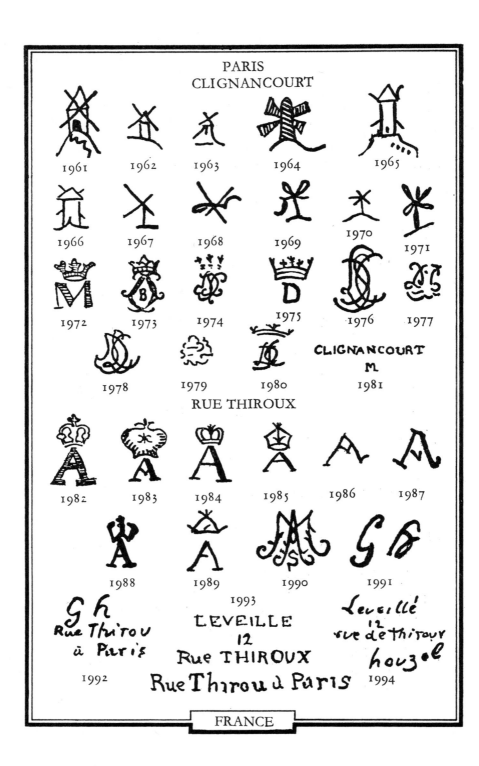

PARIS
CLIGNANCOURT

1961 1962 1963 1964 1965

1966 1967 1968 1969 1970 1971

1972 1973 1974 1975 1976 1977

1978 1979 1980

CLIGNANCOURT
M
1981

RUE THIROUX

1982 1983 1984 1985 1986 1987

1988 1989 1990 1991

1993

G h
Rue Thirou
à Paris

1992

LEVEILLE
12
Rue THIROUX

Rue Thirou à Paris

Leveillé
12
rue de thirour
houzel

1994

FRANCE

PARIS
RUE PONT-AU-CHOUX

| 1995 | 1996 | 1997 | 1998 | 1999 |

Fabrique du Pont aux Choux   *Fabrique de Pont-aux-Choux*

| 2000 | 2001 |

| 2002 | 2003 | 2004 | 2005 | 2006 |

RUE AMELOT

Lefevre rue amelot
à paris

2007

BARRIÈRE DE REUILLY

| CH | CH | | | M |
| 2008 | 2009 | | 2011 | 2012 |

2010

CH   MAP

2013   2014

RUE DE REUILLY

L   L   L

2015   2016   2017

FRANCE

PARIS
VEUVE CHICANNEAU
FAUBOURG ST. HONORÉ RUE DE LA VILLE L'EVÊQUE

2018   2019   2020

FAUBOURG ST. DENIS
FABRIQUE DU COMTE D'ARTOIS

2021   2022   2023   2024   2025

2026   2027   2028   2029   2030

2031   2032   2033   2034   2035

FAUBOURG ST. ANTOINE MORELLE

2036

PARIS PASSY

2037   2038

PARIS
RUE FONTAINE-AU-ROI

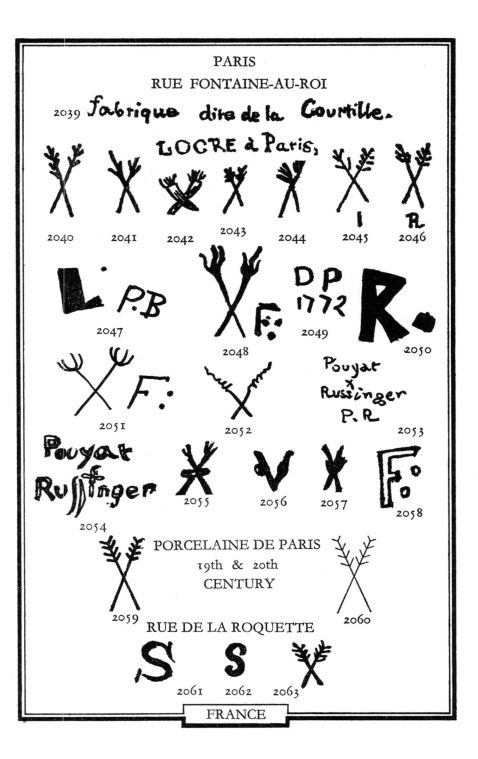

2039 *Fabrique dite de la Courtille.*

LOCRE à Paris,

2040 2041 2042 2043 2044 2045 2046

2047 2048 2049 2050

2051 2052 *Pouyat* X *Russinger* P. R 2053

2054 2055 2056 2057 2058

PORCELAINE DE PARIS
19th & 20th CENTURY

2059 2060

RUE DE LA ROQUETTE

2061 2062 2063

FRANCE

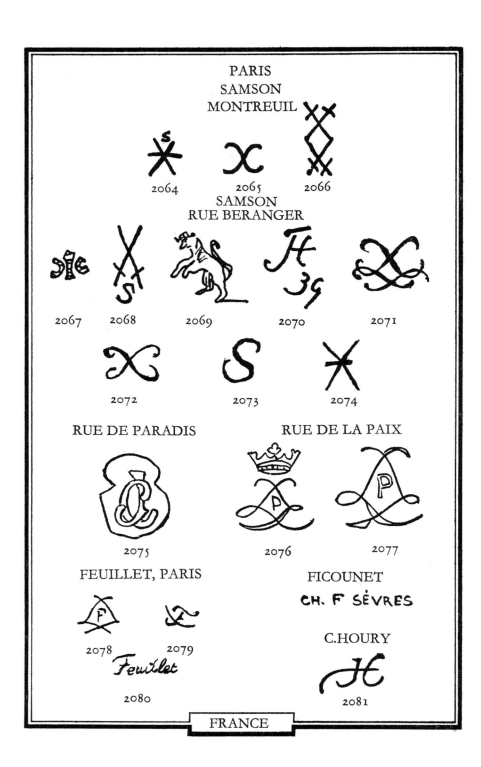

PARIS
SAMSON
MONTREUIL

2064   2065   2066

SAMSON
RUE BERANGER

2067   2068   2069   2070   2071

2072   2073   2074

RUE DE PARADIS   ## RUE DE LA PAIX

2075   2076   2077

FEUILLET, PARIS   ## FICOUNET
                            ### CH. F SÈVRES

2078   2079   ### C.HOURY

Feuillet

2080   2081

FRANCE

PARIS

RUE DE CRUSSOL   RUE ST. GILLES

Dagoty a Paris

2082

Ed HONORÉ A PARIS

2083

P. L. DAGOTY A PARIS

2084

H ç C

2085

Manufacture de S.M. L'Imperatrice P.L DAGOTY à Paris.

2086

🌙)

2087   2088

MADAME DUCHESSE D' ANGOULÊME

2089

M^bure de MADAME P. L. DAGOTY

2090

FLEURY

2091

C. H. MENARD

2092

RUE DE CRUSSOL   PETIT CARROUSSEL

DENUELLE Rue de Crussol a Paris

2093

MANUFACTURE du Petit Carousel à Paris

2094

P C G

2095

P C G

2096

RUE DE CRUSSOL

Potter.

2097

C H potter a paris

2099

RUE DES TROIS BORNES

Potter

2098

B Potter 42

2102

E. B

2103

B Potter -42

2100

B Potter 2

2101

B C q P

2104

R C· P 1

2105

FRANCE

155

PARIS
RUE DE BONDY

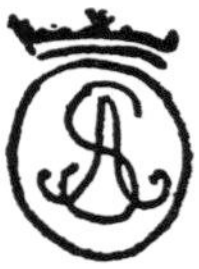

2106

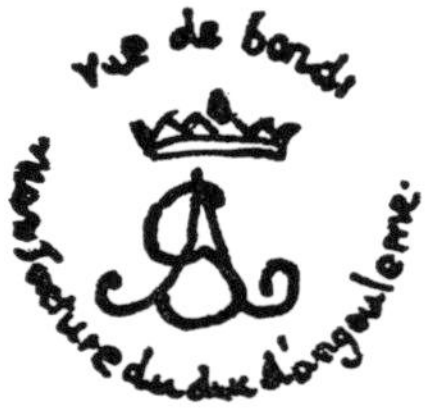

rue de bondy
Manufacture du duc d'angouleme

2107

rue de bondi

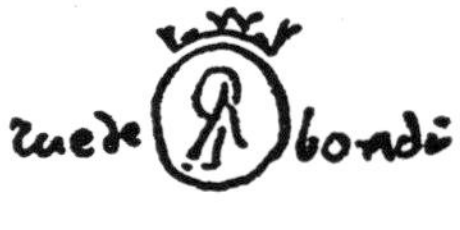

2108

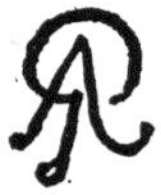

2109

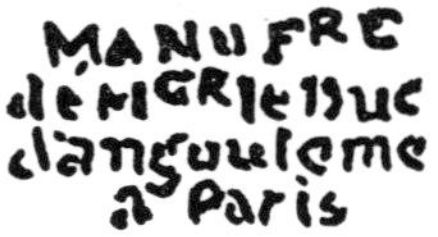

MANUFRE
de MGR le Duc
d'angouleme
a Paris

2110

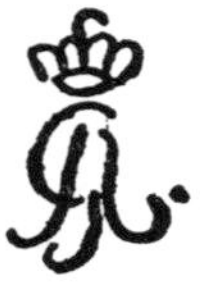

2111

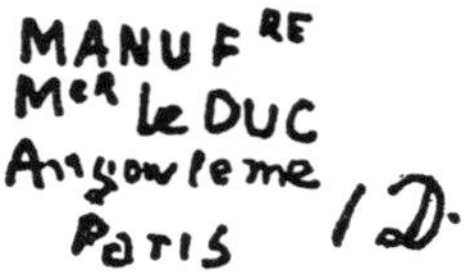

MANUFRE
MGR le DUC
Angouleme
Paris
LD.

2112

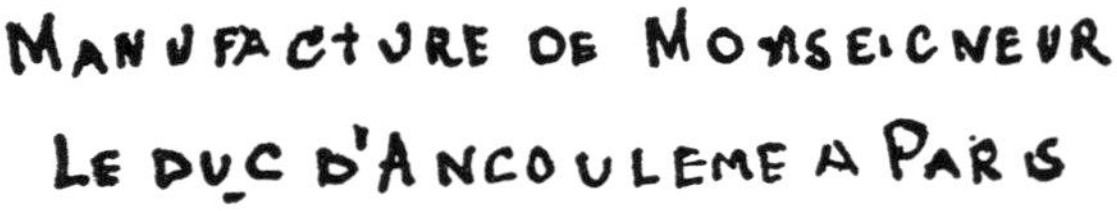

MANUFACTURE DE MONSEIGNEUR
LE DUC D'ANGOULEME A PARIS

2113

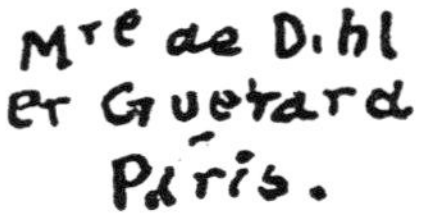

Mre de Dihl
et Guerard
Paris.

2115

Dihl.

2114

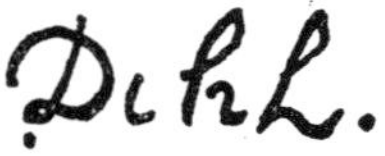

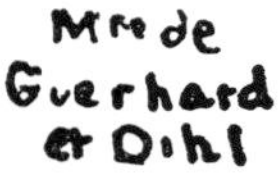

Mre de
Guerhard
et Dihl

2116

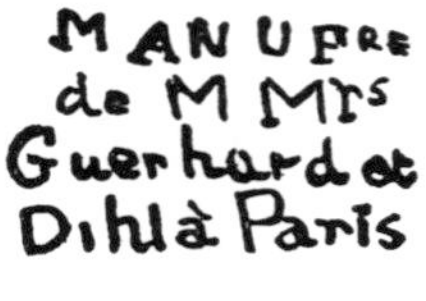

MANUFRE
de MMrs
Guerhard et
Dihl à Paris

2117

RUE MONTMARTRE

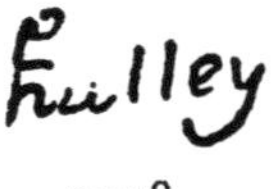

Halley

2118

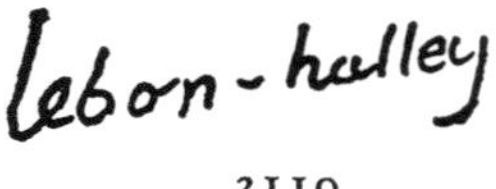

lebon-halley

2119

RUE POPINCOURT

NAST
a
Paris

2120

N

2121

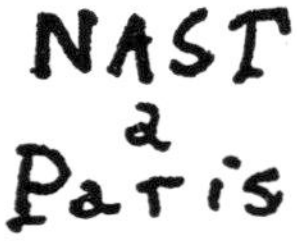

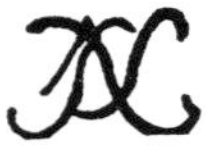

2122

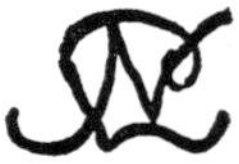

2123

FRANCE

PARIS

RUE DE RECOLLETS

OESPAEZ
Rue Des Recollets
A Paris

2124

PALAIS ROYAL

l'Escalior
de Cristal
Paris

2125

RUE DE CHARONNES

DARTE
FRERES
PARIS.

2126

DARTE
Palais Royal
n° 21

2127

MONGINOT

Monginot
20 Boulevard
des Italiens

2128

FOËSCY

Manufacture de Foëscy
Passage Violet No. 5
Rue Poissonniere à Paris

2129

CRELL

CRELL
BREVET D'INVENTION
PARIS

2130

GILLET & BRIANCHON

G.B
BREVETE
PARIS

2131

MASSON

MASSON FRERES

2132

SCHOELCHER

Schoelcher

2133

C. H. PILLIVUYT

C. H. PILLIVUYT
& Cie Paris

2134

LAHENS & RATEAU

LR

2135

A. JEAN, PARIS

2136

Jean

2137

FRANCE

BELGIUM

TOURNAY 1750–1850

This factory was established by a potter, Carpentier, who sold it to a merchant named Peterynk who enjoyed the protection of the Empress Maria Theresia. The factory produced soft paste porcelain of excellent quality, resembling the Sèvres product. Very finely modelled and decorated pieces were manufactured in the Sèvres and vieux-Saxe traditions with very good gilding. This factory also made figures which were glazed but left unpainted. Some figures were executed in biscuit porcelain.

The Tournay factory competed sucessfully with Sèvres for the service of the Duc d'Orléans, which was carried out at a cost of 60.000 florins. The best period of the factory was from 1760–1790. Among the artists employed Duvivier was famous for Italian landscapes and Mayer for decorations.

All the Tournay porcelain of the last period was in the style of Sèvres and is famous for a special blue colour and for very fine bird paintings. In 1793 the factory was destroyed by fire and later rebuilt.

The factory mark during the first period was a gate in blue. From about 1757 two crossed swords were used, surrounded by four small crosses. The marks were painted in blue, red, black, gold and violet.

In 1808 the factory belonged to Jules Hans de Bettignies and Olympe de Bettignies and was operated until 1850 when it was sold to the brothers Boch who closed the works in 1891. The moulds were bought by the Saint Amand factory and the Louvière works.

The last interesting table service was made in 1817 for Willem I, the King of the Netherlands.

MODELLERS:

Barbieux, Pierre-Ignace, 1771.
Belin.
Brasseur, Pierre Joseph, 1775–1778.
Caulier, J. B., 1775.
Decalonne, 1775.
Delmotte, 1775.
Gauron, Nicolas Joseph, 1758.
Gillis, Antoine, 1756–1771.
Lecreux, Nicolas, 1775.
Lefèbre, Jacques, 1767.
Louis, Jean-Jacques, 1754 onwards.
Noël, Jacques, 1775.
Noël, Pierre Joseph, 1775.
Willems, Joseph, dies in 1766.

PAINTERS:

Bastenaire, J. B. J., 1767.
Baudar, Marie Lucie, 1775.
Bellay, F., 1775.
Borne, Claude, 1752–1772.

Brébard, Raymond, 1775–1786.
Breunin, Ch. F. J., 1775–1786.
Brunin, Ch., 1773.
Cardon de Bertauvillet, Jean Claude, 1755, chief painter.
Crépin, J. F. J., until 1785.
Delmotte, 1775.
Duvivier, Henri Joseph, 1763.
Gaudry, Jean Baptiste.
Gilles, Jean, 1771.
Godry, Marie, 1775.
Hazard, Antoine, 1775.
Heindrix, Antoine François, 1775, has worked at St. Cloud.
Laville, L. F. 1775.
Lourdant, F., 1786.
Malaines, 1775.
Mansaux, J.
Martin.
Mayer, Jean Ghislain Joseph, famous bird painter from 1774 to 1815.
Muller, F. C.
de la Musellerie, François, chief painter, 1771.
Pels, Felix.
Roland, P. J.
Sauvage, P.
Suther, J. M., 1788.
Thiébaud, L. Joseph.
Vanové, Louis.

BRUSSELS

The first porcelain factory was established in Brussels in 1786 by Sébastien Vaume, former director of the faience factory of Arlon. In 1784 Vaume purchased the castle of Monplaisir and took into partnership Pierre Verny de Villars.

The mark of this factory consisted of the letter B in conjunction with a crown. In 1788 Biourge became director and three years later the factory was sold by auction.

Frédéric Chrétien Kühne, a German from Westphalia, established in 1787 a porcelain factory at ETTERBEEK. He was assisted by the modeller Claude Joseph Bommer from the Niderviller factory and Louis Cretté from the Bourg-la-Reine factory. Very soon artistic ware was produced. Birds painted after Buffon in Tournay style was a favourite decoration of this factory. The works was closed in 1800.

Towards the close of the 18th and the beginning of the 19th century several painters operated decoration workshops in Brussels.

Louis Cretté decorated in his workshop in the "RUE ARENBERG" porcelain of the "La Courtille" factory of Paris.

Barr and Riss operated a workshop established in the last quarter of the 18th century.

BRUSSELS

Frédéric Théodore Faber established under the patronage of King Willem I of the Netherlands a porcelain factory in 1818 at Ixelles. Pieces in imitation of Sèvres and Meissen were produced. Faber died in 1844. In 1849 his son closed the factory.

A factory of porcelain and faience was established by Cappelmans and Daboust in 1833. From 1838–1869 ware of superior quality was produced. The painters Panneel and Chappel, as well as, the painters Jacquet and Louis Nedonchelle decorated in their workshops in the 19th century white porcelain of the Sèvres factory and the Jacob Petit factory. These painters were pupils of Faber.

Jacquet and Nedonchelles excelled in flower painting and used very rich gildings.

Joseph Panneel and Edouard Chappel favoured Chinese decorations, miniatures as well as miniature copies of famous romantic pictures.

The painters G. Schmidt, G. Florin, Nique, Merkel and Wauthier have decorated porcelain in the period of 1805 to 1860.

SÈVRES. Leda and the Swan, biscuit, model by Etienne-Maurice Falconet, from a design
by François Boucher. About 1765. Ht. 32,5 cm. *Victoria and Albert Museum, London*   XIX

XX

LUNÉVILLE. "Le petit maçon", biscuit, model by Paul-Louis Cyfffé. About 1759–60
Mark – *Terre de Lorraine* impressed and script *B* incised. Ht. 16,3 cm.
Collection M. Penkala

FRANCE. Two biscuit groups. 18th century. Ht. 19 cm. and 20 cm. *Private Collection*

TOURNAY. Climbing children. From a model attributed to Nicolas Lecreux. About 1775   XXI
Victoria and Albert Museum, London

CHELSEA. Nurse and child, after "la nourrice by Palissy". Mark – an *anchor in red*. About 1755. *Victoria and Albert Museum, London*

DERBY. Sacrifice figure, "pale-colouring period", *patch-marks*. Ht. 19,4 cm. *Collection M. Penkala*

"GIRL IN A SWING". About 1751. *Victoria and Albert Museum, London*

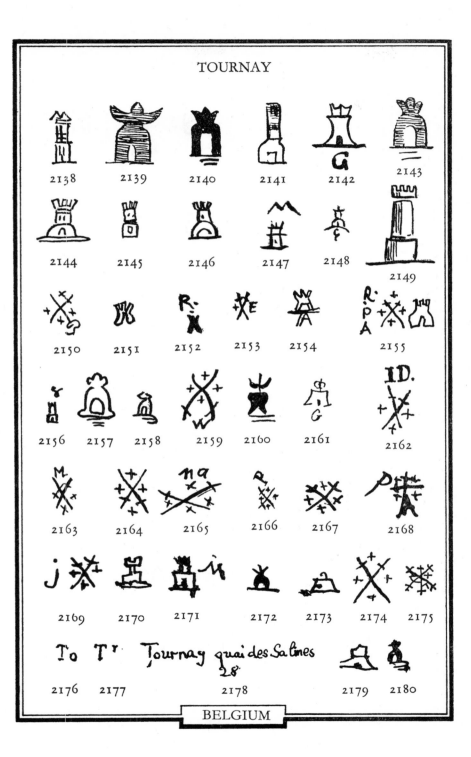

2138
2139
2140
2141
2142
2143
2144
2145
2146
2147
2148
2149
2150
2151
2152
2153
2154
2155
2156 2157 2158 2159 2160 2161 2162
2163 2164 2165 2166 2167 2168
2169 2170 2171 2172 2173 2174 2175
2176 2177 2178 2179 2180

Tournay quai des Salines

BELGIUM

TOURNAY
Marks of Painters

BELGIUM

162

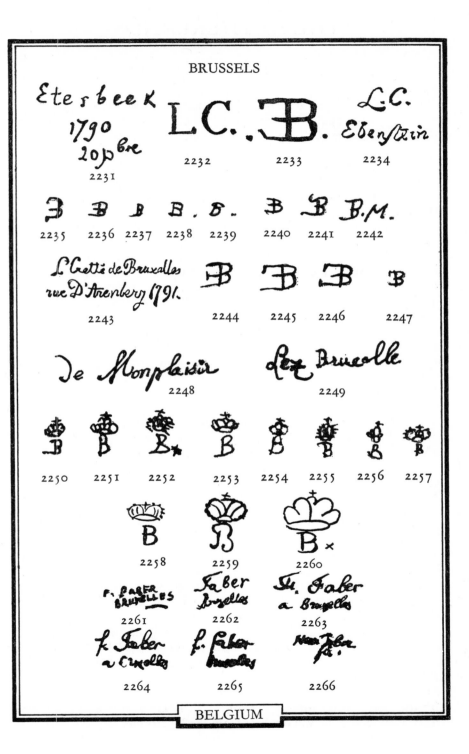

THE NETHERLANDS

The Dutch saw for the first time great quantities of porcelain in 1602, when the vessels "Zelandia" and "Langeberke" brought to Middelburg the captured Portuguese carrack "San Jago".

In 1614 J. I. Pontanus writes in the "Historische Beschrijvinge der wijt beroemde Coop Stadt Amsterdam": "The traffic with East India has brought a large amount of porcelain to the Netherlands".

In the same year an attempt had been made to manufacture porcelain at the Hague. It is recorded in the archives that the right to manufacture all types of porcelain, similar in material and decoration to those made in foreign countries, was granted for a period of five years to Claes Jansz Wijtmans of 's-Hertogenbosch.

Wijtmans was born in 1570. When very young he came to Rotterdam, where he worked as an engraver. In 1601 he was commissioned by the municipality of Rotterdam to make the glass windows for the St. Jan's Church at Gouda. The merchant Lambert de Hooch established in 1614 the so-called "Porceleyn Huis" where Wijtmans made ceramic experiments. In 1616 de Hooch got into financial difficulties and sold the workshop to Anthony de Hooch from Gorinchem.

In 1619 Wijtmans bought the "Porceleyn Huis" where besides producing his "porcelain" he made tiles. In 1616 he was commissioned to make tiles for the decoration of the Stadhouder's new yacht. In 1629 Wijtmans asked the municipality of Utrecht for a patent for himself and his son to establish a porcelain factory. The patent was granted on the 27th April 1629. The text of the patent describes Wijtmans as a resident of Rotterdam. He died in 1642, and it is assumed that the factory might have been set up in Utrecht, although the archives of Utrecht have no documents concerning Wijtmans, with the exception of the resolution of the 27th April 1629.

WEESP

Daniel Maccarthy, George Cruikshank from Aberdeen, Charles Pye from London and Daniel Muilman made an agreement for establishing a factory of China and Earthenware at Weesp in 1757.

It was stated in the English written contract that: "for better securing the secret of compounding, making, glazeing and finishing the ware it is expressly agreed that at no time more than three persons shall be admitted into any part of that secret, everyone of the concerned each for himself binding and obliging himself to the performance of this article." The factory in the Kromme Elleboogsteeg was not prosperous and the produce is not yet identified. It was sold in 1759 to Count van Gronsveld Diepenbroick for the sum of 4.500 fl. In 1762 the factory must have been already in operation, because the count had made on the 7th October of that year a contract with a Saxon ceramist, Christian Nauwerk.

With the assistance of foreign ceramists: N. F. Gauron from the Tournay factory as modeller, L. V. Gerverot from the Niderviller factory, Marchand and Th. Onkruyd, the Weesp factory made very fine white and transparent porcelain. But the factory was not prosperous and the costs being too high, Count Gronsveld was ruined and the factory publicly sold in 1771, when Ds. J. de Mol bought the materials and moulds.

The Protestant minister of Oud-Loosdrecht, De Moll, in association with capitalists at Amsterdam, reopened the factory, which he afterwards moved to Oud-Loosdrecht.

The decoration of the very rare Weesp porcelain was in the manner of Meissen.

The factory mark was the letter W and two crossed swords in blue under glaze. A rarer mark consisted of two crossed swords with three points.

OUD-LOOSDRECHT

This factory was a continuation of the porcelain works at Weesp founded by Count Gronsveldt-Diepenbroick. In 1772 it passed in the hands of the Rev. Moll, who was associated in the enterprise with I. Rendorp, I. Dedel, C. van der Hoop and the bankers G. and J. Hope. Moll moved the factory to Oud-Loosdrecht, but after his death in 1782 his partners transferred it to Ouder-Amstel, whence it was moved in 1809 to Nieuwer-Amstel.

From 1784 onwards the products of the factory are known as Amstel porcelain. The works manager was Friedrich Daeuber.

AMSTEL

The Amstel factory produced china of very fine quality, tastefully modelled and decorated with multi-coloured designs and very rich gilding, in the manner of Meissen and Sèvres. Landscape painting was of a high standard but some very good bird and flower-painting was also done. Chinese patterns and marks have also been imitated at the factory. It is known that sometimes oriental porcelain has been redecorated here.

Among the ceramists employed at the factory were: N. F. Gauron from Tournay, L. V. Gerverot, Marchand and Th. Onkruyd, chief painter. The following painters worked for the factory: d'Arest, Assenbergh, van Leen, Renaud, van Brack, van der Voort, van der Heuvel, Bruinius and Jager. Pieces made by Gerverot bear the lion mark.

From 1800 the factory belonged to the firm George Dommer and company and was moved to Nieuwer-Amstel in 1809. It was closed in 1819.

The factory mark during the Oud-Loosdrecht period consisted of the three letters M.o.L. (Moll Oud-Loosdrecht) in blue or incised under glaze. After the transfer to Ouder-Amstel the pieces were marked with the word "Amstel", or the monogram AD.

AMSTERDAM

In 1810 A. Lafond operated a decoration workshop in Amsterdam.

THE HAGUE 1775–1786

As early as 1614, it seems, an attempt had been made to manufacture china at The Hague. It is recorded in the archives that the right to manufacture all types of porcelain, similar in material and decoration to those made in foreign countries, was granted for a period of five years to Claes Jansz.

Wytmans of Bois le Duc. This would seem to indicate that a factory did at one time exist, but no further information is available.

In 1778 a porcelain factory was established in the Bagijnestraat by a German named Lynker. This factory was later moved to the Dunne Bierkade, and later to the Nieuwe Molstraat. The factory produced hard paste china of very good quality, very similar to the Meissen product, but rather more solid. The pieces were decorated with seascapes, landscapes and birds. This factory also decorated china from other sources, mostly soft paste china from Tournay. Of late years the value of Hague porcelain has greatly increased and services decorated with landscapes or fruit and flowers have fetched high prices. In 1786 the factory was closed.

The Hague mark was the stork, taken from the city arms, in blue under glaze. When foreign pieces were decorated, the mark was painted on glaze.

ROZENBURG

During the last 15 years of the 19th century the Rozenburg Delft-ware factory at The Hague made some exquisite porcelain tea-sets. These were designed by the well-known painter Colenbrander who was attached to the factory from 1883 to 1889. The factory was closed in 1916.

Rozenburg hard paste porcelain is reminiscent of oriental egg-shell china in its composition and transparency. The tea-sets are delicately decorated with flower patterns.

The following artists have worked at Rozenburg: Johan van der Vet, Brouwer, R. Sterken, D. de Ruyter, J. Schelling, D. Harkink 1884–'93, J. C. Heytze 1887–1893, W. P. Hartgring 1888–1908, F. J. Mansveld 1889–1897, J. Schelling, W. P. Hartgring, R. Sterken, M. van Rossum, Verhoog, and Jurian Kock.

MAASTRICHT

Petrus Regoût tried to make porcelain in 1836. His son, Louis, established a porcelain factory at Maastricht.

The MOSA factory, established in 1883, produces very elegant table and tea services, designed by the well-known artist Edmond Bellefroid. This works has now 900 employees.

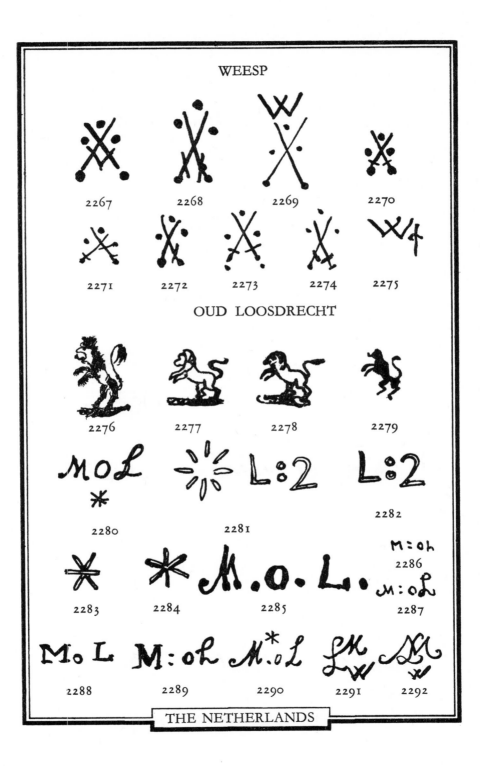

WEESP

2267   2268   2269   2270

2271   2272   2273   2274   2275

OUD LOOSDRECHT

2276   2277   2278   2279

2280   2281   2282

2283   2284   2285   2286   2287

2288   2289   2290   2291   2292

THE NETHERLANDS

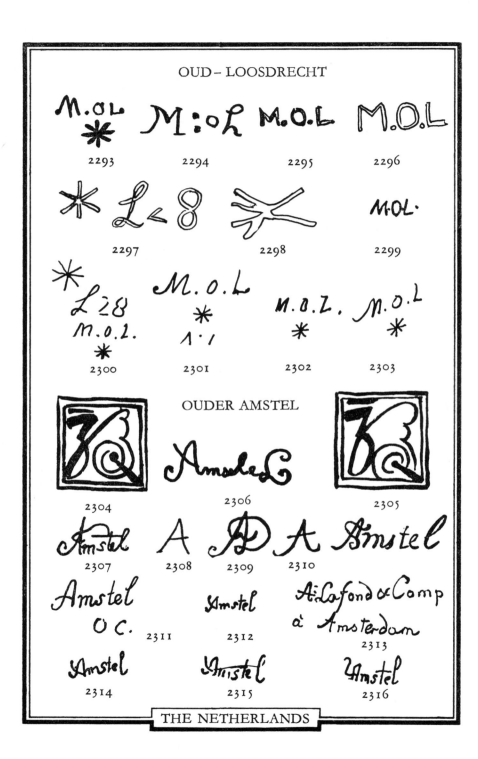

OUD – LOOSDRECHT

THE NETHERLANDS

THE HAGUE

2317   2318   2319   2320

2321   2322   2323   2324

1781

2325   2326   2327   2328   2329

2330

ROZENBURG

2331   2332

2334

20th Century

2335

2333

GOEDEWAGEN

2336

MOSA

2337

ENGLAND

BOW

The factory of Bow (Stratford-le-Bow in Essex) is the oldest in England. The site of the factory was located in the East End of London on the Essex bank of the river Lea at Stratford Langthorne. This factory was also called New Canton, because the buildings were built in the style of Canton dwellings in China. It is thought that the factory was founded in 1730. The first certain date, however, is 1744, when Ed. Heylin and Thomas Frye took out a patent for the manufacture of porcelain. The patent states that the material used to make porcelain is "an earth, the produce of the Chirokee nation in America, called by the natives –unaker".

Edward Heylin was gazetted as bankrupt in 1757, and in 1759 Thomas Frye retired. Bow belonged now to John Crowther and Weatherby, and employed c. 300 persons, of whom c. 90 were painters. In 1763 the factory went bankrupt. Crowther seems to have managed it until 1775, when the entire inventory was sold by auction to William Duesbury, who removed all the moulds and materials to Derby.

The Bow factory was the first to make bone china. Amongst the best modellers who worked for Bow were Bacon and Moser. The factory produced lovely statuettes, candlesticks, figurines of birds and animals. Imari and Chinese patterns as well as famille rose and Powder blue were copied. Some Bow specimens are decorated by over glaze transfer printing.

The oldest pieces are marked "Made at New Canton 1750".

CHELSEA

The Chelsea factory was probably established in 1742 by Thomas Bryand and Nicholas Sprimont.

We read in the "Royal Society's Journal Book for 10th February 1742": "Mr. Bryand, a stranger was present, shew'd the Society several specimens of a sort of fine white ware, made here by himself from native materials of our own Country, which appear'd to be in all respects as good as any of the finest Porcelain or China ware: and he said it was much preferable for its fineness to the ware of Dresden." It was glassy-soft paste porcelain.

Bryand seems to have worked at the Saint-Cloud factory. He was one of the many Huguenot refugees who lived in London.

Charles Gouyn, also a Huguenot, had probably financed the enterprise, whose leading spirit seems to have been Nicholas Sprimont, born in 1716 at Liège.

Sprimont, being a silversmith, derived some of his designs from silverwork. The pieces of the Gouyn and Sprimont period are often reminiscent of Sèvres. About 1750 the composition of the paste was changed. Under the influence of Meissen, figures and birds were produced. The birds were often very beautiful and life-like. According to Major W. H. Tapp, Jeffryes Hamett O'Neale (b.,c. 1734) worked probably c. 1751 for Chelsea.

About 1754 the Chelsea factory began to make toys, small trinkets, seals, snuff-boxes and scent-bottles. The manufacture of these little objects is a speciality of this factory. In 1769 Sprimont sold the works to James Cox.

Joseph Willems has worked as modeller before 1766.

In 1770 Duesbury, the owner of the Derby factory, bought the Chelsea works. Both factories were merged. The period between 1770 and 1784 is called the "CHELSEA-DERBY" period. In 1773 Duesbury received the protection of the King and Kean was taken into partnership. In 1815 the factory came into the hands of Robert Bloor, who died in 1846. In 1849 the moulds and materials were sold to Samuel Boyle of Fenton, who resold them to Copeland. The Chelsea works were abandoned in 1784.

About 1770 the Chelsea factory was producing imitations of Sèvres porcelain. The earliest mark of Chelsea is an incised triangle used from 1745–1749. A raised anchor used from 1750–1753. A red anchor used from 1753–1758, a gold anchor used from 1758–1777.

Under Duesbury a D with a crown in blue, red, violet, crimson and sometimes in gold was also used.

In the 19th century the name of Bloor was impressed in the paste on table ware and later a crown mark was again applied to the Derby products. Chelsea-Derby has produced remarkable tableware and very fine tea-sets.

PAINTERS AT THE CHELSEA-DERBY WORKS

George Complin, 1791–1795.
John Brewer, 1795–1798.
Robert Brewer, 1797–1810.
George Robertson, 1796–1826.
James Banford, 1789–1795.
Jesse Mountford, until 1821.
Mc. Lacklan, after 1800.
Richard Dodson, 1815–1825.
Philip Clavey, after 1800.
John Stanesby, worked until 1810.
Joseph and Thomas Tatlow, c. 1801.
William Wheeldon, c. 1801–1823.
Wardle, c. 1800.
Zachariah Boreman, landscapes, flowers and birds. 1779–1795.
Thomas "Jockey" Hill, landscapes, 1795–1800.
Thomas Steele, fruit, 1815–40.
Bancroft, flowers and insects. 1830–40.

THE HANCOCK FAMILY

John, born 1757–1847, until 1800 in Hanley at Spode's and Wedgwood.
John, born 1777–1840.
George, died 1850, 1819–1835, Derby.
James, at Chamberlain's Worcester.
James, manager of Worcester Royal Porcelain Works until 1862.
Moses Webster, flowers. 1815.
Edward Withers, flowers, 1780–1800.
Robinson, landscapes.
Cuthbert Lawton, hunting scenes.
S. Prince, flowers.
William Pegg, still life, 1796–1801.

Thomas Pegg, gilder.
Samuel Keys, ornaments, 1785–1830.
John Keys, flowers, 1825.
Holland, flowers.
William Billingsley, flowers, 1774–1795.
Thomas Soar, gilder.
John Haslem, figures. 1822.
Cotton & Askew, figure painters.
Richard Askew, 1794–1796.

MODELLERS OF FIGURES

Pierre Stephan, 1774–1795.
Jean-Jacques Spengler, 1790–1793.
François Hardenberg, mentioned 1789.
Charles Holmes.
George Holmes, 1765.
Catherine, 1789.
Rossi, 1788.
William Coffee, 1794–1810.
John Bacon, worked in 1769.
André Planché, born 1727, died 1809, 1755–1756, in 1756 he was mentioned as partner to be of Duesbury and Heath.
Edward and Samuel Keys until 1826 and 1830.
John Whitaker, 1818–1848.
George Cooker, until 1817.

DERBY

The first Derby factory was named the Derby Pot Works. The second factory was established by WILLIAM DUESBURY in 1751, who bought the Chelsea works in 1770. The produce might be divided into the Planché period, lasting until 1756, the light coloured period from 1755–1760 and the Patch Family from 1760–1770, so classified because of the dark patches on the bases of figures. Derby has produced biscuit figures in imitation of Sèvres.

Figures:

1750–1755: Dry edge, screw holes in bases.
1755–1760: Pale coloured family with patch marks.
1760–1770: Bright colours, elaborate gilding, patch marks.
1770: Chelsea-Derby, numbers on bases.
Derby pieces are not marked. Many early pieces are left white.
Aaron Simpson seems to have left together with some other workmen the Chelsea works ca. 1749, and had established a factory which might have produced the objects known under the collective name of **"Girl in a Swing"**, although, it is not impossible that they have been made by André

Planché at the Cockpit Hill factory, established by William Butts, John Heath and Thomas Rivett, where he is supposed to have made porcelain about 1751.

WORCESTER

In 1751 a company known as the "Worcester Porcelain Company" was founded by Dr. Wall and partners. A new company was formed in 1772 under the direction of Dr. Wall, who died in 1776.

The factory was bought by Mr. Flight and his sons in 1783 and in 1788, following the visit of King George III, the company's name was changed to the Royal Worcester Porcelain Works and a crown was added to the mark. In 1793 Mr. Martin Barr became a partner in the firm.

In 1840 Flight's son and his partner Barr joined forces with the Chamberlains who had been operating a rival factory at Diglis since 1788.

The composition of the soft paste used at Worcester was originally evolved by Dr. Wall, it was of a warm white tint and delicately translucent.

At first the factory was also engaged in the decoration of oriental white porcelain. The earliest designs were executed in blue and "powder blue". Pieces produced at Worcester during this period were decorated with Chinese and Japanese designs; later the Meissen and the Chantilly décor – particularly the blue – were imitated. From 1768 much of the porcelain was decorated in the enamelling shop of James Giles.

In the early days Chinese marks were used in blue and red. Numerous marks were used during Dr. Wall's time. A crescent mark was used in blue under glaze, in red and gold on glaze and incised. Seals impressed in moist clay were also used (these specimens are very rare). Another mark was a double letter W. Pieces decorated with Meissen designs were often marked with the crossed swords and Sèvres marks were also imitated. During the first period of the Worcester factory – it is believed as early as 1751 – transfer printing was used to decorate cheaper pieces. Minor retouching was done by painters where necessary. At a later date bat printing was used to decorate pieces with coloured prints.

The leading painters during this early period were O'Neale and Donaldson and the most notable engravers were Hancock and Richard Holdship. Under the direction of Flight and Barr some very beautiful services were made. The most remarkable of these were the services for the Emperor of Russia and the Duke of Clarence, painted by John Pennington, the service for Lord Amhearst, painted by John Bly, a service for the Imam of Mascate and a presentation service for Lord Nelson. Apart from these famous services, some very fine vases, groups and figures were also produced.

In 1819 Flight and Barr employed the following painters: John Pennington, Salomon Cole (pupil of Thomas Baxter, the famous painter of classical subjects), Charles Stinton, William Richards, Samuel Asters, Thomas Richards, and the celebrated flower painter Billingsley, who also worked for Derby and Nantgarw, William Taylor (noted for his paintings in blue), John Barker (shells), William Woods (figures), George Davis (exotic birds in the Chelsea manner), William Doe (figures and landscapes), Joseph Cottrell, Thomas Rogers, John Jones, J. C. Crowther, William Manason, Henry

Manason, Nicolas Pennings, Thomas Caradine, James Tomkins, Thomas Holloway, William Holloway, John Sead, Thomas Dobbs, Thomas Dutton Jr., Thomas Smith, Samuel Smith, Henry Stinton, Joseph Jones, John Smith, Ishmael Sherwin, Thomas Peugh, James Bradley, the celebrated Thomas Baxter, Charles Richards, John Bly, John Bly Jr., Jos. Taylor, Jos. Niblett and Jos. Dovey.

During the period 1821-1823 a series of views of Derbyshire was painted by C. Hayton.

The history of the "Royal Worcester Porcelain Works" falls into three separate periods: from 1752 to 1783; from 1783 to 1840 (Flight and Barr); and from 1840 to the present day. During the third period red, green and goldmarks were used. Many of the best specimens of Worcester porcelain are not marked and a large number bearing marks of repute are of little value. It does not therefore, follow, that, because a piece is marked it is of high value. Advantage has been taken of the demand for certain marks and they are frequently counterfeited; it is therefore, necessary that great care should be exercised in purchasing specimens represented to be "Old Worcester".

LIST OF PARTNERS AND NOTES

1751			Works founded by Doctor Wall and partners.
1756			Transfer printing introduced at Worcester.
1776			Doctor Wall died.
1783			Mr. Flight became sole proprietor.
	1786		Robert Chamberlain left and, in 1788, built a works at Diglis.
1793			Mr. Barr joined Mr. Flight—now Flight and Barr.
	1798		Humphrey and Robert Chamberlain, junior.
		1801	Thomas Grainger left Chamberlain's and built works at St. Martin's.
	1804		Humphrey and Robert Chamberlain and Ed. Boulton.
1807			Mr. Barr, junior, joined—now Barr, Flight and Barr.
	1811		Humphrey and Robert Chamberlain.
1813			Mr. George Barr joined—now Flight, Barr and Barr, until 1840.
	1828		Walter Chamberlain and John Lily.
——	1840		Old Works united with Chamberlain's.
	1848		Walter Chamberlain and John Lily.
	1850		Walter Chamberlain, F. Lily and W. H. Kerr.
	1852		W. H. Kerr and R. W. Binns.
	1862		The present Company formed.
		1889	Grainger Works acquired by Porcelain Company.
	1902	——	The Grainger manufacture transferred to the Royal Porcelain Works.
	1902		A decision given by Mr. Justice Byrne in the High Court of Chancery that the Worcester Royal Porcelain Co., Ltd., retained their exclusive right to use the word "Worcester" in connection with Ceramic goods.
	1905		Hadley Works (founded 1896) acquired by the Porcelain Company.

BRISTOL I

Soap–rock porcelain was made at Bristol at the factory of William Lowdin as early as 1750. This factory was sold to the Worcester Porcelain Company in 1752.

BRISTOL II, CHAMPION

In 1770 Champion purchased the patent rights from Cookworthy and took over the factory. The style of factory was now "The Bristol China Manufactory".

In 1772 the material of the Plymouth factory was transferred to Bristol. The hard paste porcelain produced here was of a very fine quality, lavishly decorated and very expensive. Beautiful groups and vases were made, but the porcelain could not compete with that of other factories owing to its high cost. As the models of some of Cookworthy's figures are similar with Longton Hall figures, it might be possible that he had acquired moulds of the Longton Hall factory.

The following artists have worked at the Bristol factory:

Soqui, a Frenchman.	Samuel Daw.	John Webb.
James Banford.	Samuel Lloyd.	James Sanders.
Philip James.	Jacob Alsop.	William Lyne.
John Britain.	John Garland.	John Parrot.
Tebo, alias Thiebaud.	Benjamin Lewis.	Thomas Bryand,
Henry Bone.	Samuel Peglar.	"chymist".

Marks used were in brown and blue under glaze, incised and in gold above glaze.

SPODE

In 1770 Josiah Spode bought the works of Banks & Turner, in Stoke-on-Trent. This factory was very successful. Josiah Spode died in 1797; his son Josiah II inherited the works. He took in 1799 William Copeland as partner. His son purchased the whole concern and took Thomas Garret as a partner. In the beginning the factory produced pieces which resembled those of Wedgwood. Early Spode porcelain was tastefully decorated. Later very rich patterns and gildings were used. Relief gildings were favoured by this factory. In 1910 the Grand Prix at Brussels was awarded to the Spode works. W. T. Copeland was the first to produce Parian statuary in 1842. The parian porcelain was a hard vitrified porcelain.

Copeland commissioned famous sculptors to model figures and groups for reproduction. Among those, who made models were Mrs. Mary Thorneycroft, J. H. Foley R. A.; John Gibson R. A.; William Marshall R. A.; Count D'Orsay, Baron Marochetti, Carrier-Belleuse. One of the most popular models was the "Greek Slave" by Hiram Power. At present: Chairman of Directors: C. H. Marsh. Managing Director: R. S. C. Copeland, M. A., Designer: H. Holdway.

CAUGHLEY, SHROPSHIRE

Thomas Turner began to make soft paste porcelain in 1772 and continued to manufacture until 1799. In this year John Rose, a former apprentice of

Turner's, bought the factory. Turner in his time produced very beautiful porcelain which resembled Worcester ware.

Blue and gold were used for decoration, with designs of sprays and flowers. Charming tea sets of the so-called "Salopian" ware were made here. This famous Caughley design was very popular in its time. In 1799 John Rose bought the Caughley works which he managed simultaneously with his Coalport factory.

In 1814 this factory ceased to exist.

Caughley porcelain was very famous for its blue Dragon and Willow patterns.

COALPORT (COALBROOKDALE)

John Rose, an apprentice at Caughley, established the Coalport factory in 1785 and after Turner's retirement from the Caughley works, bought up that factory which from then on came under his management. In his Coalport works John Rose imitated Sèvres porcelain and used both Meissen and Sèvres marks. About 1821 a chestnut background colour was introduced in the porcelain production of this factory. The Coalport works produced exquisitely painted china.

After the death of John Rose in 1841, the works passed to Charles Maddison, William Pugh, Thomas Rose and William Frederick Rose.

In 1845, a dessert service, sent later as a present by queen Victoria to the Czar Nicholas, was manufactured at the factory. It was coloured in Royal Blue and decorated in six bands with the badges of the various orders of the Russian Empire and the Russian and Polish eagles.

This service and a "Rose du Barry" service were to be seen at the Great exhibition in 1851.

In 1855 at the Great French Exhibition, the Coalport produce received a medal. William Frederick Rose received the permission to copy Sèvres models and Sèvres moulds were sent over to the factory. But not only Sèvres was reproduced at Coalport, Chelsea, Worcester and Meissen pieces were copied together with their marks.

In 1862 William Frederick Rose retired and William Pugh became the sole proprietor of Coalport. In 1885 the Coalport works were taken over by Peter Schuyler Bruff. In 1924 the Bruff family and their associates sold the factory to Cauldon Potteries Limited, who moved the works to Shelton in Staffordshire in 1926. In 1932 the Coalport group was acquired by George Jones and Son Ltd., and moved to the Crescent works Stoke-upon-Trent. After the war, in 1947, the Harrison company became sole proprietors of the Jones group and the Coalport China Company.

The marks used, when not imitated, were in blue or impressed.

The factory is still in operation. Directors: E. W. Brain and T. H. F. Shirley.

NANTGARW

This soft paste porcelain factory was founded by Billingsley and Walker in 1813. They first produced soft paste and later soap-rock porcelain. The products of this factory were very translucent and were decorated in imitation of Sèvres. Billingsley also tried to imitate Chantilly patterns.

SWANSEA

This factory was established as early as 1814. Soap-rock porcelain was only made after Dillwyn went into partnership with Billingsley. The quality of the products made here was equal to that of Nantgarw. The marks used by the two factories were either impressed or in underglaze blue.

In 1820 John Rose bought the Swansea factory and transferred the material to Coalport. Marks used were in red, violet and impressed.

MADELEY

Thomas Martin Randall, a former decorator at Caughley, established in 1825 a small factory at Madeley where he decorated white Sèvres porcelain and made a soft paste in imitation of Sèvres. The factory was closed about 1870.

PLYMOUTH

This factory was established in 1768 by Cookworthy with the aid and protection of Lord Camelford. Cookworthy went into partnership with Champion. Financial difficulties arose and in 1772 the material was transferred to the Bristol factory. Cookworthy retired in 1774.

Marks were impressed or under glaze. It was the first hard paste porcelain made in England.

BAYSWATER

No porcelain was manufactured, but china produced by other factories was here decorated.

BELFAST

It is believed that a porcelain factory was established in Belfast by Th. Gregg, Sam. Stephenson and S. Ashmore about 1791.

SWINTON-ROCKINGHAM

A pottery factory was established by Mr. Butler on the estate of the Marquis of Rockingham in 1757. In 1758 the factory was taken over by Thomas Bingley & Co. In 1820 Thomas Brameld started to produce soft paste porcelain of a fine quality, decorated with flowers and very rich gildings. In 1823 the Marquis of Rockingham took the factory under his protection. The marks used were in red and purple.

LOWESTOFT

Mr. Luson tried to make porcelain as early as 1756 at Gunton Hall near Lowestoft. In 1757 Walker, Browne, Aldred and Richman established a factory at Lowestoft. This small factory had a world-wide reputation for its tea sets. The earliest pieces are decorated with Chinese designs in underglaze blue. It is known that Oriental porcelain was often redecorated in Lowestoft.

Lowestoft paste closely resembles the paste used at Bow in composition, but the glaze is thinner. One of the chief decorators was Robert Allen.

Many pieces were decorated by Rose. Lowestoft porcelain bears no regular mark and many pieces are unmarked. Sometimes marks of other factories were used. Many specimens are marked: H.S.R., Z.W.R.P., these being the first letters of the names of the painters working there: Hughes, Stevenson, Redgrave, Richard Philips and two other workmen. The Lowestoft factory operated until 1803.

LONGTON HALL

According to Dr. Bernard Watney, William Jenkinson had started the factory in 1750, a year later two partners were taken into the business: one of them was William Littler. The pieces are very attractive and include beautiful dishes with relief decoration. The stock of the Longton Hall factory was sold at Salisbury when it closed down in 1760. The marks of Longton Hall are in blue under glaze. The paste was glassy and the glaze dull and waxy. Vegetable and leaf forms were favoured.

LIVERPOOL

Several factories were in operation in Liverpool: The factory of Messrs. Richard Chaffers on Shaw's Brow, which in 1765 was taken over by Philip Christian.
The produce imitated Worcester ware.
Zachariah Barnes produced in his factory pieces moulded in imitation of silver shapes.
In the factory owned by Seth Pennington artistically painted objects were made.

LONGPORT-DAVENPORT

This factory was established in the 18th century and produced excellent tableware. A very beautiful service was made for Queen Victoria.
The mark used is an anchor in red and blue under glaze.
The factory ceased to produce in 1876.

SHELTON, Cauldon Place Works.

This factory was established by G. Ridgway & Sons in 1813.
The factory produced good table ware and well decorated tea sets. In 1856 the factory was sold to Brown, Westhead, Moore & Co.

NEW HALL

This factory was founded by Samuel Hollins, Jacob Warburton, William Clowes, Charles Bagnal and Anthony Keeling in 1777. Very fine soft paste porcelain was produced and later hard paste porcelain was made. This factory worked until 1862.
In 1781 Champion sold his patent rights to the New Hall factory.
Marks used here were in red and brown and were sometimes impressed.

PINXTON (DERBYSHIRE)

This factory was established by John Lake and William Billingsley, the subsequent owner of the Nantgarw and Swansea factories, in 1796. The works closed in 1818. Specimens from this factory are very rare.

MINTON

This factory was founded at Stoke-on-Trent in 1793 by Thomas Minton, an apprentice of Thomas Turner of Caughley. In the 19th century the Minton factory acquired a world-wide reputation for its porcelain.

In 1848 Minton engaged, from France, Leon Arnoux, an artist and chemist of exceptional ability, and they proceeded to infuse new methods into the industry.

An interesting feature of the Crystal Palace Exhibition of 1851 was the introduction of Parian, which is a combination of felspar and china clay closely resembling white marble, in which figures and statuettes by some of the finest modellers and sculptors of that day were shown. Included amongst these was John Bell, one of the outstanding sculptors of that period. The Parian figure "Miranda" was one of John Bell's leading pieces.

In 1863 Minton was granted Letters Patent for a process which was to revolutionize the production of ornamental patterns in gold.

The unsettled conditions in France brought about by the Franco-Prussian war caused the exodus of a number of French artists, and it would appear that the most eminent of them were attracted to the Minton factory.

Antoine Boullemier, who arrived in 1872, was outstanding in his treatment of mythological and cupid subjects, but he was equally at home with reproductions of the Old Masters, as well as being an accomplished portrait painter and a landscape artist of great merit.

In 1870 Marc Louis Solon, sculptor and decorator of Sèvres, was engaged at Minton. He produced very artistic porcelain, beautifully decorated, closely imitating the Sèvres style and introduced many improvements in the factory. Jewelled porcelain is one of the specialities of this factory.

Present Directors are:

Mr. E. A. G. Caröe, C.B.E.

Mr. J. E. Hartill.

Mr. L. Unwin.

Mr. W. H. Whitfield

Present designer is Mr. D. H. Henson.

WEDGWOOD

The Wedgwood family was of long standing at Burslem where many members were engaged in making pottery.

The greatest of all, Josiah Wedgwood was born there in 1730. After many years of experimentation, in 1770, he invented a kind of black ware with decorations in relief, which he called "Basaltes of Egypt". In 1773 he succeeded in making a fine white terracotta of great beauty, suitable for cameos, portraits and basreliefs. In 1776 he invented solid jasper, the most beautiful of all his wares.

In 1773 he began making a large service for the Empress Catherine II of Russia, each piece being decorated with a green frog. The price paid for this service was 3000 pounds sterling.

The artistic products of Wedgwood consist for the most part of very fine hard stoneware which contains some kaolin, but which is not real porcelain. It is a far harder and finer substance than bone china. The factory was established at Burslem in 1753 but was moved to Newcastle (Etruria) by Wedgwood & Bentley in 1769.

The earlier products were cream ware, later called Queensware, made of pale yellow paste and glazed in the same colour. All kinds of table ware etc. were made from this material and the pieces were sometimes painted. Jasper-ware was made of fine, white paste resembling biscuit porcelain.

The pieces were painted blue and decorated with relief figures in white, and of a remarkable beauty and fineness. These very gracefull modelled reliefs were applied on all sorts of vases, boxes, etc. Very rarely any colour other than blue was used, but some pieces were executed in green, yellow, violet, grey and black. Jasper-ware has been imitated by many Continental factories in biscuit porcelain.

The factory mark was the word "Wedgwood" or "Wedgwood & Bentley" impressed in small print in the paste. Mark Number 3 with the word "Etruria" was fixed in the corner inside the plinth of old basalt vases. Mark Number 6 appears on bone china or porcelain made during the years 1812–1815 and is always printed in red, blue or gold. Mark Number 7 printed in sepia and other colours has been used for fine bone china dating from 1878 until the present day. Mark Number 9 printed in colour has been used since 1940.

The best imitations of Wedgwood are made by Turner at Longton and Adams at Tunstall.

WEDGWOOD ARTISTS & MODELLERS

> John E. Goodwin, Art Director until retirement 1935.
> Victor Skellern, A.R.C.A., M.S.I.A., N.R.D., Art Director.
> Keith Murray, R.D.I., F.R.I.B.A., Designer.
> Millicent Taplin, M.S.I.A., N.R.D..
> Arnold Machin, A.R.C.A., Sculptor.
> Eric Ravilious, A.R.C.A., Designer.
> Alfred Powel, Artist & Designer.
> Louisa Powel, Artist & Designer.
> S. Wedgwood, Designer.
> Arthur Dale Holland, Painter.
> Arnold Austin, D.C.M., Modeller.
> Herbert Choleston, Crest Painter.
> Paul Hulme, Engraver.

IRLAND

BELLEEK

The Belleek pottery was established in 1857 at Fermanagh county by M'Burney and R. W. Armstrong. They very soon evolved a beautiful, ivory-tinted, nacrous Parian porcelain used for statuary. Elegant, delicately modelled baskets ornamented with flowers were produced, as well as cabinet cups and saucers covered with nacrous lustre. All pieces are marked. After 1890 the name Ireland was used in conjunction with the Belleck mark.

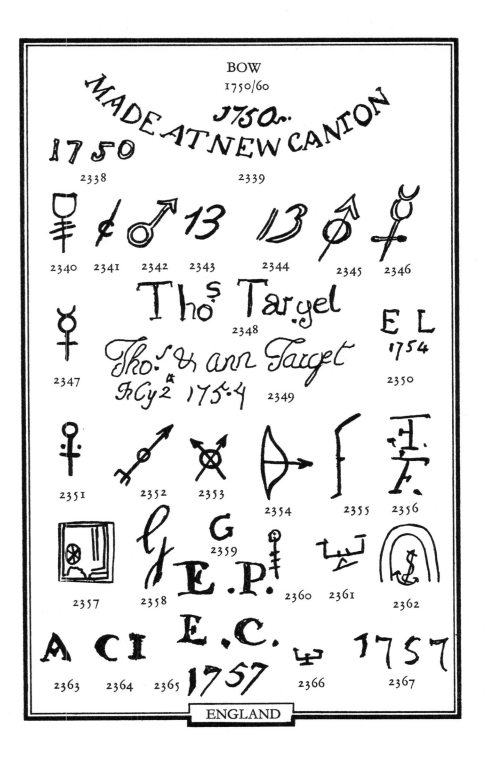

BOW
1750/60

ENGLAND

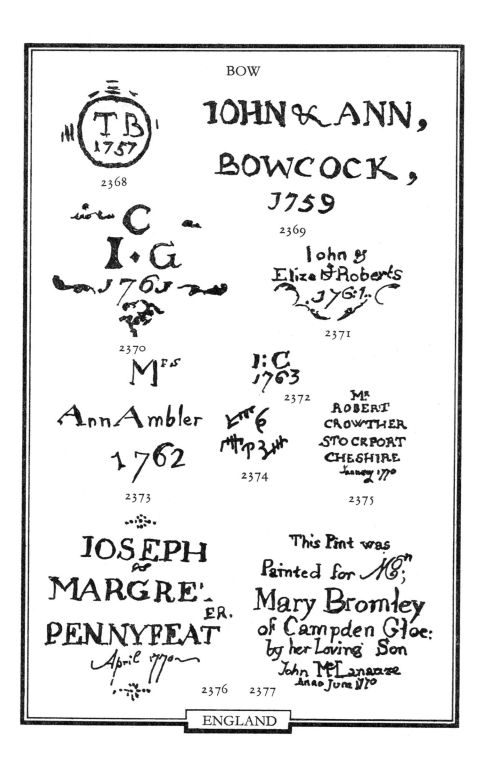

2368

IOHN & ANN, BOWCOCK, 1759

2369

I·G 1763

2370

Iohn & Eliza & Roberts 1761

2371

M^{rs}

AnnAmbler 1762

2373

I:C 1763

2372

2374

Mr ROBERT CROWTHER STOCRPORT CHESHIRE January 1770

2375

IOSEPH & MARGRE^T ER. PENNYFEAT April 1770

2376

This Pint was Painted for M^{rs}: Mary Bromley of Campden Gloe: by her Loving Son John McLanaaze Anno June 1770

2377

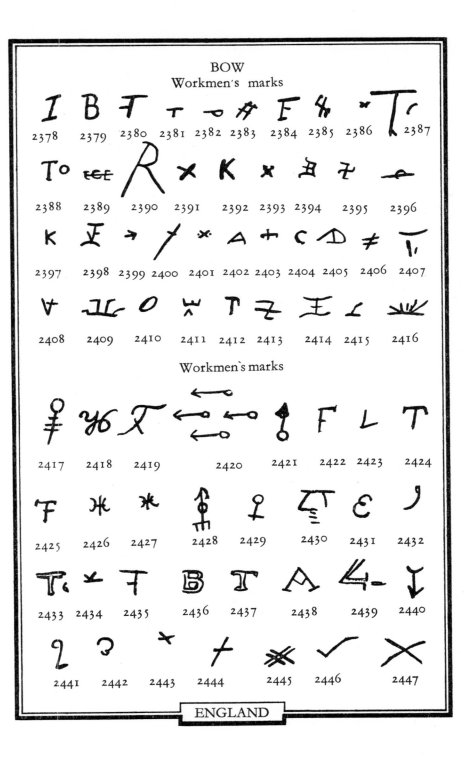

BOW
Workmen's marks

2378 2379 2380 2381 2382 2383 2384 2385 2386 2387

2388 2389 2390 2391 2392 2393 2394 2395 2396

2397 2398 2399 2400 2401 2402 2403 2404 2405 2406 2407

2408 2409 2410 2411 2412 2413 2414 2415 2416

Workmen's marks

2417 2418 2419 2420 2421 2422 2423 2424

2425 2426 2427 2428 2429 2430 2431 2432

2433 2434 2435 2436 2437 2438 2439 2440

2441 2442 2443 2444 2445 2446 2447

ENGLAND

BOW

1760–1776

2448

2449

2450

2451

2452

2453

2454

2455

2456

2457

2458

2459

2460

2461

2462

2463

2464

2465

2466

2467

2468

2469

2470

2471

2472

2473

2474

2475

2476

2477

2478

ENGLAND

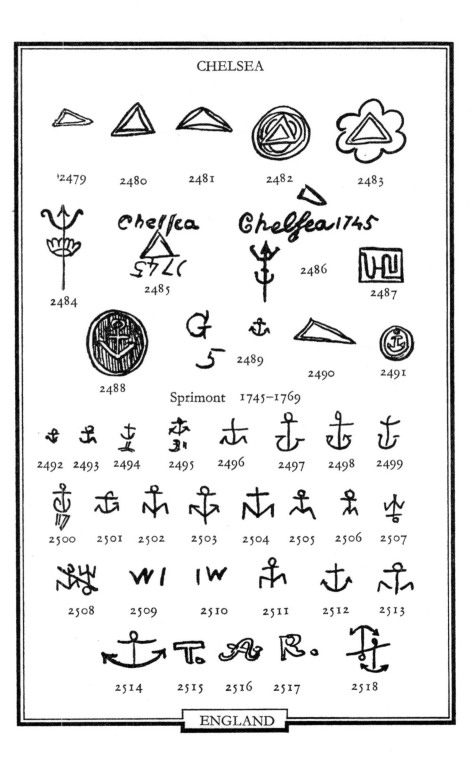

2479 2480 2481 2482 2483

2484 2485 2486 2487

Sprimont 1745–1769

2488 2489 2490 2491

2492 2493 2494 2495 2496 2497 2498 2499

2500 2501 2502 2503 2504 2505 2506 2507

2508 2509 2510 2511 2512 2513

2514 2515 2516 2517 2518

ENGLAND

DERBY

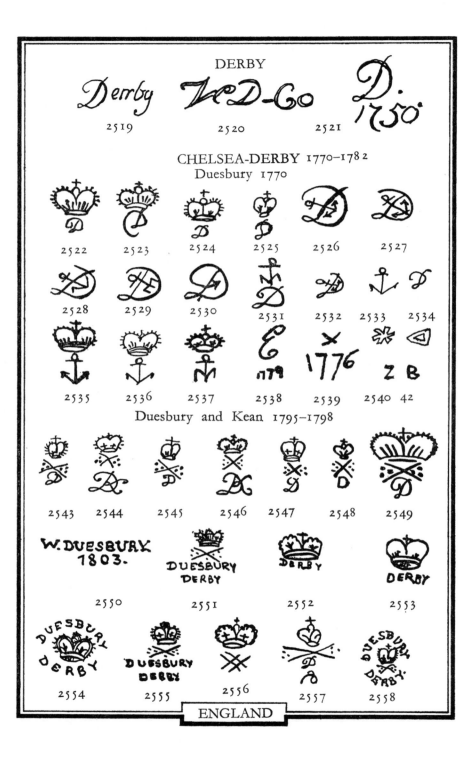

2519   2520   2521

CHELSEA-DERBY 1770–1782
Duesbury 1770

2522   2523   2524   2525   2526   2527

2528   2529   2530   2531   2532   2533   2534

2535   2536   2537   2538   2539   2540   42

Duesbury and Kean 1795–1798

2543   2544   2545   2546   2547   2548   2549

2550   2551   2552   2553

2554   2555   2556   2557   2558

ENGLAND

186

DERBY
Bloor 1811-1844

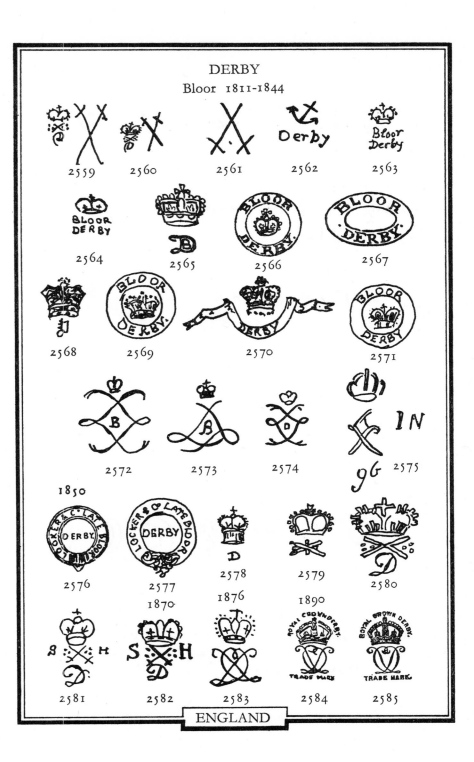

2559   2560   2561   2562   2563

2564   2565   2566   2567

2568   2569   2570   2571

2572   2573   2574   2575

1850

2576   2577   2578   2579   2580

1870   1876   1890

2581   2582   2583   2584   2585

ENGLAND

WORCESTER
Dr. Wall 1751–1783

2586 2587 2588 2589 2590 2591 2592 2593 2594 2595

2596 2597 2598 2599 2600 2601 2602 2603 2604 2605

2606 2607 2608 2609 2610 2611 2612 2613 2614 2615

2616 2617 2618 2619 2620 2621 2622 2623 2624

2625 2626 2627 2628 2629 2630 2631 2632 2633 2634

2635 2636 2637 2638 2639 2640 2641 2642 2643 2644 2645

2646 2647 2648 2649 2650 2651 2652 2653 2654 2655 2656

2657 2658 2659 2660 2661 2662 2663 2664

2665 2666 2667 2668 2669 2670

2671 2672 2673 2674 2675 2676 2677

ENGLAND

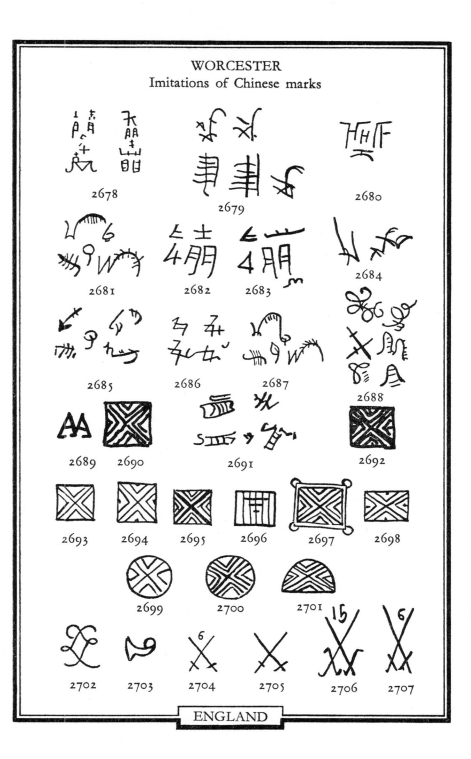

2678　2679　2680

2681　2682　2683　2684

2685　2686　2687　2688

2689　2690　2691　2692

2693　2694　2695　2696　2697　2698

2699　2700　2701

2702　2703　2704　2705　2706　2707

ENGLAND

2708

2709

2710   2711   2712   2713   2714   2715

1756–1774 on transfer prints

2716   2717   *R Hancock, fecit*   2718   *RH Worcester*   2719   *RH*

1783–1793 impressed blue under glaze

FLIGHTS   *Flight*   2722 *Flight*

2720   2721   Service of
Duke of Clarence

1793–1807

B   *Flight & Barr*

2723   2724

BFB   FBB

2725   2726

WORCESTER
London House
No. 1 Coventry Street   BARR FLIGHT & BARR
Royal Porcelain Works

2727   2728

1813–1840

Flight Barr & Barr

2729

WORCESTER

1788–1808

1814

Chamberlain's

Chamberlain's Worcester & 63. Piccadilly, London

2730

2731

1814–1820

1820–1840

Chamberlain's Regent China **Worcester** *& 155 New Bond Street, London.*

Chamberlain's Worcester & 155 New Bond Street, London.

Royal Porcelain Manufacturers

2732

2733

2734

1840–1845

CHAMBERLAIN & CO.,
WORCESTER
155, NEW BOND STREET
& NO. 1,
COVENTRY ST
LONDON

Chamberlain & Co; Worcester.

2735

2736

1847–1850

CHAMBERLAINS

1850–1851

1852–1862

1889

2737

2738

2739

2740

1900–1905

1862–1946

2741

2742

2743

2744

ENGLAND

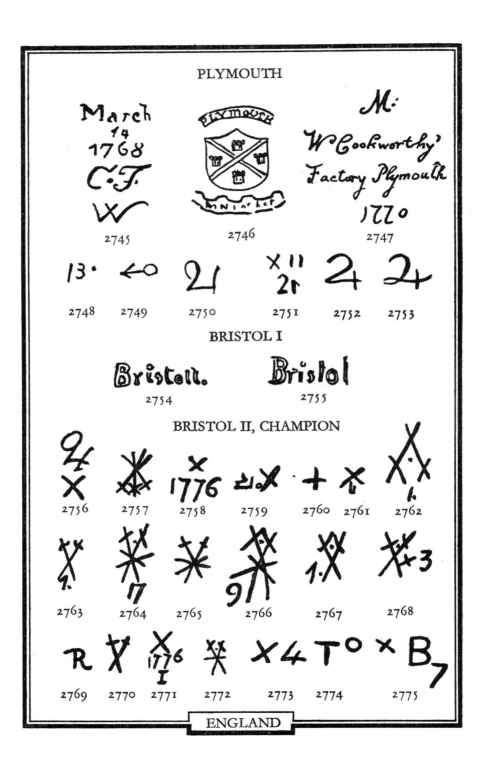

PLYMOUTH

2745

2746

2747

2748 2749 2750 2751 2752 2753

BRISTOL I

2754

2755

BRISTOL II, CHAMPION

2756 2757 2758 2759 2760 2761 2762

2763 2764 2765 2766 2767 2768

2769 2770 2771 2772 2773 2774 2775

ENGLAND

CHELSEA. The music lesson, after an engraving by René Gaillard, 1758, from a painting   XXIII
by Boucher (1750). About 1765. *Victoria and Albert Museum, London*

XXIV   DERBY. Chinaman and boy. About 1755. *Victoria and Albert Museum, London*

LONGTON HALL. Figure
of a goatherd. About
1955. *Victoria and
Albert Museum, London*

XXV

WEESP. Oil and vinegar set. About 1766. *Rijksmuseum, Amsterdam*

WEESP. Cup and saucer decorated with moulded sprigs. About 1764
    Rijksmuseum, Amsterdam

WEESP. Venus
About 1765

XXVII

AMSTEL, Vase. About 1790. Ht. 43,5 cm.
Rijksmuseum, Amsterdam

AMSTEL. Salad bowl, Japanese decoration.
About 1784. *Rijksmuseum, Amsterdam*

XXVIII

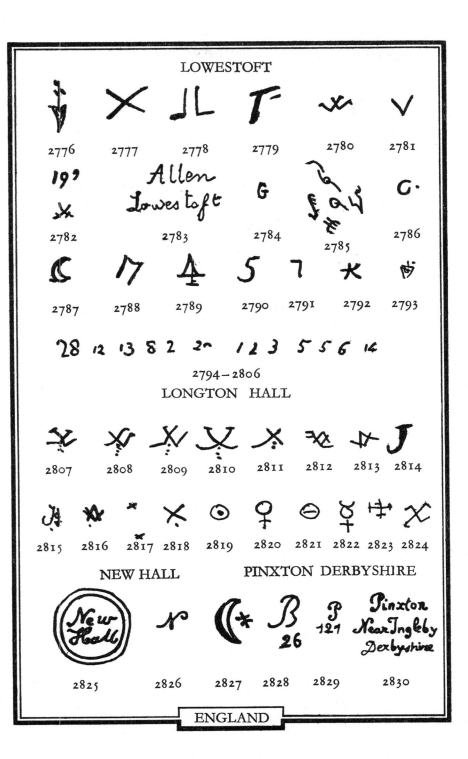

LOWESTOFT

2776 2777 2778 2779 2780 2781

2782 2783 2784 2785 2786

2787 2788 2789 2790 2791 2792 2793

2794–2806

LONGTON HALL

2807 2808 2809 2810 2811 2812 2813 2814

2815 2816 2817 2818 2819 2820 2821 2822 2823 2824

NEW HALL   PINXTON DERBYSHIRE

2825 2826 2827 2828 2829 2830

ENGLAND

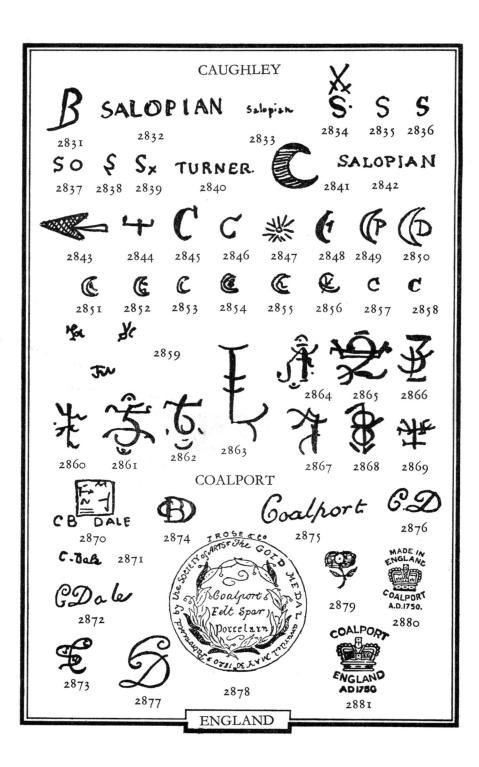

CAUGHLEY

COALPORT

MINTON
19th century

MINTON

2882 2883 2884 2885 2886

2888

2887

2889 Improved Stone China

2890

2891

CAULDON POTTERIES, LTD.
RIDGWAYS (BEDFORD WORKS), LTD.

2892 2893 2984

CAULDON ENGLAND John Ridgway & Co CAULDON ENGLAND
Cauldon Place
Potters to her Majesty

CAULDON CHINA
ENGLAND

2895 2896 2897

Royal Cauldon
England
Est 1774

J. W. R.

2898 2899 2900 2901 2902

ENGLAND

195

SPODE
W. T. COPELAND & SONS, LTD

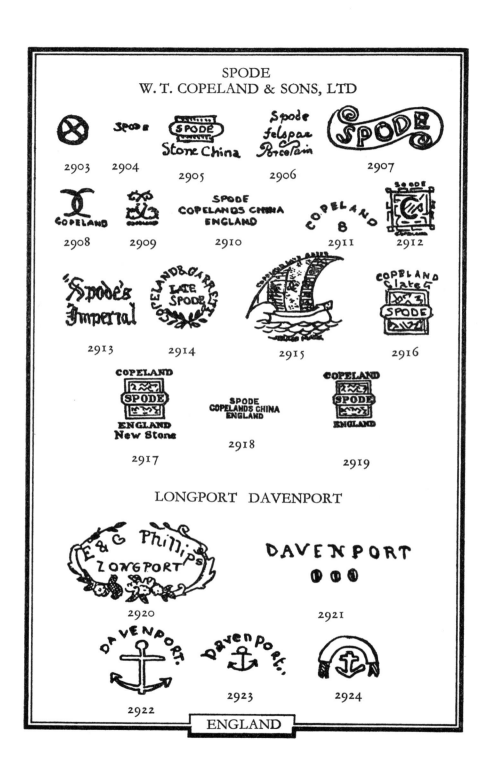

2903   2904

2905

2906

2907

2908   2909

2910

2911

2912

2913   2914   2915   2916

2917

2918

2919

LONGPORT   DAVENPORT

2920

2921

2922

2923

2924

WEDGWOOD

2925

 WEDGWOOD

2926

2927

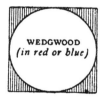

2928

2929

2930

2931

2932   Marks of Modellers and Painters   2933

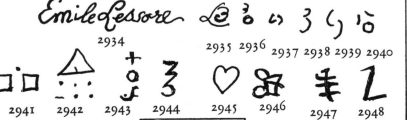

2934

2935 2936 2937 2938 2939 2940

2941   2942   2943   2944   2945   2946   2947   2948

SWANSEA

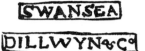

SWANSEA

2949   2950   2951   2952

2953   2954   2955

2956   2957   2958

NANTGARW

NANTGARW
C.W.

NANT GARW

Nantgarw

2959   2960   2961   2962

ROCKINGHAM

BRAMELD

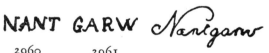

2963   2964   2965

19th & 20th CENTURY
DOULTON & CO., LTD. (BURSLEM)
DOULTON & CO., LTD. (LONDON)

2966

2967

DOULTON LAMBETH ENGLAND

2968

2969

2970

2971

NEW CHELSEA PORCELAIN CO., LTD.

2972

2973

2974

CHARLES ALLERTON & SONS

2975

2976

2977

2978

2979

2980

2981

ADDERLEYS, LTD.

2982

2983

ENGLAND

2984

199

IRELAND
BELLEEK POTTERIES, LTD.

DONOVAN

Donovan's
Irish Manufacture

2985

2986

2987

Dublin
Donovan's Irish
Manufacture

2988

Dublin

2989

$\mathcal{X}$
M
DONOVAN

2990

FINLAND

2991

ARABIA
Helsingfors

2992

ARABIA
HS

2993

YY
ARABIA

2994

ARABIA

2995

2996

2997

Porsgrunds
Porselæns

2998

49

2999

3000

NORWAY

DENMARK

COPENHAGEN

The Frenchman, Louis Fournier, former modeller of the Chantilly factory established a soft paste porcelain factory at Copenhagen about 1760. In 1772 a factory for hard paste porcelain was founded by the apothecary Müller with the assistance of Baron von Lang who had previously been attached to the Fürstenberg factory.

During the first years of its existence the artists Gylding, Leipsius and Ruck worked at Copenhagen. Later A. C. Luplau from Furstenberg worked here. Under the direction of Müller, the factory reached the peak of its fame. Müller secured the services of J. C. Bayer from Nuremberg who undertook the decoration of the famous Flora Danica Table Service which was intended for the Empress Catherine II of Russia, who, however, died in 1796 before the service was completed.

The porcelain was of very fine quality. Very beautiful table ware, services, vases, table ornaments etc. were manufactured for the Court. In 1779 the factory was given Royal patronage and thereafter it flourished rapidly. The products of Copenhagen were modelled and decorated in the manner of Meissen, Fürstenberg and Berlin. The factory was famous for its egg-shaped vases with cover and handles, shaped like masks.

Figures of high artistic merit were made, following the style of Meissen, but not quite achieving the elegance and graceful lines of the German products. Very well modelled small biscuit figures were also made. The classical style was only introduced at the very end of the 18th century. In 1868 the factory came into private hands, and since 1888 it has been operated by a limited company. Since that time its artistic achievement has steadily improved.

The pioneer of the modern period of Copenhagen porcelain was Philip Schou, who took over the management of the factory in 1884. The factory mark from the date of its foundation to the present day has consisted of three parallel waves.

The colour most used by the Royal Copenhagen Factory is a milky pale cobalt blue. In recent years craquelé porcelain glaze of a greenish grey tint has been used for large vases, ornamented with gold.

The sculptor Carl Martin-Hansen modelled among other objects a series of figures in Danish national costumes which together with an artistic centre-piece were presented to the Danish Royal Couple on the occasion of their Silver Wedding Jubilee in 1923 by the women's associations.

In 1925 the Grand Prix was awarded at the Paris Exhibition to the "Joachim Table Service".

C. F. Ludwigsen had worked out a process for making craquelé porcelain which was perfected about 1920. After Ludvigsen's, retirement P. Proschowsky resumed experiments with "Crystalline Glazes" and achieved striking results; whilst H. Madslund initiated the Solfasara Glaze with a metallic oxide as its foundation.

DIRECTORS:

Arnold Krog 1885–1915
H. C. Joachim 1915–1922

C. A. Poulsen.. 1922–1944

PAINTERS UNDER GLAZE:

Jenny Meyer 1892–1927
Oluf Jensen 1885–1934
Stefan Ussing.. 1894–1929
V. Th. Fischer... 1894–1928
G. Rode 1896–1936
Niels Munk Plum 1912–1931
Benjamin Olsen.. 1917–1935
Th. Kjølner 1913
R. Bøcher... 1912

PAINTERS ON GLAZE:

Thorkild Olsen 1917
N. Tidemand.. 1918–1943
Nils Thorsson 1912
Kai Lange... 1934
N. Sylvest-Pedersen 1910

SCULPTORS AND MODELLERS

Patrick Nordström 1912–1922
Jais Nielsen 1920
Knud Kyhn 1904
Hans Hansen.. 1908
Holger Christensen..................................... 1910
Bode Willumsen 1925
Gerhard Henning 1909
Arno Malinowsky...................................... 1921–1935
Georg Thylstrup....................................... 1911–1923
Olaf Mathiesen 1924
C. Halier... 1913

COPENHAGEN – BING & GRÖNDAHL

This factory was established in 1853. Per Krohn, a former director of the museum at Copenhagen, was one of the first directors. From the very beginning the products of this factory were of high artistic merit. A large staff of skilled painters and modellers was employed. At first attempts were made to reproduce groups and busts by Thorwaldsen. Afterwards new methods were sought and very soon the factory developed a new and individual style. The colours and glaze are very harmonious and the groups and figures produced are exquisitely modelled. Many vases with floral designs have been made. The marks used are usually three towers and the letters B G with the words Danish China Works. The pieces often bear the artist's signature. The factory is now under the directorship of O. and P. Simonsen.

COPENHAGEN – DAHL JENSEN

A factory was established here in 1945 by Dahl-Jensen. The produce follows the style of the Copenhagen factory Bing and Gröndahl where Dahl Jensen had worked for several years.

COPENHAGEN
Fournier
1760–1766

3001 3002

ROYAL MANUFACTORY
Franz Heinrich Mueller 1775–1802

3003 3004 3005 3006 3007 3008

3009 3010 3011 3012

3013 3014

Marks of Modellers and Painters

3015 3016 3017 3018

3019 3020 3021 3022

3023 3024 3025 3026

3027 3028 3029 3030 3031 3032

DENMARK

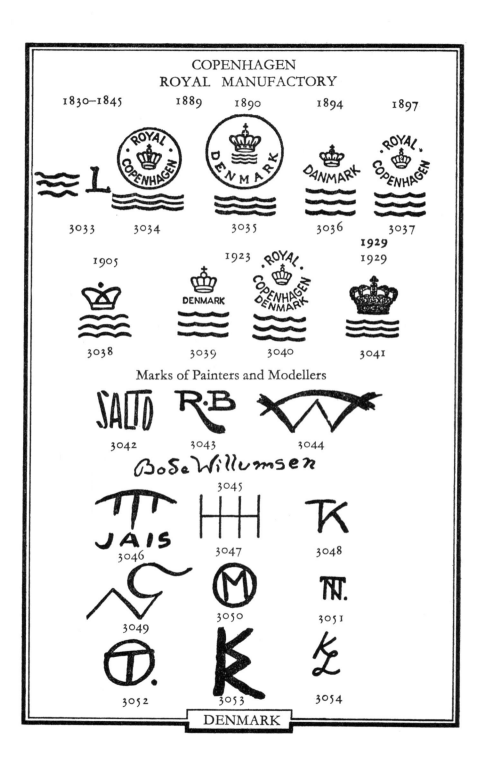

COPENHAGEN
ROYAL MANUFACTORY

1830–1845   1889   1890   1894   1897

3033   3034   3035   3036   3037

1905   1923   **1929**
1929

3038   3039   3040   3041

Marks of Painters and Modellers

3042   3043   3044

3045

3046   3047   3048

3049   3050   3051

3052   3053   3054

DENMARK

COPENHAGEN
BING & GROENDAHL

Danish China Works
B&G
COPENHAGEN

B & G

3055

B&G

3056

1854/94

DANISH CHINA WORKS

B & G

3057

3058

B&G

3059

B&G

3060

1915

B&G

3061

B&G
KJØBENHAVN

3062

Marks of modellers and painters

J.F.W.

3063

SALTO

3064

3065

Carl Petersen

3066

3067

3068

3069

K K

3070

Jo.

3071

ED EDK

3072

Nielz **n**

3073

HM

3074

S.j.

3076

DENMARK

205

COPENHAGEN
BING & GROENDAHL
Marks of Painters

3077

3078

3079

3080

3081

3082

3083

3084

3085

3086

3087

3088

3089

3090

3091

3092

3093

3094

Axel LOCHER
3095

Clara Nielsen
3096 a

Am. Schou
3096 b

3097 a

Dahl Jensen
3097 b

Th. L.
3098

DAHL JENSEN
COPENHAGEN
3100

KAI NIELSEN
3099

DENMARK

SWEDEN

MARIEBERG

It is not known with certainty when porcelain was first manufactured at Marieberg. In 1768 a Frenchman named Berthevin was engaged in producing the rare first pieces of soft paste porcelain. Two years later another Frenchman, Huret, and in 1777 a third Frenchman, Dortu, joined the factory and assisted in the production. Fleurot, a modeller, also worked here about that time. In 1780 the factory commenced production of hard paste porcelain. In 1782 the factory was sold to Major Nordenstople who merged it with the Rörstrand works and in 1788 it was closed. Nine years later, in 1797, it was acquired by some merchants who reopened it and appointed Geijer as manager. During its first period finely decorated table ware was produced which closely resembled china from the Mennecy factory. The hard paste porcelain was painted in the manner of Berlin. As mark the factory employed the monogram MB and in 1780 three small crowns were added. Henrik Sten (1759–1788) made some pieces in white soft paste porcelain. The Marieberg porcelain was sometimes decorated only with a gilt edge and slight gold decoration. Polychrome flowers are often found on pieces from this factory. The paintings are very tasteful. Besides mythological groups and Italian comedy figures, subjects for groups and figures were also taken from scenes of everyday life. Marieberg porcelain is very rare.

RÖRSTRAND

The Rörstrand faience factory was founded in 1726. On June 13, 1726, a group of 20 persons (5 of them members of the Kommerskollegium, all merchants) signed an "Association Contract" to erect at Stora Rörstrand a plant for the Manufacture of "Delft Pottery".

The first firing at Rörstrand was carried out in August 1727 in the presence of King Frederick I. The works manager was Johan Wolff, a native of Holstein. He came to Sweden via Copenhagen where, in 1722, he had been successful in obtaining a concession to manufacture faience in a factory at Store Kongens Gade, which he was obliged to leave in 1725.

Wolff left Rörstrand at the end of 1728. From 1730–40 the position of works manager was filled by three more Germans. In 1729 Kristoph Conrad Hunger from Vienna, who had formerly worked at Meissen, was engaged and worked at Rörstrand for five years until he was dismissed in 1733.

The fifth works manager at Rörstrand was Anders Fahlström, a Swede who had received his training at the factory. He assumed the technical and artistic management in the summer of 1740 and remained in office until his death in 1760. Even prior to the Fahlström era, the factory around the old castle near Lake Karlberg had grown to the extent of becoming a village on its own. According to a staff register compiled in January 1741 there were, in addition to Fahlström, 2 journeyman painters, 4 painters' mates, 6 apprentices, 6 journeyman turners, 2 turners' mates, 4 firers, 1 joiner, 1 glazier, 1 clay stamper, 6 general labourers, 1 manservant, 1 porter, 1 book-keeper. 37 persons, of whom 34 were engaged in actual production. In 1750 the number had risen to 93.

The years 1750 and 1751 saw a severe economic crisis. However, the liquidation was prevented by the establishment, in 1753, of a new company – Rörstrands Porcellaine Werks Bolag; with Elias Magnus Ingman, raised later to the peerage under the name of Nordenstolpe, as manager. He soon became the sole owner of the factory. He was assisted by Anders Fahlström and his younger brother Erik.

One of Rörstrand's liveliest competitors throughout the 18th century were Chinese imports, a trade fostered since about 1730 by the Swedish East India company (between 1768–1786 a total of almost 8 million pieces of teaware alone were imported via Gothenburg).

The purchase by the Nordenstolpe heirs of its competitor, Marieberg, in 1782 did little to alleviate the crisis. Bengt Reinhold Geijer purchased the factory in 1797, and after he took over the management in 1798 the manufacture of hard paste porcelain was introduced. In 1801 a German craftsman, Christian August Ehms, was engaged and remained with the factory until 1818.

After Geijer's death in 1815 the factory was managed by his heirs, who were destined to witness the end of a half-century period of decline. One of the main reasons for the lack of success of Rörstrand-Marieberg, and later Rörstrand alone, was the competition of British flintware. The Swedish factories were denied supplies of English clay. However, towards the end of 1828 the export of clay, which had previously been prohibited, was resumed. The re-introduction of English clay was accompanied by the adoption of English production methods, and a number of English craftsmen were now employed at Rörstrand. By 1830 Rörstrand had succeeded in producing flintware of a quality that could compete with the English produce.

The Gustavsberg factory was established in 1827, and became a competitor up to the commencement of the 20th century. The next era of expansion began twenty years later, during the period of ownership by Nils Wilhelm Stråle af Ekna.

After his death in 1853 the factory passed to his heirs who, in 1858, sold the concern to Gustaf Holdo Stråle, Robert Almström and N. C. Claëson. The title of the firm was still "B. R. Geijers Arfingar" (Heirs of B. R. Geijer), but, in 1867, a limited company was founded under the title of "Rörstrands Aktiebolag". With Stråle as the administrative manager and Ahlström as the technical executive Rörstrand became a major concern with a turnover reckoned in millions. At the close of the 19th century the number of employees totalled 1,000.

In 1875 a Finnish subsidiary was established. However, this was not a successful venture and the Arabia factory passed into Finish ownership in 1916. Two years previously the company had acquired "Göteborgs Porslinsfabrik".

From 1910 the factory was managed by Harald and Knut Almström. Harald Almström was succeeded in 1923 by Tore Grönwall who, in his capacity as managing director, was responsible for the closing-down of the 200-years-old factory and the transfer of the establishment to the subsidiary factory in Gothenburg in 1926.

After the Swedish Cement Group, via AB Iföverken, had acquired an interest in Rörstrand in 1929, Grönwall was succeeded by J. Magnus Bernström. In the same year the company had initiated collaboration with AB Lidköpings Porslinsfabrik (discontinued during the war) and, after Frederik Wehtje had assumed the position of managing director in 1932, the business was gradually transferred to Lidköping. The feldspatic porcelain works there was extended by the addition of modern premises for the manufacture of flintware (1934–1936) and, after further extensions in 1951–1953, the factory is the largest in Scandinavia engaged in the manufacture of domestic pottery (about 1,100 employees).

The Rörstrand factory received a new impetus when Frederik Wehtje became a director in 1932, and Gunnar Nyland was engaged as chief modeller. He is an artist of great skill who has produced many very finely modelled groups and figures.

Besides Gunnar Nyland many well-known painters have worked for the factory. Vicken von Post has modelled figurines in a graceful and charming manner. Gertrud Lönegren has designed beautiful tea sets. The best painter of the factory is Isaac Grünewald who specialises in flowers.

At LIDKÖPINGS PORSLINSFABRIK, Louise Adelborg, Oscar Dahl, Tyra Lundgren, and at RÖRSTRANDS PORSLINSFABRIKER, Gothenburg; Tyra Lundgren, Louise Adelborg, Ilse Claësson, Yngve Berg, E. Böckman and Nils Lundström have worked as modellers and decorators. Rörstrand's contribution to modern Swedish industrial art can be dated from the year 1917.

NORWAY

OSLO

The Porsgrunds Porselaens factory was established in 1887. The production is very artistic. Tea and table services are manufactured. A table service was made for President Roosevelt after World War II.

FINLAND

HELSINKI – ARABIA

The factory was opened in 1875. In recent years the Arabia factory has produced excellent and artistic porcelain ware.

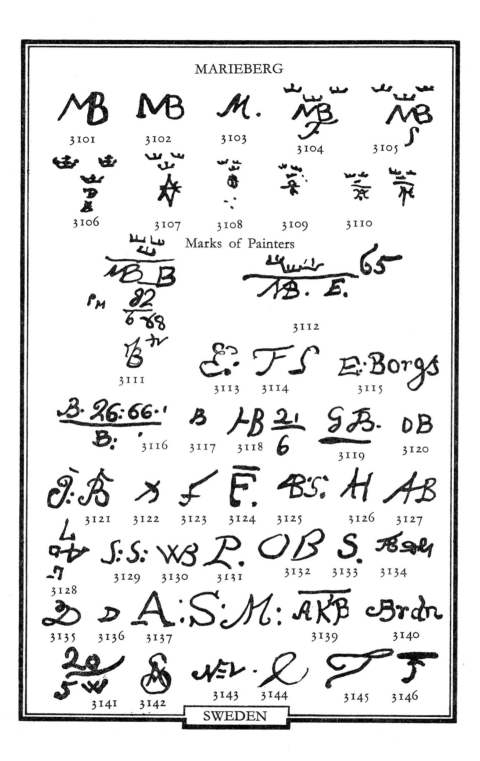

MARIEBERG

3101 3102 3103 3104 3105

3106 3107 3108 3109 3110

Marks of Painters

3111 3112

3113 3114 3115

3116 3117 3118 3119 3120

3121 3122 3123 3124 3125 3126 3127

3128 3129 3130 3131 3132 3133 3134

3135 3136 3137 3139 3140

3141 3142 3143 3144 3145 3146

SWEDEN

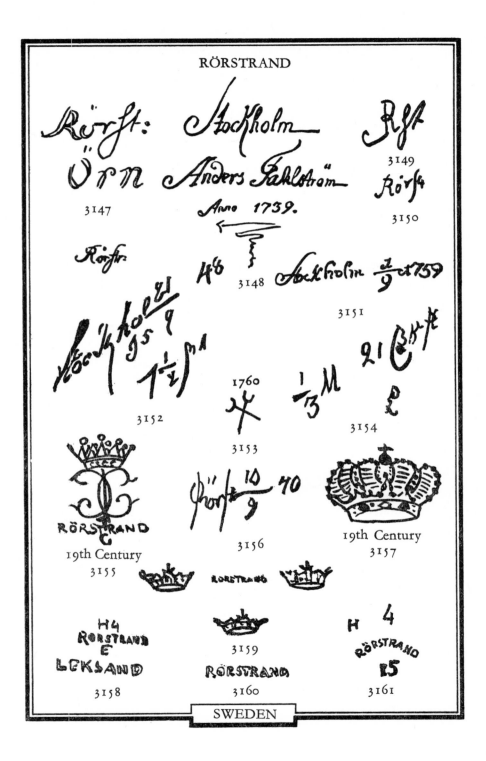

3147

3149

3150

3148

3151

3152

3153

3154

3155
19th Century

3156

3157
19th Century

3158

3159

3160

3161

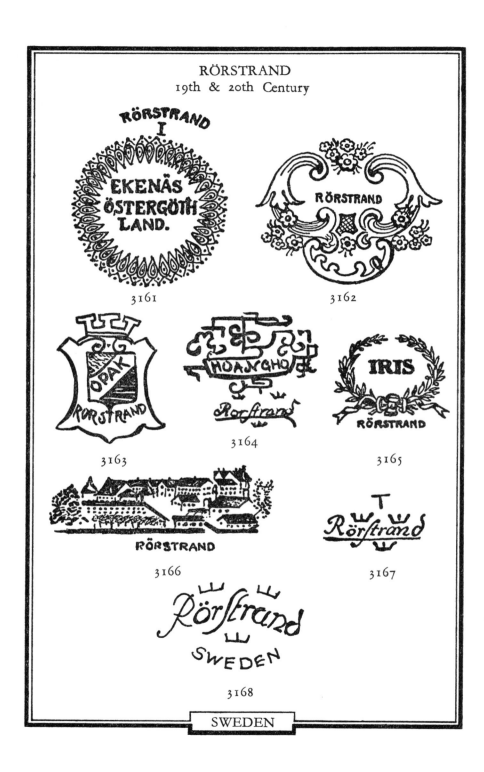

3161

3162

3163

3164

3165

3166

3167

3168

RÖRSTRAND
Marks of painters

3169   3170   3171   3172   3173

3174   3175   3176   3177   3178   3179

3180   3181   3182   3183   3184   3185   3186

3187   3188   3189   3190   3191   3192

3193   3194   3195   3196   3197   3198   3199   3200

3201   3202   3203   3204

3205   3206   3207   3208   3209   3210   3211   3212

3213   3214   3215   3216   3217   3218   3219   3220

SWEDEN

RÖRSTRAND
Marks of painters

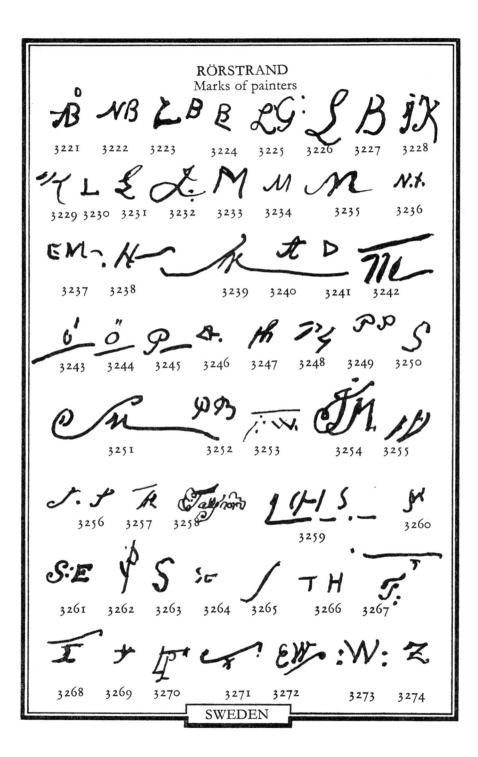

SWEDEN

214

SWITZERLAND

ZÜRICH 1763–1803

The Zürich factory was established by Salomon Gessner, Heinrich Heidegger, Johann Konrad Heidegger, Hans Martin Usteri and Heinrich Lavater. For a short time after its establishment the Zürich factory produced soft paste porcelain, but soon it began to manufacture hard paste porcelain of a creamy colour. It produced ordinary table ware and very beautifully painted services in the style of Meissen. Its best period was from 1775 to 1790. The landscape painting on the products of this factory was particularly good. The leading painters were Gessner and Füszli (1771–1778). Figures were less well executed and were mostly imitations of Ludwigsburg.

The factory used as mark the letter Z in underglaze blue, sometimes incised or impressed in the moist clay. Pieces bearing this mark are often imitations. Tea sets and services in Sèvres style were also made at Zürich.

The following painters and modellers have worked there:
Nees, Joseph, 1768, previously at the Ludwigsburg factory; Sonnenschein, Johann Valentin, 1775–1779, previously modeller at the Ludwigsburg factory; Klein, Gabriel, 1768, previously at the Wallendorf factory; Maurer, Caspar, painter; Spengler, Johann Jakob, modeller, 1770–1790; Thommen, Heinrich, 1770–1786, painter; Bleuler, Heinrich, 1761–1780, painter; Herliberger David, modeller, 1770; Bleuler, Johann, 1778, painter; Bonland, Johann, 1773, painter; Daffinger, Johann, painter, 1760–1796; Frei, Karl, painter; Füszli, Heinrich, painter.

NYON 1781–1813

This factory, established by Jacques Dortu and Ferdinand Müller, made hard paste porcelain exclusively. It produced very well decorated services and vases in the more restrained, classical manner, usually after French models. The figures are not very good and, on the whole, uninteresting. They were painted or executed in biscuit porcelain.

The factory mark was a fish in underglaze blue. This mark has often been forged on modern porcelain. Dortu had previously worked in Berlin at the Royal factory, from 1777–1778 he was in Sweden in the Marieberg Factory and later at Marseille. After a short time he left Nyon.

In 1787 he returned to Nyon and took over the directorship of the factory. The style of the firm was changed first to Dortu, Finckenagel and Cie, and later to Dortu, Soulier, Doret and Cie. The factory was in operation until 1813.

GENEVA

Pierre Mülhauser established in 1805 an enamelling shop in Geneva, where he mainly decorated Nyon porcelain assisted by 10 painters. Pierre Mülhauser left Geneva in 1818.

LANGENTHAL

This factory was established in 1906 and soon developed into a flourishing enterprise producing utilitarian objects and artistic ware.

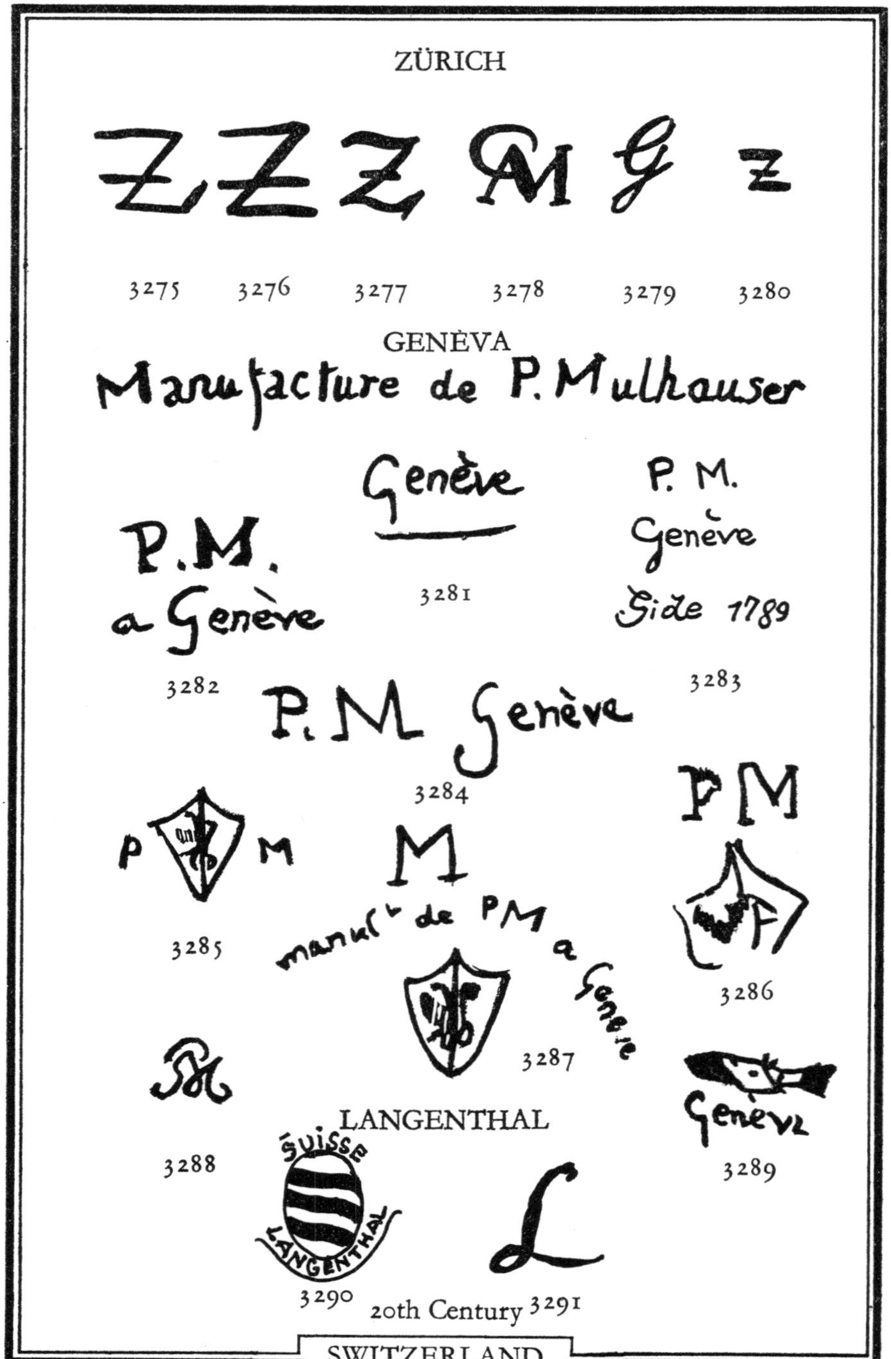

Z Z Z M G z

3275   3276   3277   3278   3279   3280

GENÈVA

Manufacture de P. Mulhauser

Genève

P. M.
Genève

3281

P. M.
a Genève

Side 1789

3282

3283

P. M Genève

3284

P M

P   M

3285

M

3286

manuf^r de PM a Genève

3287

3288

Genève

3289

LANGENTHAL

SUISSE
LANGENTHAL

3290   20th Century   3291

L

SWITZERLAND

SWITZERLAND

RUSSIA

ST. PETERSBURG

After his return from Holland Czar Peter tried to introduce the manufacture of Delft faience in Russia. In 1718 a Dutchman by the name of Eggebrecht, who owned a small factory at Dresden, was invited to come to Russia and accepted the offer. At the same time emissaries were sent to Meissen to find out the secret of the manufacture of hard paste porcelain. Many unsuccessful attempts were made. In 1744, many years after Peter's death, new attempts were made to find out the secret of the composition of hard paste porcelain in China. These attempts were also fruitless.

A Meissen porcelain painter, Hunger, who had worked both in Meissen and Vienna, boasted of knowing the secret of the Meissen porcelain mixture and in consequence the Russian Government, who had an envoy in Saxony, resolved to kidnap him. Hunger was brought to St. Petersburg, where he made many unsuccessful attempts to produce porcelain ware. He accused his Russian collaborators of spoiling his work and finally left. The personality of Hunger is interesting because he also succeeded in deceiving the Danish and Swedish governments by promising to reveal the secret of the manufacture of porcelain.

In 1750 the Russian scientist Winogradov succeeded in making genuine hard paste porcelain. The china clay used by him was of Russian origin and came from Gjiel near Moscow. Later it was brought from Orenburg where a better-grade material was found.

At first the factory produced coffee- and tea-sets. These were delicately painted in the manner of Meissen or Sèvres. The Empress Elizabeth ordered many snuffboxes which were used as presents for the Imperial entourage. Attempts were also made to model groups and figurines.

The predominant colours used were pale mauve, green, brick-red, pale blue and yellow; gold was also frequently used, particularly for borders and ornaments. Some pieces were gilded all over leaving only a white space for initials or a painted scene. Of the products of that period only one dinner service, known as the "Private Service of Her Majesty", is still known to exist. The plates are decorated with a raised trelliswork in pale mauve, and the baskets are pierced with moulded wreaths of flowers.

The intricate problem of the marks used at the Imperial factory between 1747 and 1770 demands detailed particulars. No dated objects of the year 1747 are known. The earliest dated piece known to exist is a heartshaped sugar-bowl. It is dated 1748 and is marked with a W in blue (for Winogradov). Bearing the same mark and the date 1749 in blue, is a small round cup with no handle, slightly misshaped. There are also in existence a very small number of pieces bearing the dates 1751 and 1752.

In 1752 Winogradov's health began to deteriorate and from that time the activity of the factory declined. After his death in 1758 a new mark appeared, namely an imperial eagle impressed in the paste and painted black, followed, somewhat later, by an arrow and then a small circle. This last was in blue. Another mark used by this factory (exceedingly rare) consisted of two anchors crossed (arms of St. Petersburg). This mark, too, was in blue. It is possible that all these marks were only tentatively used. They were discontinued when the Empress Catherine II ordered the first letter of her name to be adopted. The Empress reorganized the factory in 1763 and workmen and modellers from Meissen were brought in.

Catherine was very fond of porcelain, and ordered many services and vases. She also placed large orders with Sèvres and Meissen, as well as with Wedgwood, and these foreign pieces were often used as models for the production of her own factory. Towards 1760 the output steadily improved in quality. On the order of the Empress the factory made an important dinner-service for Count Gregory Orlov. A considerable number of pieces of the service are still in existence, including a hors d'oeuvre set, and, a tea-set with small porcelain spoons. A toilet-set including a mirror fitted with a clock is preserved. This service is richly embellished with gold and silver and painted with battle-scenes, military emblems and the initials G.G.O. which are in some instances surmounted by a coronet. Above the mirror are two Cupids sitting astride two cannons which gives a clue to the probable date of manufacture, namely the year 1765, when Orlov was appointed Master in Chief of Ordnance.

The figures of that epoch bear the same characteristics as the dinner-services. Their enamel is bluish grey, often showing defects caused by the firing, and slight distortions. The Oriental figures are supposed to have been modelled between 1752 and 1754 by Dunker, a wood-carver who was attached to the factory for a time.

After 1770 many dinner-services and tea-sets were made, partly under the inspiration of Meissen models. Various attempts were made to secure foreign artists, but without success.

In 1797 a Frenchman, Jean Dominique Rachette, was engaged as modeller and he remained at the head of that department for many years. He executed a large number of figures, groups, busts and reliefs of outstanding merit. Among his most important works were numerous Russian types inspired largely by prints from John Georgi's book, "Description of all the Nationalities who inhabit the Russian State" (1776–1777). He was also responsible for the table-ornaments in biscuit for the service called Arabesque, which was one of the remarkable services produced after 1780. This service, which was made in 1784, was designed for sixty persons and consisted of 978 pieces, its cost being 25.000 Rubles. It got its name from the arabesques in the Pompeian style, with which the pieces are decorated.

The Yacht service, somewhat similar to the Arabesque in the details of its ornamentations, differs from it in colouring as well as in its general plan. The end of the 18th century saw no notable changes in the products of the factory. The shapes became less florid and more directly inspired by antique art. Of dinner-services the best-known of that period is the one made for Prince Youssoupov, which was designed for eighty persons.

During the following reign of Paul I, when the Meissen style was imitated, and during the reign of Alexander I, when the empire style was most successfully adapted to the Russian taste, the factory achieved worldrenown.

During the reign of Alexander II the style and quality of decoration deteriorated and at the beginning of the reign of Nicholas II an attempt was made to raise the artistic level of production.

During the 19th century many foreigners were attached to the works, including German technicians, French gilders and painters, such as Denis Joseph Moreau, decorator and gilder, and the painters Swebach, Desfontaines, and Ferdinand Davignon. The Russian national style, however, was never entirely abandoned in favour of the classical style.

At the beginning of the 20th century the well-known Russian painter Konstantine Somov, who was one of the greatest connoisseurs of rococo, designed a number of figurines and groups which are unequalled in the precision of the costume detail and the frail grace of their composition. These groups and figurines were very delicately painted.

Another Russian painter, Leon Bakst, who lived in Paris, where he was famous for his stage decorations, inspired the porcelain factory. Some of his famous costume designs, such as the yellow sultana, were modelled by the Imperial Factory.

After the revolution of 1917 the Imperial Porcelain Factory was taken over by the Soviet Government. New artists gave a revolutionary impulse to the production. Very few of the Soviet specimens have been brought out of Russia. After the end of the Second World War many Commemoration vases bearing portraits of Stalin and military heroes were produced by the factory.

From 1754 onwards the initial of the ruler in underglaze blue, often with a crown but sometimes alone, was used as mark.

The initial of the Empress Catharine II was used until 1796, that of the Emperor Paul from 1796 to 1801 and the initial of the Emperor Alexander I from 1801 to 1825. From 1825 to 1855 the porcelain of the Imperial Factory bears the initial of Nicolas I, from 1855 to 1881 that of Alexander II, from 1881 to 1894 the initial of Alexander III and from 1894 to 1917 the initial of Nicolas II, the last Russian Emperor.

The Soviet Government uses the Soviet emblem, in underglaze blue. The name of factory is now Farforovy Zavod Imeni Lomonosova.

GARDNER

In 1746 an Englishman, Francis Gardner, came to Russia, where for the next ten years he was engaged in business. He then turned his attention to the manufacture of porcelain and between 1754 and 1756 established himself in the province of Moscow, where he spent the ensuing ten years in making various experiments in the manufacture of porcelain. In 1765 he erected a factory on land belonging to Prince Urusov in the village of Verbilki and two years later he bought the land on which the factory stood. Gardner was a very economical man and during all his years of experimentation his total expenditure did not exceed a thousand pounds.

During the first ten years from 1755 to 1765 Gardner manufactured statuettes, small teasets, wine-coolers etc., none of them marked with the letter G, which he later adopted, but having a barely discernible circle impressed in the paste (some of the pieces do not bear this mark) and a mark in blue. The latter, however, is very rarely found. His pieces were painted in a delicate colour scheme, which is found on no other porcelain. The colours used were apple-green, a very light raspberry-red and yellow.

Gardner's factory developed rapidly and soon received orders from the Court. From 1777 to 1780 he made three dinner services commissioned by the Empress, the services for the Knights of St. George for eighty guests, for the Knights of St. Alexander for forty, and for the Knights of St. Andrew for thirty guests. For the three services he recieved 16.000 Rubles.

In 1783 the Empress commissioned yet another service, the most important of the four, for twice the number of guests as that of St. George. This service, known as the St. Wladimir service, was completed in 1785 at a cost of 15.000 Rubles.

In the 19th century the Gardner factory increased its output and mostly produced tea- and coffee-sets as well as small figures. These are similar to those turned out by other factories up to 1830, but the figures have a certain character of their own. These figures, which are rather clumsy and naïve and often out of proportion, invariably preserve a Russian popular style, born of the expansion of national pride after the Napoleonic wars.

The Gardner factory, after being in the hands of the family for 136 years, passed into the possession of M. S. Kuznetsov in 1891.

KUZNETSOV

Kuznetsov 1818–1886	at Liszovo.
Kuznetsov T.L. 1830–1840	at Dulevo.
Kuznetsov T.L. 1840–1850	at Novokharitonovka.
Kuznetsov M.S.	at Riga.
Kuznetsov M.S.	at Kharkov.
Kuznetsov M.S.	at Budy.

The Kuznetsov factories produced porcelain of the highest quality. They made exquisite tea-sets with transparent cups in pale blue and pale rose porcelain, decorated with beautifully painted flowers and birds in the Russian style. Among their specialities were toilet-sets, bottles, and powder-boxes in dark blue porcelain with rich gildings and in pale blue without gildings. These sets were made at all the factories and their paintings and colourings differ very little. The marks were printed in blue on glaze. Kuznetsov porcelain made at Dulevo is rare.

DULEVO

The Dulevo factory is now in operation and the output belongs to the best porcelain produced in Soviet Russia. Artistic figurines and pretty tea-sets are made.

AUERBACH 1809

This factory produced table-services and coffee-sets of good quality, decorated in empire style. The Imperial eagle in blue under glaze was used as mark.

POPOV 1811–1850

This factory was established by Alexander Popov at the village of Gorbunovo near Moscow. It turned out a large quantity of table-ware and table-ornaments and produced china for restaurants and many other pieces of excellent quality and design, using a fine paste and decorations of rich gilding and brilliant colours.

The factory successfully competed with the Imperial factory. Its best period was about 1830. The predominant colours, used by Popov, were a chestnut brown and a light blue, the decorative forms being borrowed from the rococo style. The figures and groups were imitations of 18th century Dresden models.

KIEV 1798–1880

The municipality of Kiev established this factory at the nearby village of Mejogoriye, which afterwards became Crown property. At this time the factory was merged with the Imperial factory and administered from St. Petersburg. It produced an excellent paste from clay found locally and during the reign of Nicholas I good porcelain was made there. Owing to bad management, however, the business failed and the works were closed in 1880.

POSKOTCHIN 1817

This factory was established by a man named Poskotchin in the village of Morye near Schlüsselburg. Here some of the finest figures, produced in Russia, were made. Both the modelling and the enamel colours (mostly apple-green, chestnut-brown and yellow) display an unusually advanced technique.

However, the number of the models is small, the principal examples being a seated Chinese figure with movable hands and head in imitation of Meissen, and a hawker carrying a sack on his head. Some of the products of this factory closely resemble English cream-ware or Queen's ware. Some of the pieces, such as tea-sets and similar articles, were painted to imitate marble.

ARKHANGELSKOYÉ 1814–1831

In 1814 Prince Yousoupov opened a workshop for painting porcelain at his country home at Archangelskoyé near Moscow. Here French painters decorated white porcelain which was mostly obtained from Sèvres, the supplies being brought from Sèvres to Moscow by road on the Prince's own wagons. White porcelain was also brought from the Popov factory. The finished products, which are invariably of high quality, were not sold, but were used for presentation purposes. In 1831 the workshop was closed.

ST. PETERSBURG 1831

This factory was established by the brothers Kornilov at the capital. Several foremen from the Imperial factory were employed as well as a Frenchman, Auguste Darte, who worked there in 1844. Between 1830 and 1850 this factory created several figures representing popular Russian types. These, notably one representing a vendor of engravings, show very delicate workmanship. This factory continued operating until the revolution of 1917.

VOLOKITINO 1839

In the village Volokitino a porcelain factory was established by Miklashevsky and was managed by a Frenchman, Auguste Darte till 1851. The distinctive feature of this factory's products was a creamy white glaze, while the painted decorations were noticeably restrained. The favourite motifs were flowers, which also appear on vases and trellis-work baskets. Some very good figures were also made representing a variety of subjects: Jesus Christ, Joan of Arc, knights and figures of Ukrainian peasants in picturesque costumes. Besides these more commonplace articles very ambitious work was undertaken for the church at Volokitino, where icons, frames, pillars and enormous chandeliers were executed in porcelain.

In addition to the larger factories to which reference has been made in the text, a large number of less important factories existed, which produced common table ware and figurines, which, though rather crude, are very amusing. These smaller factories include: P. KOZLOV, BATENIN, NOVY, SAFRONOV, TERIKHOV, KISSELEV, KHRAPUNOV, KHRAPU-NOV-NOVY, VSEVOLOJSKI, POLIVANOV and many others.

The smaller works copied the pieces of the Gardner, Kuznetzov or Kornilov factories. They sometimes produced figurines representing officers, ladies and gentlemen, peasants and children. The production of these figurines was small and they are to-day interesting pieces for collectors. The marks of all these factories are given.

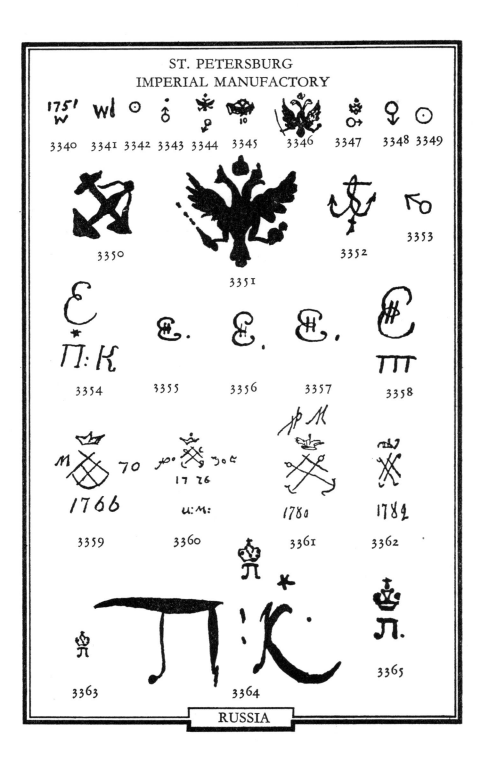

ST. PETERSBURG
IMPERIAL MANUFACTORY

3340 3341 3342 3343 3344 3345 3346 3347 3348 3349

3350 3351 3352 3353

3354 3355 3356 3357 3358

3359 3360 3361 3362

3363 3364 3365

RUSSIA

THE HAGUE. Punch Bowl.
Mark – *stork*.
Rijksmuseum, Amsterdam

THE HAGUE. Ewer and basin.
Rijksmuseum, Amsterdam

THE HAGUE. Tournay porcelain decorated at the Lynker factory. *Rijksmuseum, Amsterdam*

XXIX

COPENHAGEN. Ganymedes and the Eagle, biscuit, after a sculpture by Bertel Thorwaldsen. About 1830. Ht. 10,5 cm. *Private Collection*

GARDNER. The bootseller. About 1830. Ht. 21,3 cm. *Collection M. Penkala*

GARDNER. Peasant boy with flute. Ht. 16,2 cm. *Collection M. Penkala*

Lorenz Hutschenreuther. White
Parrot. Ht. 38 cm. *Private Collection.*

ROZENBURG. Small vase, cup and
saucer. About 1898. *Private Collection*

The dancer Loïe Fuller, biscuit. Model by Agathon Leonard van Weydefeldt. Ht. 29,2 cm. About 1900. *Private Collection.*

BERLIN. Lady with a snowball. Model by the sculptor Rudolf Marcuse, Jugend Stil. Ht. 40.5 cm. *Collection M. Penkala*

Lady in an armchair. Incised *K. Arnoaller Private Collection.*

ST. PETERSBURG
IMPERIAL MANUFACTORY

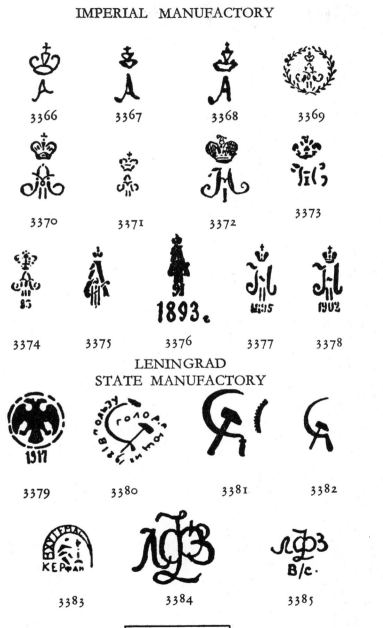

3366 3367 3368 3369

3370 3371 3372 3373

3374 3375 3376 3377 3378

LENINGRAD
STATE MANUFACTORY

3379 3380 3381 3382

3383 3384 3385

RUSSIA

GARDNER MANUFACTORY MOSCOW
VERBILKI

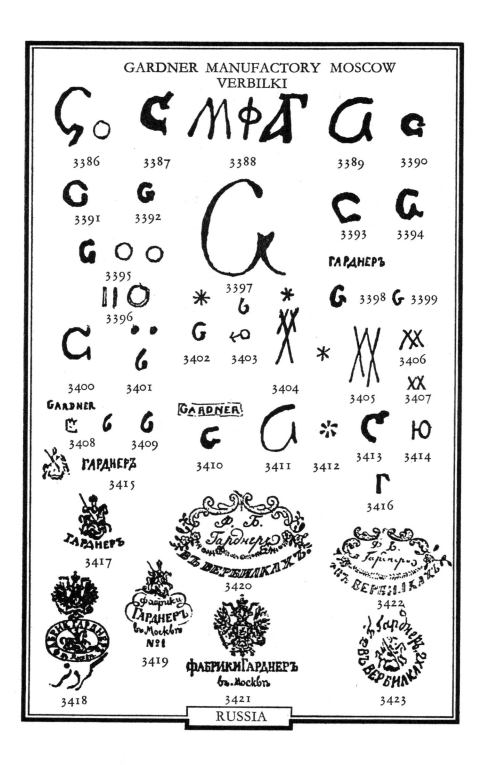

ГАРДНЕРЪ

GARDNER

GARDNER

ГАРДНЕРЪ
3415

ГАРДНЕРЪ
3417

3386 3387 3388 3389 3390
3391 3392 3393 3394
3395 3397 3398 3399
3396 3402 3403 3404 3406 3407
3400 3401 3405
3408 3409 3410 3411 3412 3413 3414
3416
3418 3419 3420 3421 3422 3423

RUSSIA

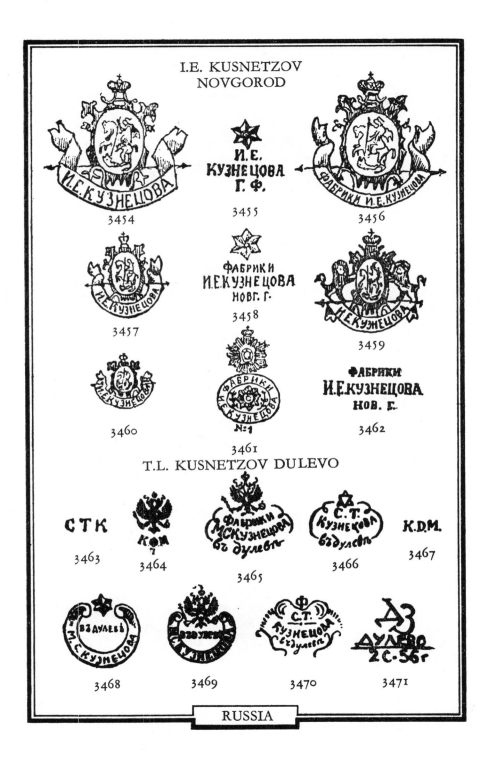

I.E. KUSNETZOV
NOVGOROD

3454

3455

3456

3457

3458

3459

3460

3461

3462

T.L. KUSNETZOV DULEVO

СТК

3463

3464

3465

3466

K.D.M.

3467

3468

3469

3470

3471

M. S. KUSNETZOV, RIGA

С.Т.К.
РИГА
3472

ЗАВОДА
С.Т.КУЗНЕЦОВА
РИГА
3474

ТВА
М.С.КУЗНЕЦОВА
Р.Ф
3475

ФАБРИКИ М.С.КУЗНЕЦОВА ВЪ РИГѢ
3473

М.С.К
3476

ВЪ РИГѢ
М.С.КУЗНЕЦОВА
3477

ФАБРИКИ М.С.КУЗНЕЦОВА ВЪ РИГѢ
3478

Фабрики
М.С.Кузнецова
въ г. Ригѣ
3479

ФАБРИКЪ
М.С.КУЗНЕЦОВА
ВЪ РИГѢ
3480

С.Т. КУЗНЕЦОВА ВЪ РИГѢ
3481

Т-ВА Т-ГФ
М.С. КУЗНЕЦОВА
ВЪ РИГѢ
3482

M. S. KUSNETZOV
BUDY

KHARKOV

Т-ВА М.С.КУЗНЕЦОВА
БУДЫ.
3483

ВЪ ХАРЬКОВѢ
М.С. КУЗНЕЦОВА
3485

Т-ВА М.С.КУЗНЕЦОВА
въ Будахъ.
3486

KHARKOV

М.С.К
3484

М.С.
КУЗНЕЦОВА
въ Харьковѣ.
3487

RUSSIA

KORNILOV, St. PETERSBURG

3488

3489

3490

3491

3492

3493

3494

POPOV

3495

3496

3497

АГ

3498

ПОПОВЫ

3499

5 Р

3500

5 Р

3501

ZHAIDIN

FA BRICK
ZHAIDIN

3503

3502

3504

ISSAYEV   ISSAYEV

3505

3506

3507

3508

3509

3510

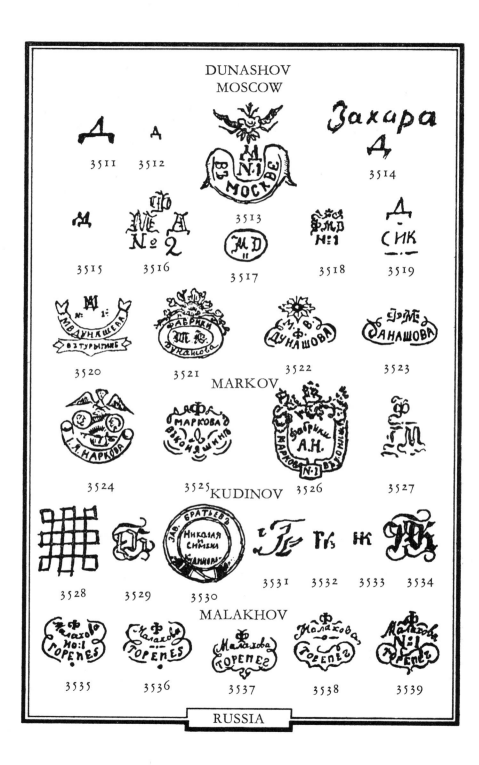

DUNASHOV
MOSCOW

3511   3512   3513   3514

3515   3516   3517   3518   3519

3520   3521   3522   3523

MARKOV

3524   3525   3526   3527

KUDINOV

3528   3529   3530   3531   3532   3533   3534

MALAKHOV

3535   3536   3537   3538   3539

RUSSIA

232

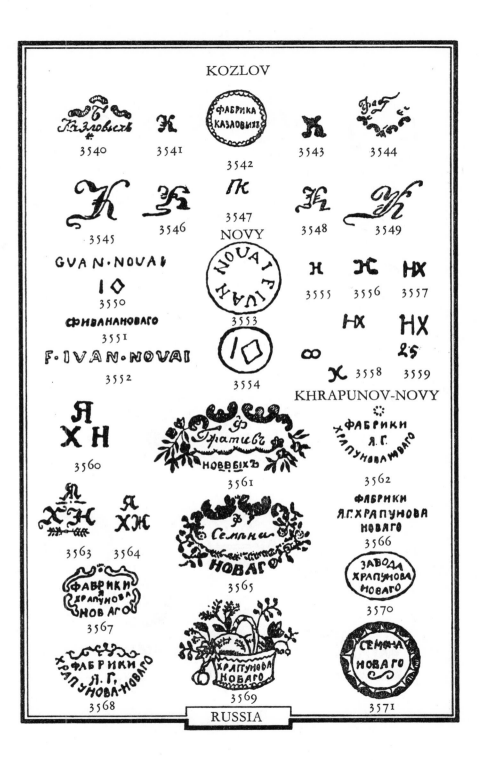

KOZLOV

3540 3541 3542 3543 3544

3545 3546 3547 3548 3549

NOVY

GVAN·NOUAI
3550

3553

3555 3556 3557

ФИВАНАНОВАГО
3551

F·IVAN·NOVAI
3552

3554

3558 3559

KHRAPUNOV-NOVY

3560

3561

3562

3563 3564

3565

3566

3567

3569

3570

3568

3571

BARMIN

3572

3573

3574

3575

3576

3577   3578

3579

STUPIN

3580

TERIKHOV-KISSELEV

3581

3582

3583

3584

3585

3586

3587

3588

RUSSIA

WELIKANOV

DREYLINGSBUSCH

VALAAM

3589

3590

3591

POSKOTCHIN

3592 3593

3594

3595

3596

3597

MORYE-KOUTOUZOV

MIKLASHEVSKI

1851—1862

3598

3599

3600

3601

3602

3603

IKONNIKOV

3604

3605

3606

3607

3608

RUSSIA

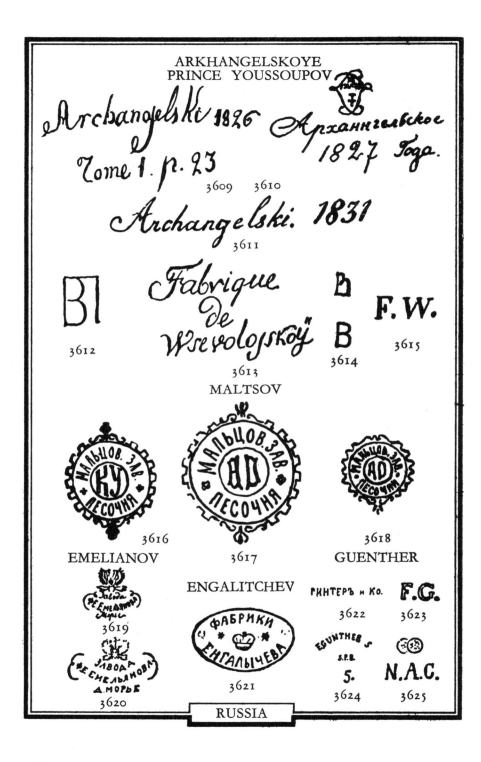

ARKHANGELSKOYE
PRINCE YOUSSOUPOV

Archangelske 1826

Tome I. p. 23

3609

Архангельское 1827 года.

3610

Archangelski 1831

3611

BI

3612

Fabrique de Wsevolojskoy

3613

MALTSOV

B

3614

F.W.

3615

3616

3617

3618

EMELIANOV

3619

3620

ENGALITCHEV

3621

GUENTHER

ГИНТЕРЪ и КО.

3622

F.G.

3623

EGUNTHER S
S.P.B.
5.

3624

N.A.C.

3625

RUSSIA

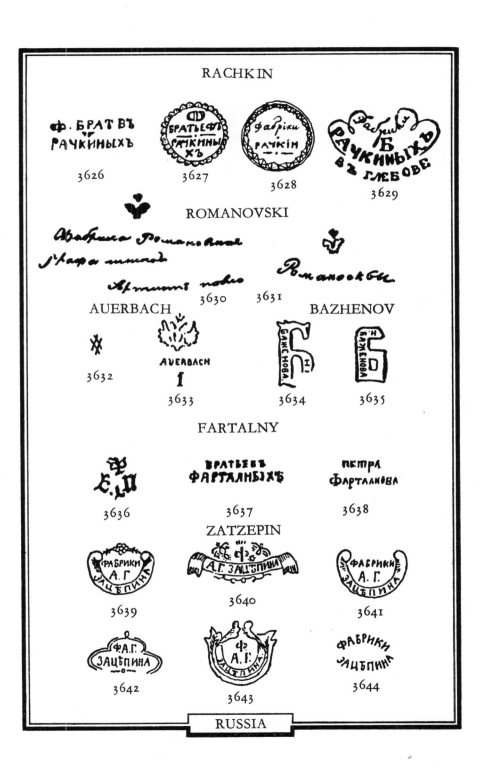

RACHKIN

3626 3627 3628 3629

ROMANOVSKI

3630 3631

AUERBACH BAZHENOV

3632 3633 3634 3635

FARTALNY

3636 3637 3638

ZATZEPIN

3639 3640 3641

3642 3643 3644

RUSSIA

SABANIN

3645 3646 3647 3648 3649

SAFRONOV

САФРОНОВА

САФРОНОВА

3650 3651 3652 3653

SAMSONOV

3654 3655 3656 3657 3658 3659

SIPYAGIN

3660 3661 3662 3663 3664

GULIN

3665 3666 3667 3668 3669 3670

RAKHMANOV

3671 3672 3673

RUSSIA

POLAND

BARANOWKA

Michel de Mézer established this factory in 1804 on the estate of prince Adam Lubomirski. He was assisted by artists and workmen from the Korzec factory which was destroyed by fire in 1797. The produce of the factory was of high quality between 1804 and 1833.

CMIÉLÓW

This factory was established by Woitos at the end of the 18th century. Count Jacques Malakhowski acquired the works in the beginning of the 19th century. At first only faience was produced. In 1848 the factory was sold to prince Xavier Drucki-Lubecki. From now on artistic porcelain was produced. The plant is still in operation.

TOMASZÓW

The factory at Tomaszów (near Lublin) was established by count Zamoyski in 1795. From 1805 the factory produced porcelain. Franciszek Mezer was appointed as director. The produce was of high artistic quality and often decorated with historical portraits. In 1834 the plant was closed. In 1842 the factory was sold to Robert Wendler and Joseph Bentkowski who operated it until 1846.

KORZEC 1793

A hard paste porcelain factory was established by Prince Chartoryski at Korzec with the object of imitating the table services of Sèvres. The factory made beautifully decorated tea-sets and vases and became one of the best-known in Poland. The Korzec mark is an eye in a triangle, in red or blue under glaze. The word "Korzec" is often used with the mark. Korzec porcelain has been imitated by small factories established at Lubartow and by the factory of Count Zamoyski at Tomaszow.

BELVEDÈRE

This hard paste porcelain factory was established in Warsaw about 1774. It specialised in products of superior quality and no cheap porcelain was made there. During the reign of the last Polish King, Stanislas Poniatowski (1764–1795), the Belvedère factory produced very beautiful vases, some of which were one meter high. Pieces in imitation of Chinese and Japanese ware were also produced. Groups and bowls were also made. The Belvedère specimens were decorated in the Sèvres style and some of the big vases are ornamented in blue and red. Four extremely rare vases have been presented by the Szlenkier family to the National Museum at Warsaw.

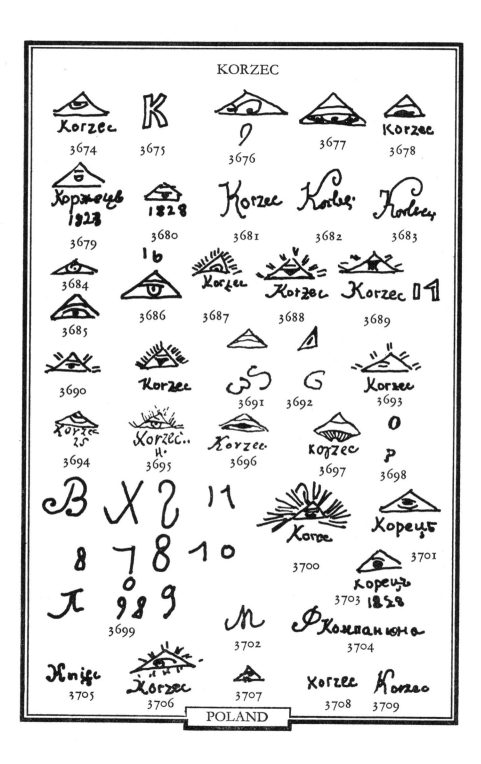

KORZEC

HORODNITZA

POLAND

241

BELVEDÈRE WARSAW

3736   3737   3738   3739

BARANÓWKA

3740   3741   3742   3743

3744   3745   3746   3747

3748   3749   3750   3751   3752

CMIELÓW

CPM

3753   3754   3755   3756

3757

3758   3759

POLAND

242

TOMASZÓW

TOMASZÓW

3760   3761   3762   3763

WTOMASZOWIE
1802

3764

Tomaszow

22 — 6

2   11.

3765

Jomaszów Mezer

3766

Jomaszow

3767

Jomaszów

3768

Mezer

3769

G m θ
31 2

EC

3770

PRUSZKÓW

P   P   P   P   K4   B

3771   3772   3773   3774   3775   3776

POLAND

243

LIST OF ILLUSTRATIONS

VIENNA. Solitaire, Sorgenthal period. Marks, *beehive* in blue underglaze. About 1785. *Collection J. Morpurgo, Amsterdam* (XIV)

SAINT-CLOUD. "Chinaman". About 1720. Ht. 22,7 cm. *Pâte tendre. Victoria and Albert Museum, London* (XVIII)

MENNECY-VILLEROY. "Chinaman." About 1740. Ht. 22,2 cm. *Pâte tendre. Victoria and Albert Museum, London* (XIX)

CHANTILLY. Jug, Imari decoration. About 1738. *Rijksmuseum, Amsterdam* (XX)

CHANTILLY. Four-lobed vase decorated with moulded prunus sprigs. About 1730. *Bayerisches Nationalmuseum, Munich* (XX)

SÈVRES. Leda and the Swan, biscuit, model by Etienne-Maurice Falconet, from a design by François Boucher. About 1765. Ht. 32,5 cm. *Victoria and Albert Museum, London* (XXII)

LUNÉVILLE. "Le petit maçon", biscuit, model by Paul-Louis Cyfflé. About 1759–60. Mark, *Terre de Lorraine* impressed and script *B* incised. Ht. 16,3 cm. *Collection M. Penkala* (XVII)

FRANCE. Two biscuit groups. 18th century. Ht. 19 cm. and 20 cm. *Private Collection* (XVII)

TOURNAY. Climbing children. From a model attributed to Nicolas Lecreux. About 1775. Ht. 30 cm. *Victoria and Albert Museum, London* (XXI)

CHELSEA. Nurse and child, after "la nourrice by Palissy." Mark – an *anchor in red*. About 1755. *Victoria and Albert Museum London* (XXIII)

DERBY. Sacrifice figure, "pale-colouring period", *patch-marks*. Ht. 19,4 cm. *Collection M. Penkala* (XXIII)

"GIRL IN A SWING". About 1751. *Victoria and Albert Museum, London* (XXIII)

CHELSEA. The music lesson, after an engraving by René Gaillard, 1758, from a painting by Boucher (1750). About 1765. *Victoria and Albert Museum, London* (XXV)

DERBY. Chinaman and boy. About 1755. *Victoria and Albert Museum, London* (XXVI)

LONGTON HALL. Figure of a goatherd. About 1955. *Victoria and Albert Museum, London* (XIV)

WEESP. Oil and vinegar set. About 1766. *Rijksmuseum, Amsterdam* (XXVIII)

WEESP. Cup and saucer decorated with moulded sprigs. About 1764. *Rijksmuseum, Amsterdam* (XXVIII)

WEESP. Venus. Model ascribed to Nicolas Gauron. About 1765. Ht. 20,3 cm. *Rijksmuseum, Amsterdam* (XXVII)

AMSTEL. Vase. About 1790. Ht. 43.5 cm. *Rijksmuseum, Amsterdam* (XV)

AMSTEL. Salad bowl, Japanese decoration, about 1784. *Rijksmuseum, Amsterdam* (XV)

THE HAGUE. Punch Bowl. About 1790. Ht. 27 cm. Mark – *stork, Rijksmuseum, Amsterdam* (XXIX)

THE HAGUE. Ewer and basin. *Rijksmuseum, Amsterdam* (XXIX)

THE HAGUE. Tournay porcelain decorated at the Lynker factory. *Rijksmuseum, Amsterdam* (XXIX)

GARDNER. The bootseller. About 1830. Ht. 21.3 cm. *Collection M. Penkala* (XXX)

GARDNER. Peasant boy with flute. Ht. 16.2 cm. *Collection M. Penkala* (XXX)

COPENHAGEN. Ganymedes and the Eagle, biscuit, after a sculpture by Bertel Thorwaldsen. About 1830. Ht. 10.5 cm. *Private Collection* (XXX)

Lorenz Hutschenreuther. White Parrot. Ht. 38 cm. *Private Collection* (XXXI)

ROZENBURG. Small vase, cup and saucer. About 1898. *Private Collection* (XXXI)

The dancer Loïe Fuller, biscuit. Model by Agathon Leonard van Weydefeld. Ht. 29.2 cm. About 1900. *Private Collection* (XXXII)
Lady with a snowball. Model by the sculptor Rudolf Marcuse, Berlin. *Mark, Scepter* Ht. 40.5. cm. *Collection M. Penkala* (XXXII)
Lady in an armchair. Incised *K. Arnoaller. Private Collection* (XXXII)

BIBLIOGRAPHY

AGUILERA, E. DE: La porcelana dei Buen Retiro en el Museo Municipal de Madrid, 1934.

ALBIKER, CARL: Die Meissner Porzellantiere im 18. Jahrh. Berlin, 1935.

AUSCHER, E. S.: History and Description of French Porcelain. London, 1905

AVERY, C. LOUISE: Masterpieces of European Porcelain. New York, 1949.

BARBANTINI, N.: De porcellane di Venezia et delle Nove. Col. catalogo degli esemplari esposti a ca. Rezzonico. Venezia, 1936.

BAYER, A.: Ansbacher Porzellan. Geschichte und Leistung der Ansbacher Brückberger Porzellan Manufakturen 1757–1860. Ansbach, 1933.

BEAUCHAMP, OCTAVE: Céramique. La porcelaine. Paris, 1900.

BEMROSE, W.: Bow, Chelsea and Derby Porcelain. London, 1898. Longton Hall Porcelain. London, 1906.

BEMROSE, G.: 19th Century English Pottery and Porcelain. London, 1952.

BERLING, KARL: Das Meissner Porzellan und seine Geschichte. Leipzig, 1900.

Festschrift der Kgl. Sächs. Porzellan Manufaktur Meissen. Dresden, 1911.

BINNS, R. W.: Century of potting in the City Worcester, 1865.

BONCZ, CLARA – KAROLY GINK: Herender Porzellan. Budapest, 1962.

BRÜNING, ADOLF: Handbücher, der Kgl. Museen zu Berlin, Porzellan. Berlin, 1907.

BRYANT, G. F.: Chelsea Porcelain Toys. London, 1925.

BURTON, WILLIAM: A General History of Porcelain. London, 1925. A History and Description of English Porcelain. London, 1902.

CAHIERS de la céramique et des arts de feu. Sèvres, 1955—

CAROLSFELD, LUDWIG SCHNORR VON/KÖLLMAN: Porzellan der europäischen Fabriken. Braunschweig, 1956.

CASEY, ELIZABETH TEMPLE: The Lucy Truman Aldrich Collection of European Porcelain Figures of the 18th Century. Providence, 1965.

CHAVAGNAC, DE et DE GROLLIER: Histoire des Manufactures françaises de Porcelaine. Paris, 1906.

CHRIST, HANS: Ludwigsburger Porzellanfiguren. Stuttgart-Berlin, 1921.

CHURCH, A. H.: English Porcelain. London, 1911.

COOK, CYRIL: The life and work of Robert Hancock. London, 1948.

DAVILLIER: Les origines de la Porcelaine en Europe. Paris, 1882.

DOENGES, W.: Meissner Porzellan. Berlin 1921.

DUCRET, S.: Zürcher Porzellan. Zürich 1958/59.

Fürstenberger Porzellan bis 1800. Braunschweig, 1965.

ENGLISH CERAMIC CIRCLE TRANSACTIONS 1933—

ENGLISH PORCELAIN CIRCLE TRANSACTIONS 1928—

THE ENGLISH CERAMIC CIRCLE: Commemorative Catalogue of an Exhibition of English Pottery and Porcelain held at the Victoria and Albert Museum, 1949.

ESSER, KARL HEINZ: Höchster Porzellan. Königstein, 1962.

Höchster Fayencen und Porzellane (Catalogue). Mainz, 1964. (K. H Esser und H. REBER).

FALKE, O. V.: Deutsche Porzellanfiguren. Berlin, 1919.

FISHER, S. W.: English Blue and White Porcelain of the 18th Century. London 1947.

The Decoration of English Porcelain. London, 1954.

FOLNESICS, J.: Die Wiener Porzellan Sammlung Karl Mayer. Wien, 1914.

FOLNESICS, J. and BRAUN, E. W.: Geschichte der Kaiserl. Köningl. Porzellan Manufaktur Wien. Wien, 1907.

GARNIER, EDOUARD: La porcelaine tendre de Sèvres. Paris, 1890.

Dictionnaire de la Céramique.

GATTY, C. T.: The Liverpool Potteries. Liverpool, 1882.

GELDER, H. E. VAN: Catalogus van de verzameling Haagsch porcelein. 's Gravenhage, 1916.

GIACOMOTTI, J.: Faïences Françaises. Paris, 1963.

GILHESPY, F. BRAYSHAW: Derby Porcelain. London, 1965.

GODDEN, GEOFFREY A.: Encyclopaedia of British Pottery and Porcelain Marks. London, 1964.

GRAUL, RICHARD und KURZWELLY ALBRECHT: Altthüringer Porzellane. Leipzig, 1909.

GROLLIER, CHARLES DE: Manuel de l'amateur de porcelaines, manufactures européennes. Paris, 1914.

HACKENBROCH, YVONNE: Meissen and other continental Porcelain, Faience and Enamel in the Irwin Untermyer Collection. London, 1956.

HASLEM, J.: The Old Derby China Factory. London, 1875.

HAYDEN, A.: Royal Copenhagen Porcelain. London, 1911.

HAYDEN, A.: Spode and his successors. A history of the pottery, Stoke-on-Trent, 1765–1965. London, 1925.

HAYWARD, J. F.: Viennese porcelain of the Du Paquier period. London, 1954.

HERNMARCK, CARL och GYLLENSVÄRD, BO: Rörstrand under tre århundraden. Stockholm, 1943.

HIRTH, HERBERT and HELBRING, HUGO: Deutsche Tanagra, Porzellanfiguren des 18. Jahrhunderts. München-Leipzig, 1896.

HOBSON, R. L.: Catalogue of the English Porcelain in the British Museum. London, 1905.

HOFFMANN, FRIEDRICH: Das Porzellan der Europäischen Manufakturen im XVIII. Jahrhundert. Berlin, 1932.

HOFMANN, FRIEDRICH: Frankenthaler Porzellan. München, 1911.

HOFMANN, FRIEDRICH: Geschichte der Bayerischen Porzellan Manufaktur Nymphenburg. Leipzig, 1923.

HOFMANN, FRIEDRICH: Johann Peter Melchior (1742–1825). München, 1921.

HURLBUTT, FRANK: Bow Porcelain. London, 1926.

Old Derby Porcelain and its Artists and Workmen. London, 1925.

Chelsea China. Liverpool, 1937.

Bristol Porcelain. London, 1928.
HYAM, E. E.: The English Period of Derby Porcelain. London, 1926.
JACQUEMART, A.: Les Merveilles de la Céramique. Paris, 1868–71.
JEWITT, L.: Ceramic Art of Great Britain. London, 1878.
JOHN, W. D.: Nantgarw Porcelain. London, 1948.
KING, WILLIAM: English Porcelain Figures of the 18th century. London, 1925.
KÖLMANN, ERICH: Berliner Porzellan. Braunschweig 1966.
KRAUS, JOHANN: Die Marken oder Fabrikzeichen der Porzellanmanufaktur in Frankenthal. Frankenthal, 1899.
LA MANUFACTURE IMPERIALE DE PORCELAINE À ST. PETERSBOURG, 1744–1904. St. Petersbourg, 1906.
LANDAIS, HUBERT: French Porcelain. London, 1961.
LANDENBERGER, MECHTHILD: Katalog Alt-Ludwigsburger Porzellan. Ludwigsburg, 1959.
LANE, ARTHUR: English Porcelain figures of the XVIIIth century. London, 1961.
LECHEVALLIER-CHEVIGNARD: La manufacture de porcelaine de Sèvres. Paris, 1908.
LENZ, G.: Berliner Porzellan. Die Manufaktur Friedrich des Grossen, 1763–1786. Berlin, 1913.
LESSING: Berliner Porzellan des XVIII. Jahrhunderts. Berlin, 1895.
LILL, GEORG: Ludwigsburger Figurenplastik in Amberger Ausformungen. Festsehr. Altert. Ver. München, 1914.
Europäische Porzellanfiguren des XVIII. Jahrhunderts. München.
LORM, DE A. J.: Arnhems Aardewerk. Arnhem, 1961.
LUKOMSKY: Russisches Porzellan (1744–1923). Berlin, 1924.
MAC ALISTER MRS. D. ED.: William Duesbury's London Account Book (1751–1753). London, 1931.
MACKENNA, F. SEVERNE: Cookworthy's Plymouth and Bristol Porcelain. Leigh-on-Sea, 1946.
Champion's Bristol Porcelain. Leigh-on-Sea, 1947.
Worcester Porcelain. Leigh-on-Sea, 1950.
Chelsea Porcelain. Leigh-on-Sea, 1948.
MARIËN-DUGARDIN, A. M.: Faïences fines (Catalogue). Bruxelles, 1961.
MARSHALL, H. RISSIK: Coloured Worcester porcelain of the first period (1751–1783). Newport, 1954.
MAURI, L. DE: Vinovo and its porcelain. Milano, 1923.
MAYER, J.: History of the Art of Pottery in Liverpool. Liverpool, 1855.
MEAGER, K. S.: Swansea and Nantgarw Potteries.
MEDEDELINGENBLAD Vrienden van de Nederlandse Ceramiek, Amsterdam.
MEISTER, P. W.: Figürliche Keramik aus zwei Jahrhunderten. Frankfurt-Main, 1964.
Porzellan des 18. Jahrhunderts; Sammlung Pauls, Riehen, Frankfurt-Main, 1967.
MEW, EGON: Old Bow China. London, 1909.

MITTEILUNGSBLATT, Freunde der Schweizer Keramik. Zürich.
MORAZZONI, GIUSEPPE SAUL LEVY: Le Porcellane Italiane. Milano, 1960.
MORTON, A. E.: Lowestoft China. London, 1932.
MOUFANG, N.: Alt-Berlin in Porzellan. Berlin, 1927.
NANCE, MORTON: The Pottery and Porcelain of Swansea and Nantgarw. London, 1943.
NICAISE, H.: La Porcelaine de Bruxelles. Bruxelles, 1936.
NIGHTINGALE, J. E.: Contributions towards the History of early English Porcelain from contemporary Sources. Salisbury, 1881.
OWEN, HUGH: Two Centuries of Ceramic Art in Bristol. London, 1875.
PAZAUREK, G. E.: Deutsche Fayence und Porzellan Hausmaler. Leipzig, 1925.
Meissner Porzellanmalerei des XVIII. Jahrhunderts. Stuttgart, 1929.
PENKALA, MARIA: European Porcelain. Amsterdam-London. 1947.
European Pottery. Hengelo-London, 1952.
Far Eastern Ceramics, marks and decoration. The Hague/Vermont/Tokyo, 1963.
PEYRE, R.: La céramique française. Paris, 1911.
RÖDER KURT und OPPENHEIM, MICHEL: Das Höchster Porzellan auf der Jahrtausend Ausstellung in Mainz 1925. Mainz, 1930.
RÖDER, KURT: Das Kelsterbacher Porzellan. Darmstadt, 1931.
ROMANO, ELENA: La Porcellana di Capodimonte. Napoli, 1959.
ROZEMBERGH, ALEXANDRE: Les Marques de la Porcelaine Russe. Paris, 1926.
RÜCKERT, RAINER: Bustelli. München, 1963.
Meissener Porzellan 1710–1810. Katalog. München, 1966.
RUST, W. J.: Nederlands Porcelein. Amsterdam, 1952.
SAUERLANDT, MAX: Deutsche Porzellanfiguren der XVIII. Jahrhunderts. Köln, 1923.
SAVAGE, GEORGE: 18th Century English Porcelain. London, 1952.
SAVAGE, GEORGE: Seventeenth and Eighteenth century French Porcelain. London, 1960.
SCHERER, CHRISTIAN: Das Fürstenberger Porzellan. Berlin, 1909.
SCHMIDT, ROBERT: Early European Porcelain as collected by Otto Blohm. München, 1953.
SELIVANOV, A. W.: Porcelain and Earthenware of the Russian Empire. Vladimir, 1903. (Russian).
SEVERANI, G.: Catalogo delle Porcellane dei Medici. Faenza, 1936.
SOIL DE MORIAMÉ, E. J.: and DELPLACE DE FORMANOIR (L.), La Manufacture impériale et royale de Porcelaine de Tournay. Paris, 1937.
SPELMAN, W. W. R.: Lowestoft China. London and Norwich, 1905.
STEGMAN, H.: Die Fürstlich Braunschweigische Porzellan Manufaktur zu Fürstenberg.
SYPENSTEYN, C. A. C. H. VAN: Het Loosdrechtsche Porcelein. Hilversum, 1927.
Het Oud-Hollandsch porcelein. Hilversum, 1933.

TAIT, HUGH: Bow Porcelain 1744–1776. Exhibition Catalogue. London, 1959.

TAPP, W. H.: Jefferyes Hamett O'Neale. London, 1938.

TILMANS, EMILE: Porcelaines de France. Paris, 1950.

VALENTE, VASCO: Porcelana Artistica Portuguesa. Porto, 1949.

WALCHA, OTTO: 250 Jahre Staatliche Porzellan Manufaktur Meissen. Leipzig, 1960.

WANNER-BRANDT: Album der Erzeugnisse der ehem. Württembergischen Manufaktur Alt-Ludwigsburg. Stuttgart, 1906.

WARE, GEORGE W.: Deutsches und Österreichisches Porzellan. Frankfurt a/Main.

WATNEY, BERNARD: Longton Hall Porcelain. London, 1957.

ZIMMERMANN, ERNST: Erfindung und Frühzeit des Meissener Porzellans. Berlin, 1909.

ZIMMERMANN, ERNST: Meissner Porzellan. Leipzig, 1936.

APOLLO, London.

CHRISTIE, MANSON and WOODS, Ltd., London, Catalogues.

LONDON ILLUSTRATED NEWS, London.

POTTERY GAZETTE, London.

SOTHEBY AND CO., London, Catalogues.

THE BURLINGTON MAGAZINE, London.

THE CONNOISSEUR.

THE TIMES, London.

INDEX